Fighters and Singers

Fighters and Singers

The Lives of Some Australian Aboriginal Women

Edited by

Isobel White
Diane Barwick
Betty Meehan

George Allen & Unwin
Sydney London Boston

©Isobel White, Diane Barwick and Betty Meehan and the several authors, each in respect of the paper contributed by her.

This book is copyright under the Berne Convention. No reproduction without permission. All rights reserved.

First published in 1985 by
George Allen & Unwin Australia Pty Ltd
8 Napier Street, North Sydney 2060, NSW, Australia

George Allen & Unwin (Publishers) Ltd
Park Lane, Hemel Hempstead, Herts HP2 4TE, England

Allen & Unwin Inc.
Fifty Cross Street, Winchester, Mass 01890 USA

National Library of Australia
Cataloguing-in-Publication entry:

Fighters and singers: the lives of some Aboriginal women.

Bibliography.
ISBN 0 86861 612 5.
ISBN 0 86861 620 6 (pbk.).

1. Aborigines, Australian — Women — Biography.
I. White, Isobel. II. Barwick, Diane.
III. Meehan, Betty.

920'.00929915

Typeset by Ruskin Press, Melbourne
Printed by Singapore National Printers (Pte) Ltd

For
Shirley Andrew Rosser,
who knows about books and
cares about people.

Contents

Contributors — viii

Maps — xi

Preface — xvi

'Two Dreamtimes' — *Judith Wright* — xix

1. Topsy Napurrula Nelson: Teacher, Philosopher and Friend — 1
    Diane Bell

2. Mondalmi: One of the Saltwater People — 19
    Catherine Berndt

3. A Teacher's Life — 40
    Pearl Duncan

4. Utopian Women — 55
    Jenny Green

5. Eileen McKenzie — 68
    Luise Hercus

6. I Was a Drover Once Myself: Amy Laurie of Kununurra — 76
    Amy Laurie and Ann McGrath

7. Lorna Dixon — 90
    Janet Mathews

8. Emily Margaret Horneville of the Muruwari — 106
    Lynette Oates

9. Inyalangka — 123
    Helen Payne

10	My Sister Who Mothered Me *Janice Reid*	129
11	Running Free: Three Kugu-Nganychara Women *Diane Smith*	142
12	Two Women of Jigalong *Myrna Tonkinson*	161
13	Aunty Ellen: The Pastor's Wife *Diane Barwick*	175
14	Bandeiyama: She Keeps Going *Betty Meehan*	200
15	Mangkatina: Woman of the Desert *Isobel White*	214

Contributors

Diane Barwick is an anthropologist who has done years of research on the history of Aboriginal administration in Victoria and New South Wales, described in many articles and the forthcoming book *Rebellion at Coranderrk*. She has edited the first six volumes of *Aboriginal History, A handbook for Aboriginal and Islander history,* and a memorial volume honouring the anthropologist W.E.H. Stanner.

Diane Bell is an anthropologist with extensive fieldwork experience in Northern Australia. In *Daughters of the Dreaming* she writes of the ritual life of Aboriginal women of Warrabri, where she lived for eighteen months and, in *Law, the old and the new,* of their role in the maintenance of customary law. She has acted as consultant to the Aboriginal Land Commissioner, the Australian Law Reform Commission, Aboriginal Land Councils and Legal Aid Services. At present she is a research fellow in the Research School of Social Sciences, Australian National University.

Catherine Berndt is an anthropologist at the University of Western Australia. She has spent a number of years living in Aboriginal communities in South Australia, the Northern Territory and the Western Desert. She has made a special study of Aboriginal women, about whom she writes from almost life-long experience. She has published a number of books and articles about Aborigines, some by herself, some with her husband Ronald Berndt. Their major joint publication *The World of the first Australians* is widely read and highly acclaimed.

Pearl Duncan was the first Aborigine to become a trained teacher in Australia and has taught in New South Wales, North Queensland, the Torres Straits Islands, and New Zealand. She is a former member of the National Aboriginal Education Committee and is at present studying for a B. Litt. in anthropology at the Australian National University.

Jenny Green is an artist who was employed for some years by the Northern Territory Education Department to encourage art and craft of high quality, produced by adults and children, at the Aboriginal-owned Utopia Station. There she was instrumental in setting up the thriving batik industry. Successful exhibitions of the women's craft work have been held in several capital cities and one is planned for overseas. She is now consultant to the Central Land Council on various matters associated with Aboriginal land tenure and land claims.

Luise Hercus is a linguist, teaching Sanskrit in the Faculty of Asian Studies, Australian National University. She also studies Aboriginal languages, particularly those spoken by only few survivors. She has published two volumes on the languages once spoken in Victoria and one on the Barkindji language of the Darling River people. She is preparing for publication a grammar of the Wangkanguru-Arabana language of South Australia.

Ann McGrath is a tutor in the history department at Monash University, after some years as a lecturer in the School of General Studies, Darwin Community College. She has collected oral histories from Aboriginal people and has contributed historical information for several Aboriginal land claims. She has written a PhD thesis entitled 'We Grew up the Stations: Europeans, Aborigines and Cattle in the Northern Territory'.

Janet Mathews has used her training in music to record many rare songs and some other aspects of music from various parts of New South Wales. She has also recorded for the Australian Institute of Aboriginal Studies the last surviving speakers of a number of languages now no longer spoken at all. She has written a number of books about Aborigines, including the widely-read *The two worlds of Jimmie Barker* and a series of informative books for children.

Betty Meehan is an anthropologist who has lived at intervals over the last twenty years with the Anbarra community in Arnhem Land. Her book *Shell bed to shell midden* and several articles describe some of her experiences with the women of that community. For five years she was a research fellow in Prehistory in the Research School of Pacific Studies, Australian National University. She is now a consultant working on Aboriginal land claims in the Northern Territory.

Lynette Oates is a linguist who has worked with the Summer Institute of Linguistics in several countries. She has published work on a number of hitherto unwritten languages, and, together with her late husband, produced a survey of Australian Aboriginal languages, *A revised linguistic survey of Australia,* as well as a later updated *Survey.* She is currently working on two New South Wales languages, and is also engaged in secondary teaching.

Helen Payne is an ethnomusicologist who has made a depth study of the music of Aboriginal women's ceremonies in the Western Desert. While she lived at Ernabella she learnt to sing this music and to dance in the ceremonies. She is now a part-time research assistant and lecturer in the Elder Conservatorium, University of Adelaide.

Janice Reid is a medical anthropologist who has lived with the Yolngu people of Yirrkala in Arnhem Land. There she studied attitudes to illness and death and indigenous healing practices. She now lectures in the Commonwealth Institute of Health at the University of Sydney. She is editor of *Body, land and spirit,* a collection of papers on health and healing in Aboriginal society, and author of *Sorcerers and healing spirits,* a study of change in the medical system of the Yolngu.

Diane Smith is an anthropologist who made a special study of the lives of Aboriginal women and their families while staying on an outstation of Aurukun, Cape York Peninsula. She has studied at the University of Queensland and at the Australian National University, and worked for a short time for the Northern Land Council. She is now a consulting anthropologist recording Aboriginal sites of significance and helping to sort out problems of land tenure.

Myrna Tonkinson is an anthropologist who has lived with Aboriginal people in Western and Central Australia. She has made a special study of healing practices in Aboriginal communities. For some years she was research co-ordinator for the Australian Institute of Aboriginal Studies and is now research assistant to Mr Justice Kearney, Land Claims Commissioner for the Northern Territory.

Isobel White is an anthropologist who has lived with Aborigines in South Australia while studying women's social and ceremonial life, about which she has written a number of articles. Since her retirement from Monash University she has been a visiting fellow in the Research School of Pacific Studies at the Australian National University. She is editing for publication the manuscript of *The native tribes of Western Australia* written by Daisy Bates in the 1900s.

Maps

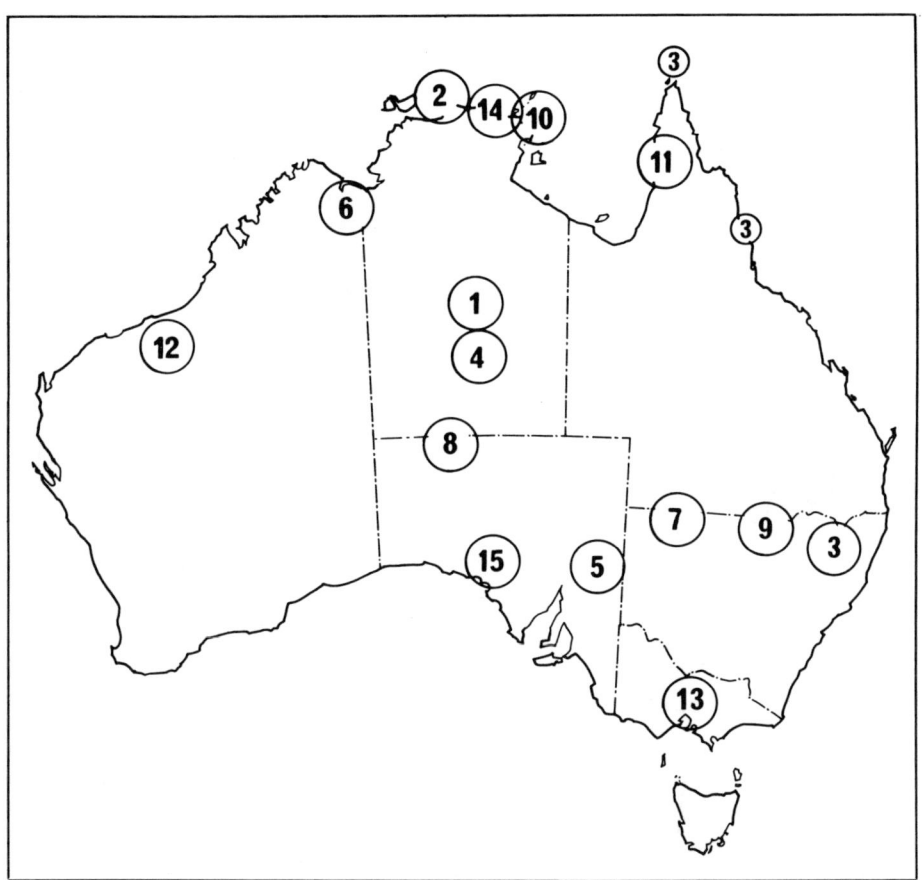

1 Numbers in circles refer to relevant chapters

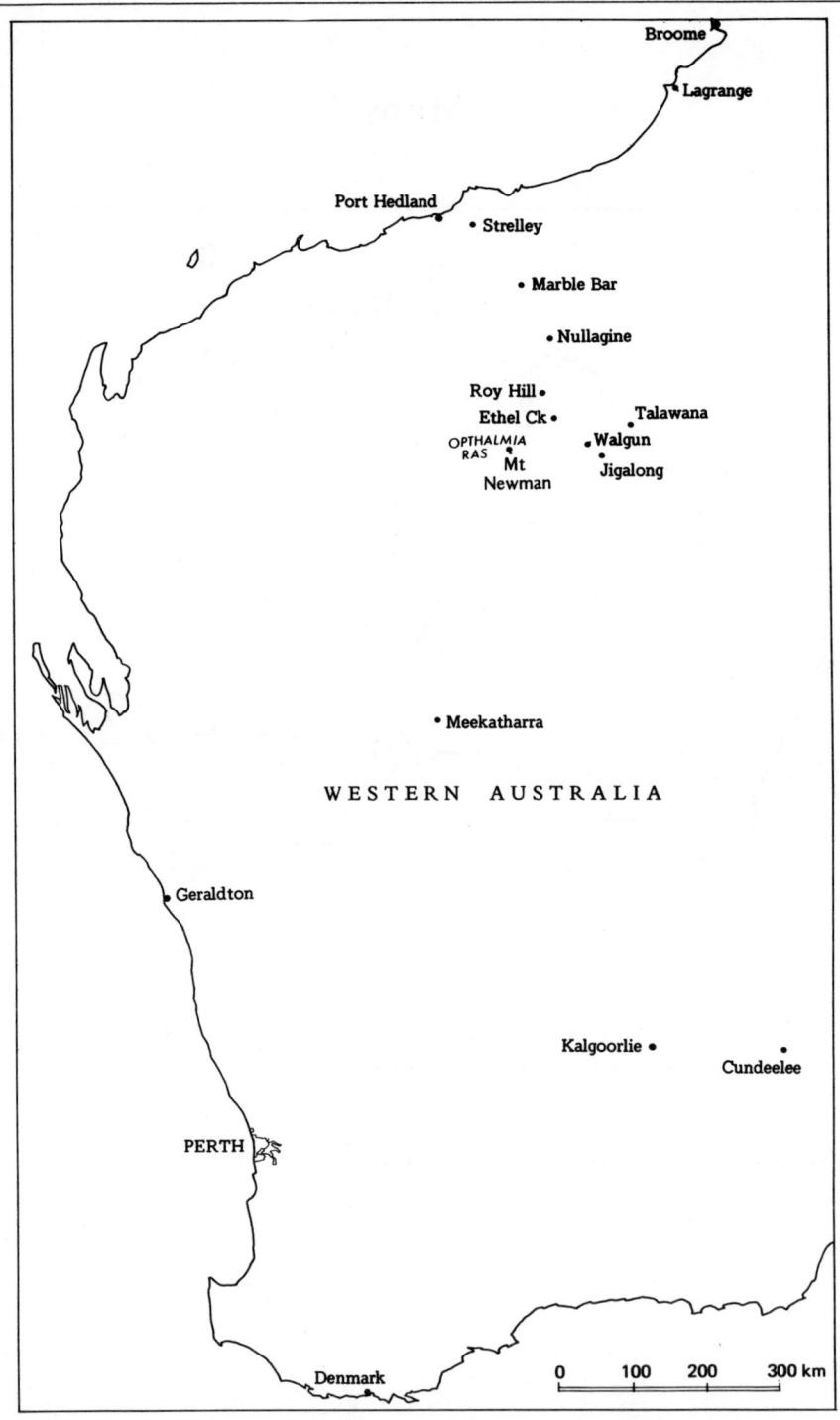

2 Shows places mentioned in Chapters 12 and 15

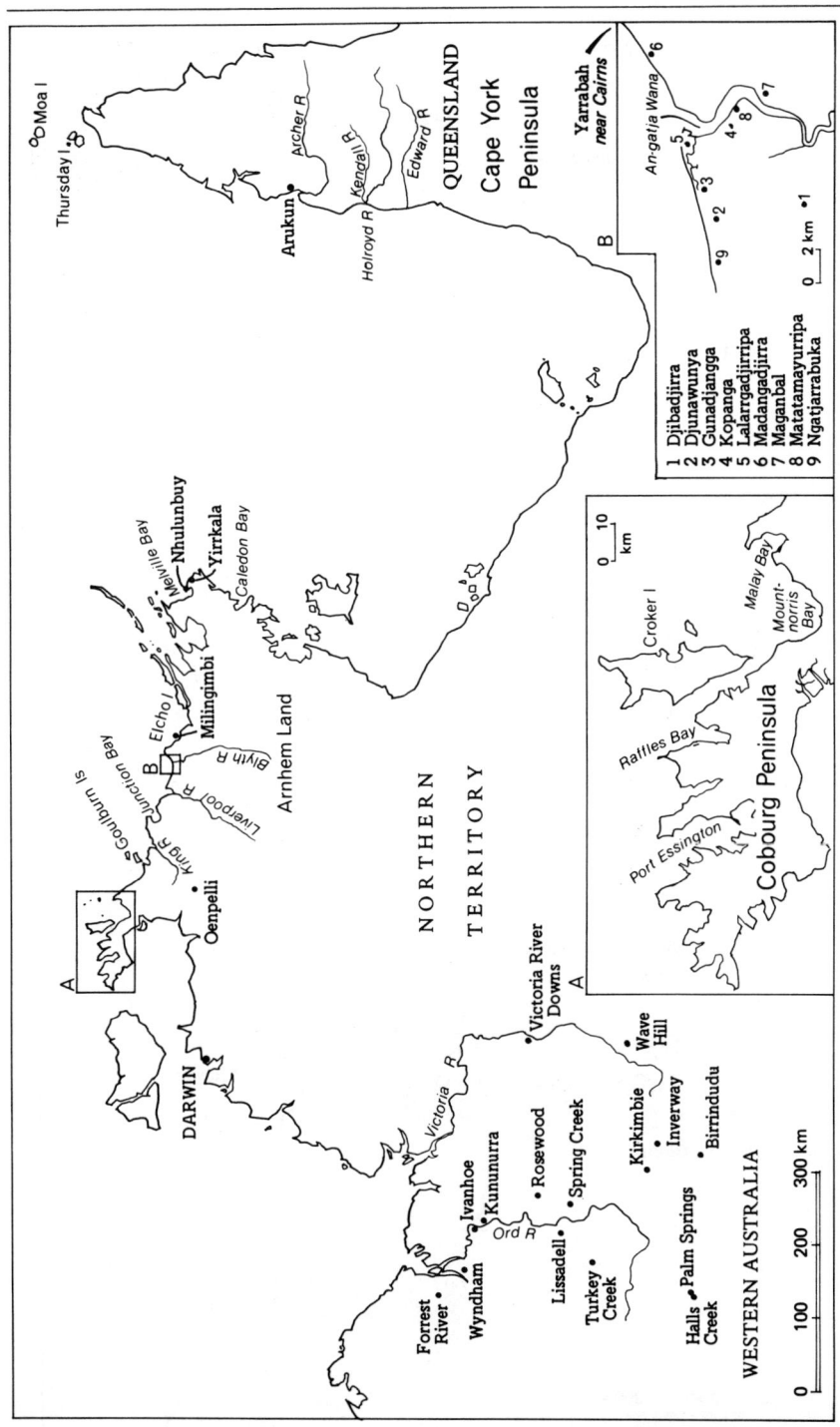

3 Shows places mentioned in Chapters 2, 3, 6, 10, 11, & 14

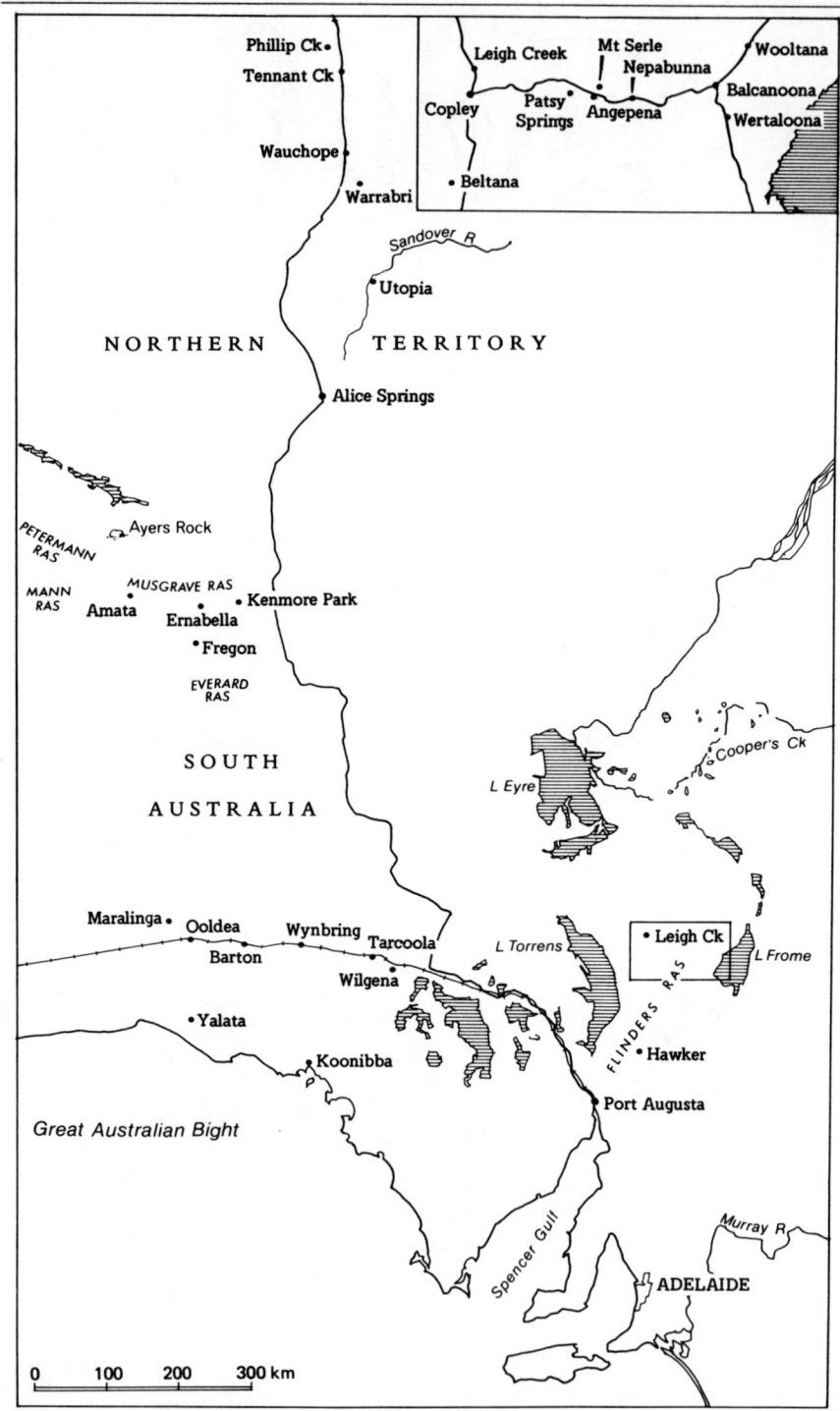

4 Shows places mentioned in Chapters 1, 4, 5, 8 & 15

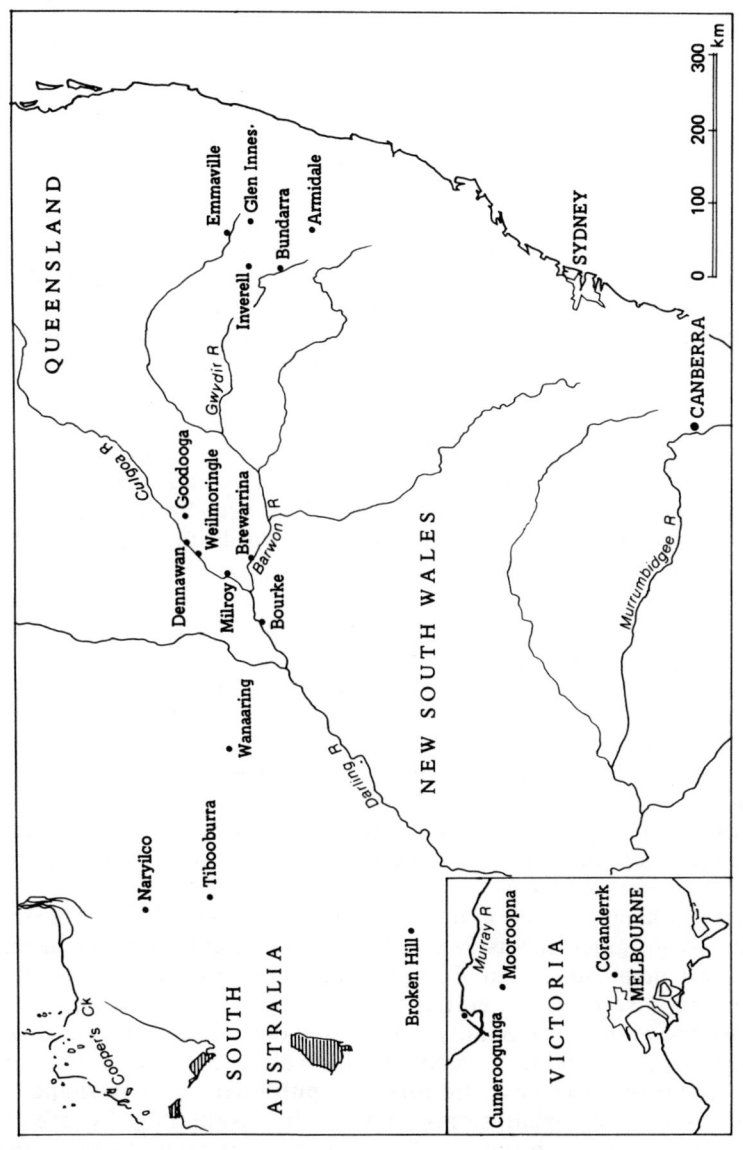

5 Shows places mentioned in Chapters 3, 7, 9 & 13

Preface

The literature on Australian Aborigines is vast. But much of it is curiously depersonalised and strangely silent about the experience and activities of women. The life stories sketched in this book offer a more intimate view of the Aboriginal heritage. The lives of these women span a century of experience in fifteen communities scattered from Cape York, Arnhem Land and East Kimberley to the Western Desert, the Centre, South Australia, Victoria and New South Wales.

Some women recall their impressions of the first time they saw a European in their land; others tell how Europeans had influenced their communities generations before they themselves were born. Every sketch contains transcriptions or translations of the words in which a woman told of her life, but only one is an autobiography. Other reminiscences were written by friends — anthropologists, archaeologists, historians, linguists, ethnomusicologists — who wished to share with a wider audience their knowledge of women they admired.

This is not a book about research, although the stories in fact tell readers more about the ethics and practice of various disciplines than is usual in academic tomes. This volume is a record of friendships which formed despite differences of background, experience and age. The collection is unorthodox primarily because it focuses on the experience of women, but also because the authors attempt to convey what Aboriginal women considered relevant when describing their lives to friends who were both strangers and kin.

In most anthropological and historical narratives about Aboriginal society the Aborigines themselves are nameless. Published life histories are rare, and most adhere to European conventions about biographical literature: reminiscences are edited to fit a chronological format which emphasises individual personality but omits the wealth of genealogical information and commentary on community values intrinsic to Aboriginal styles of recounting the past. Editors and publishers who re-shape such narratives by excising what seems to them irrelevant may believe their attempts to portray Aboriginal lives in a European fashion make Aborigines more intelligible to outsiders. But the style is part of the story. Such omissions may impoverish the portrayal so that readers cannot perceive why Aboriginal life, however different, has its own satisfactions.

Allegiance to family and familiar territory shapes the personal histories of Aborigines in ways scarcely appreciated by people reared in nuclear family households in cities. Family and community loyalties are the source of Aboriginal identity. Such bonds endure, despite decades of official intervention aimed at promoting individual assimilation. Although ancient ways have been transformed — by force and by choice — Aboriginal communities survive because their members feel pride in their historic identity and find security in their staunch allegiance to forebears, family and friends.

We solicited these life stories from a circle of women researchers who share our belief that the dignity and strength of Aboriginal communities could be more widely understood through reading about the women who contribute so much to the maintenance of those communities.

We tried not to dictate how contributors should depict the friends they called grandmother or aunt, sister or daughter. Some authors have said little of their own involvement with the subjects of their stories or the communities in which they lived, relying instead upon notes or tape-recordings of autobiographical statements. Other chose to describe their own experiences when composing portraits of their friends. Age, temperament and historical chance influenced the relationships that led to the writing of these stories; ties of affection and the conventions of respect and courtesy appropriate to specific relationships in particular communities also shape the way in which the stories are told. The variety of approaches in these biographical essays illustrates the rich complexity of human relationships. Because of the time lapse between the writing of some of the stories and the publication of this book, there have naturally been changes in the lives of some of the women. We were grieved to hear of the recent death of Inyalangka.

As editors we encouraged variety of approach and presentation. We were overborne in our efforts to achieve consistency in certain matters of terminology and orthography. Some authors objected to our preference for the term 'Europeans' because 'whites' was the usual term used by Aborigines themselves. Some argued that the women they portrayed always spoke of miles, thus measurement of distance in kilometres would be anachronistic. Opinions about the transcription of Aboriginal words necessarily varied as there are many systems of orthography. Usage differs across the continent, and it seemed sensible to accept authors' advice about the words and spellings most appropriate in particular communities.

Indigenous systems of kinship terminology also vary, and this may influence usage when Aborigines 'translate' their understanding of relationships. Readers may find certain passages puzzling because English kinship terms are used to describe relationships which obviously are not biologically derived. Many Aboriginal communities still use what is called classificatory kinship terminology. All persons regard themselves as related, even if they cannot trace actual genealogical links. Terms for mother, father, sister, brother and so on are extended to include other members of the society. Where a distinction is relevant some authors have marked classificatory relationships by enclosing kin terms in quotation marks.

This book is the work of many people. The essays acknowledge indebtedness to particular women and a sense of kinship which makes the contributors feel both entitled and obliged to share their understanding of Aboriginal life. Other friends, too many to name here, helped with this publication. The editors owe special thanks to Patricia Croft, May McKenzie, members of the ANU typing pool and the staff of ANU Press.

It was Shirley Andrew Rosser, professional editor of many pioneering works in Aboriginal studies, who first suggested we prepare this book; our dedication acknowledges her contribution. We are grateful to Judith Wright, poet and fighter for Aboriginal rights, for allowing us to reprint the poem which inspired our title. 'Fighters and singers' seemed a fitting description of the countless Aboriginal women whose words and actions have celebrated life and enriched the lives of others.

Isobel White
Diane Barwick
Betty Meehan

Two Dreamtimes

(For Kath Walker)

Kathy my sister with the torn heart,
I don't know how to thank you
for your dreamtime stories of joy and grief
written on paperbark.

You were one of the dark children
I wasn't allowed to play with—
riverbank campers, the wrong colour,
(I couldn't turn you white.)

So it was late I met you,
late I began to know
they hadn't told me the land I loved
was taken out of your hands.

Sitting all night at my kitchen table
with a cry and a song in your voice,
your eyes were full of the dying children,
the blank-eyed taken women,

the sullen looks of the men who sold them
for rum to forget the selling,
the hard rational white faces
with eyes that forget the past.

With a knifeblade flash in your black eyes
that always long to be blacker,
your Spanish-Koori face
of a fighter and singer,

arms over your breast folding
your sorrow in to hold it,
you brought me to you some of the way
and came the rest to meet me,

over the desert of red sand
came from your lost country
to where I stand with all my fathers,
their guilt and righteousness.

Over the rum your voice sang
the tales of an old people,
their dreaming buried, the place forgotten . . . .
We too have lost our dreaming.

We the robbers robbed in turn,
selling this land on hire-purchase;
what's stolen once is stolen again
even before we know it.

If we are sisters, it's in this —
our grief for a lost country,
the place we dreamed in long ago,
poisoned now and crumbling.

Let us go back to that far time,
I riding the cleared hills,
plucking blue leaves for their eucalypt scent,
hearing the call of the plover,

in a land I thought was mine for life.
I mourn it as you mourn
the ripped length of the island beaches,
the drained paperbark swamps.

The easy Eden-dreamtime then
in a country of birds and trees
made me your shadow-sister, child,
dark girl I couldn't play with.

But we are grown to a changed world:
over the drinks at night
we can exchange our separate griefs,
but yours and mine are different.

A knife's between us. My righteous kin
still have cruel faces.
Neither you nor I can win them,
though we meet in secret kindness.

I am born of the conquerors,
you of the persecuted.
Raped by rum and an alien law,
progress and economics,

are you and I and a once-loved land
peopled by tribes and trees;
doomed by traders and stock exchanges,
bought by faceless strangers.

Two Dreamtimes

And you and I are bought and sold,
our songs and stories too
though quoted low in a falling market
(publishers shake their heads at poets).

Time that we shared for a little while,
telling sad tales of women
(black or white at a different price)
meant much and little to us.

My shadow-sister, I sing to you
from my place with my righteous kin,
to where you stand with the Koori dead,
"Trust none—not even poets."

The knife's between us. I turn it round,
the handle to your side,
the weapon made from your country's bones.
I have no right to take it.

But both of us die as our dreamtime dies.
I don't know what to give you
for your gay stories, your sad eyes,
but that, and a poem, sister.

Judith Wright

Acknowledgement
'Two Dreamtimes' has been reprinted from Judith Wright's collection *Alive: Poems 1971-72*, Angus & Robertson, Sydney, 1973, by kind permission of author and publisher.

1

Topsy Napurrula Nelson: Teacher, Philosopher and Friend

Diane Bell

I'm sitting down in Tennant Creek now, at this Blueberry Hill camp. My father is not too well. He's getting old, getting weak. I reckon we'll wait here with him, all the families. There's my mother and her sisters, Mompy [Topsy's father's mother's younger sister], my brothers Mick and Johnny and their kids, and Glenda and Roberta [two of the three children of her brother's daughter, fostered by Topsy. Dion, the eldest, was away at school in Alice Springs]. We're all here with this old man. He's happy now. He knows his country is safe. My country too. (You went there in the cool time [winter], eh, Diane?) It's good country. I reckon we'll move back there.

Topsy's words, that morning in September 1979, brought to my mind memories of the trip I had taken with several of her close relatives earlier that year in July. Because she had wished to devote her attention to her sick father, she had not accompanied us. I had missed her company. I recalled the splendid trips we had taken together over the three years I'd known her. Sometimes we went in search of a particular plant, animal or ochre; sometimes we sought a particular site of religious significance.

But always Topsy explained patiently the significance of the country and its bounty. She would remember questions I had asked on previous occasions and draw my attention to matters which might clarify her earlier answers. Constantly Topsy 'cross-referenced' for me things and experiences in the classificatory system of her own culture and indicated parallels in my own experience and in white Australian culture. Once, when searching for a way to convey the strength of the power imparted by the use of body paint and song during 'business' (religious rituals), she had likened the experience to a blood transfusion: 'It's life, our life blood, but it comes from another.'

For my tape recorder, that morning in 1979, Topsy continued to speak of the two most important things in her life — family and country:

> That country, Diane, that Pawurrinji — we're going back there. My father told me about it when I was a child, and all my aunties too [father's sisters]. They taught me the business, the songs and the painting-up for that country. We went into that country before with you, lots of times, but there was too much long grass, too much no road. We had to turn back all the time. We couldn't get right up close to that really place at Pawurrinji, where the *jintirrpiri* [Willie wagtail] and *kurlukuku* [diamond dove] dreamings come through.
>
> But they told me about you — you got there. They told me here, where I'm sitting now. That country, it's all right now. They been burn it and make it clean. Now you can get right up to that Pawurrinji place. They were telling me and my father about when you got to that Pawurrinji, and he was happy. Rosie, his sister, was singing for that country. She was teaching me about that business, like before.

Rosie had also taught me, and I reminded Topsy that Rosie Nakamarra had been the first person in Central Australia to call me 'sister'. Through this classifactory relationship to Rosie I was incorporated within the kinship system and regarded as a close member of certain families, and a more distant member of others: Topsy's father (who was Rosie's brother) also called me 'sister'. My initiation into the intricacies of Aboriginal social organisation began in 1976 when, as a post-graduate student of the Australian National University, I first came to Warrabri, a government settlement 375 km north of Alice Springs. I came to ask Aboriginal women to teach me about their ritual life but discovered that first I needed to understand the dynamics of the settlement. Warrabri, I found, was home to four different linguistic groups — Warlpiri, Warramunga, Alyawarra and Kaititj — each of whom maintained separate camps and thereby reinforced their distinctively different cultural heritages. Topsy, with a Warlpiri father and a Kaititj grandmother, was one of the privileged few at home in several camps. As a chaperone she was invaluable.

But Topsy, I soon realised, was more than a wonderful guide, she was also an expert on ritual matters. Aboriginal women do not pass on knowledge in a haphazard fashion, and Topsy had long ago been selected by her close relatives as a suitable candidate for instruction in matters of ritual and country. She was of scholarly mind, free from the responsibilities of caring for small children, the eldest daughter of an important man of the desert and the granddaughter of a highly respected knowledgeable woman, now dead. Like many desert people, Topsy had a vast and rich dreamtime heritage on which to draw and would emphasise different aspects at different times.

From her father, and all his fathers before him, Topsy held the rights and responsibilities of *kirda* for the country of Pawurrinji (south-west of

Tennant Creek) and for the rituals which maintain the harmonious relationship of people to land according to the *jukurrpa* (dreaming). She shared her *kirda*ship with all the other men and women who traced a direct relationship through their patriline to the dreamtime ancestors of Pawurrinji. In explaining it to me, Topsy often said: 'I call that country "father". I hold it from my father, and from my grandfather'. In another 'country', further to the south, Topsy held the rights and responsibilities of *kurdungurlu* through her mother from her mother's father. Of this country Topsy would say: 'I call it "mother". I am the child of that country'. Topsy also enjoyed certain other privileges in the country of her mother's mother (*jaja*) because she was born there. To mark this relationship, Topsy was endowed with a special 'bush name', which was never spoken in her presence.

When I met Topsy in 1976 she was in her ritual prime. Although only in her early forties, she had access to an extensive range of dreaming knowledge, was respected by other women, and her participation was sought on many ritual occasions. Further, because she had borne no children of her own, she had not spent years in the time-consuming and emotionally demanding task of child-rearing. Consequently, Topsy had been able to devote her time and energy to acquiring knowledge and ritual expertise.

After I had been at Warrabri some three months, Topsy selected me as a pupil. It was only after a year of working with her, and the Kaititj women with whom she was at that time camped, that I began to understand the complexities of our teacher–pupil relationship. In that initial period I was tested, cross-examined and watched. I was allowed certain privileges, but I was expected also to take increasing responsibility for my actions. On arrival at Warrabri, various women asked why I had come, whether I would take women out hunting, and whether I could handle a rifle. I had undertaken an intensive language course in Warlpiri before entering the field and answered in my broken Warlpiri that I had come to learn of women's lives from women, that I was delighted to take women hunting, but that I was wary of guns.

My faltering speech was greeted with a mixture of pleasure and amusement and prompted more questions about my 'skin'. In Aboriginal English the term 'skin' refers to the subsection names which desert people employ. In this all-encompassing system of classification, every member of the society is known by one of eight subsection terms. Knowledge of a person's subsection affiliation, which is determined by birth, immediately provides other members of the society with important clues about how they should behave properly towards another. Finer distinctions are made within the kinship system but, in the first instance, the subsection system, the 'skins', operate as a sort of short-hand of social relationships. I explained that in Alice Springs, at the language course, they had called me Nakamarra. 'We'll see,' old Rosie Nakamarra answered. On the basis of my experience in that course I was able to give a semblance of correct behaviour for a Nakamarra. It was a fortunate choice for it gave me potential membership of several strong ritual groups, and made me a possible younger sister of Rosie. By the end of the week I was declared to be a Nakamarra, the younger sister of Rosie, and thereby related to everyone in the Warlpiri camp, and, through her niece Topsy, to many within the Kaititj camp.

The next round of questions concerned more personal issues: where was my husband; how did I support myself; how long would I stay? I explained that I was supported by the University in Canberra and that, as a divorced woman, I received a pension from the government. 'In that case, you are just like us,' Rosie had said. Being 'just like us' entailed the emotional and financial independence I enjoyed as a 'widow' (i.e., a woman without the support of a man) and the social status I enjoyed by virtue of my two children (aged seven and nine when I first arrived at Warrabri).

I had access to the women's camps, where no man may trespass. I was trusted with women's secrets because I was told that, unlike many married white women, I did not deem it necessary to confirm with a man everything I learnt. My children were past the stage of dependence: my daughter was seen to be nearing the age of marriage and my son approaching initiation. I was determined to learn for myself, and although my progress was slow in some respects (I still confuse the tracks of a goanna and a snake at the entrance of the hole in which they sleep during the day) I was 'just like them' — independent, and proud to be a woman. When one day I complained of my greying hair as a sign of ageing, Topsy smilingly corrected me with, 'That's your dreaming; you're properly old woman.'

Topsy led me by the hand (sometimes physically) through the maze of knowledge required of me as an adult woman in a desert community. It was she who either nodded approvingly at my response or moved to protect me from dangers of which I was unaware when we found ourselves in unfamiliar situations. On reflection I now can see turning points when, having demonstrated competence at one level, I was permitted to proceed to another.

Learning retrospectively from one's mistakes is a dangerous way of acquiring knowledge in a society where an error may constitute an unforgivable breach of etiquette or may endanger life. Gently, but unremittingly, I was taught to whom I could speak directly, to whom obliquely, and those I must avoid; where I could visit freely, where with caution and where I should not trespass. In this society, showing respect for kinsfolk is a complex and serious concern: scant allowance is made for blundering fools. I quickly learnt to identify my primary kin, always reckoned through my relationship as 'sister' to Rosie Nakamarra, but I needed constant assistance in identifying more distant relatives. In time I came to understand how, within a kinship system which is fixed by birth, much is negotiable and subject to adjustment. I also learnt to 'play the game', and much to Topsy's pleasure, was able to suggest possible kinship statuses for visiting whites.

Many women taught me, corrected me and sat with me; yet I always felt it was Topsy who was overseeing the entire process. I learnt that she would test me to decide when new doors should be opened. I saw her glow when I displayed increasing competence in unravelling the intricacies of desert life. On one memorable occasion she sternly reprimanded another woman for having given me misleading information. 'Tell her straight,' Topsy cautioned, 'she is learning the law.'

'Yes' Topsy continued. 'I taught you all right. When you arrived here you were *missisus* [often translated as 'white woman'], but now you are Nakamarra, my *pimirdi* [father's sister]. We're all *kirda* together for that country.'

'That's true,' I replied. 'You taught me a lot about this country, about how to hunt and to call people's names. You taught me *yawulyu* [women's rituals] and language. Topsy, do you remember telling me about when you lived at the old mission at Phillip Creek? We were camped there one night and you were telling me about when you were a little girl.'

'I remember. We laughed about that one.'

'Do you remember telling me about when you lived at Greenwood Station?'

'Yes. I was a kid then with my family.'

'Topsy, could I write all that down and make one big story?'

'All right. But I'll tell it from the beginning, like *papulanji* [white people] do.'

'What, like once upon a time,' I teased.

'No. Like "first I lived with my grandmother" — like that. Mompy can listen too. She is old now but she remembers it all. She really travelled through this country when she was young.'

On this and other occasions, my tape-recorder was not intrusive: its use was something the women controlled. They particularly enjoyed replaying songs and discussed their performance with the fervour of connoisseurs. When recording her story, Topsy was not self-consciously providing 'answers' to my queries; she was deliberately creating for me a structured story which would be intelligible to outsiders.

Listening to stories of their own people's past told in this sequential fashion is a rare treat for Aboriginal children. On this occasion the youngsters of the camp approached shyly and were incorporated warmly into the listening group. Mompy, the oldest member of the group, began the proceedings by opening the topic.

> When I was young we travelled from here to Newcastle Waters. We were following the business. We danced all the way. We were making young mans [initiating youths]. We danced and sang all the way, like this . . .

Mompy flicked out her hands in imitation of the dancing legs of women at initiation time and began intoning songs from that country. Her face was immediately alive; her eyes sparkled. For a moment it was hard for me to remember that Mompy was over seventy, a frail great-grandmother almost blind with trachoma.

Mompy continued:

> We were travelling for months and months, that business man [ritual leader] was in front, and all the old mothers, aunties and wives were

coming behind. We carried water in a *mardu* [wooden water-carrier] — no billy-can then. I saw that white fella for the first time when I was at the Seven Mile [the Overland Telegraph Station, 7 miles north of Tennant Creek, where a police ration-depot operated in the 1920s]. All the Jingili, Mudbura, Warlmanpa, Warramunga and Warlpiri, they all came together for that business. Those women had really big business.

Graciously Mompy turned to Topsy, whose turn it now was to tell her story:

Mompy travelled all through that country, with my father's mothers. There were three of them, all sisters. They went from Pawurrinji (where you visited, Diane) to Miyikampi, a bit to the south. Mompy was taking the place for her sisters. They only had one son, that Jakamarra. Those sisters were all gone first.

Mompy took me hunting in that Miyikampi country when I was little. Once she left fat in a tree, and when we came back for it all the birds had eaten it. I was about eleven then, bigger than Roberta [Topsy's foster-daughter, then aged eight].

Every Sunday she used to take me hunting. Remember, old woman? You took me out hunting this side [west] of Phillip Creek [34 km north of Tennant Creek]. Once you had a mother pussy-cat. You didn't give it to me. You ate it all yourself. I had the two baby ones. ['I was hungry bugger,' Mompy interjected]. All that was when I was living at the mission [the Phillip Creek Native Settlement was known locally as a mission], before I was at Greenwood station [90 km south of Tennant Creek] with my family, my grandmother and grandfather. I had one live grandmother first. Then I was travelling this way. I was born at Ngapajinpi [on Dixon Creek, near Greenwood Station], in my grandmother's country. We ate all that *ngarlu* [wild honey]. The swallow eats it too. That's the song Mompy is singing now. *Ngarlu* from that *piraru* [acacia] and *wirrpinyaru* [grevillea]. Look, Mompy is showing you how she dances for that one. [Mompy pinched her fingers together and gave the sign for the swallow, one of the major dreamings of her father's country.] She's *kirda* for that one; but that Pawurrinji country she calls 'mother', she's *kurdungurlu* for that one. We look after it together.

We stayed at Greenwood until I was about four or five — when I was still a baby, still not walking, at that station, when Mr Curtis was owning it. You know that Mary Curtis who lives up here at Blueberry Hill? Well, that family now — that Mr Curtis. He was good to us people. He had a lot of goats, cattle, bullocks, sheep. He was making all the killers [killing meat for consumption] for the Aboriginal people. He was a good fella. We moved around that country, down to Jalyirrpa [32 km north-west of Greenwood] and back. I don't really remember all this, my old fella was telling me, that's all. After a while we'd go right up to Wakulpu and then travel back this way and maybe get some *yarla* [bush potato — *Ipomea*], and *yakajirri* [bush currant — *Solanum*]. We'd never stay there very long — just keep moving. That way I was learning the country all along. That Wakulpu was straight *kalarra* [west] from the old station. Must be about like that Phillip Creek from here [34 km]. We'd sleep half-way and get there the next morning. (We might be able to get that place again. It's outside the fence. Must be all right, eh, Diane?)

Topsy breaking *yarla* (bush potato), December 1976 (Photograph by D. Bell)

Many of the women with whom I worked at Warrabri had impressed upon me the significance of the Wakulpu site, but I had not yet visited it. I knew that its exact location might be of special importance to Topsy's people: if it were on vacant Crown Land, they might be able to claim it under the *Aboriginal Land Rights (Northern Territory) Act 1976*. Topsy's statement that Wakulpu lay outside the boundary fence of a pastoral station showed her awareness of this possibility.

People involved in preparing land claims in this region of the Northern Territory must accurately identify sites such as Wakulpu on maps. Phrases such as Topsy's concerning boundary fences are often important in determining whether a site is on alienated or unalienated Crown land. Although the Aborigines of the Central Australian desert may not be familiar with ordinance survey maps, they are unerringly accurate in direction and orientation of their own sites to geographical features such as ranges of hills, soakages, and introduced land marks such as fences or station homesteads.

I asked Topsy who the appropriate person was to assist me in locating and mapping the site of Wakulpu.

> Ask that Johnny Nelson, my brother. When he was a young man, he was making a fence around from Singleton Station [i.e. west of Wauchope]. Ask him about Wakulpu. It's really outside the fence. It's straight down from that Pawurrinji, *kurlirra* [south]. It's straight *kalarra* [west] from that Wauchope. There's water there, a big waterhole with spring water. Wakulpu points straight to Wauchope. They were telling me. I was only a little kid. My mother would carry me in a *parraja* [wooden coolamon]. My granny, my mother's mother, and her brothers, that's their really country there.
>
> My grandmother, she was just like a man — tall and straight. Molly [Topsy's mother's brother's child] was like that. That's her nanna, my mother's side. She was a really tall one. You see Molly's face? Well, just like my mother. My mother carried me in a *parraja* in Wakulpu country. Then, when I was a little girl, I went walking in that country. Once we was stealing berries: my grandmother was making a bough shade and putting berries in the *parraja*. They used to tell us mob, 'Right, you kids, you stay home. We'll go and get some more'. I was shaking the fire-stick [to keep it alight]. I saw my grandmother's lot of food in the top of that tree in the bough shade. I didn't see my grandmother was walking back. You know what she did? She hit me with that digging stick. But my grandmother was too late, I had eaten it.
>
> When I was a bit bigger, maybe four, I was stealing *yakajirri* and *nganjawarli* [bush tomato — *Solanum*]. When I was really big and my grandmother was digging for *yarla* [bush potato], I kept watching her and she kept telling me, 'Watch out for the digging stick. It'll poke your eye out.' I kept looking at it and she threw the *yarla* at me.
>
> I never left my grandmother [mother's mother] alone. I used to be there always. I loved her very much. I always followed her — never my mum. She was still with us at the Six Mile [a ration depot operated from 1943 to 1945 by Mr and Mrs W.A. Long of the Aboriginal Inland Mission at a site 6 miles east of the Telegraph Station north of Tennant Creek]. She passed away there at that old place. Then we went to Phillip Creek [the settlement established by the Native Affairs Branch in 1945 but staffed by missionaries of the Australian Inland

Mission until 1951. Four years later, when the water supply proved inadequate, the mission was abandoned.] The missionary there taught us to read and write. Mr Long was there then. Remember, Diane. I was telling you about the frogs there? You caught that one [recorded it]? [I told Topsy I had.] Well, put it into my story here. It belongs here now.

On several occasions I have taken Warrabri women on nostalgic trips to their former home at Phillip Creek. In May 1977, while strolling through the mud-brick ruins of the mission, Topsy had shared her bittersweet memories of her life there with her foster children, Glenda and Roberta, and with my children, Genevieve and Morgan. During the daylight hours, Topsy moved confidently through the crumbling walls of the old dormitories, kitchen, bake-house and laundry. She spoke lightly of the official regime which had separated children from parents. However, after dark, as we cuddled into swags spread within the shelter of our improvised windbreak and tended our smoky mosquito-repelling fires, Topsy spoke again of missions and missionaries:

We had two missionaries, *yapa* [Aboriginal] ones here. We'd go in a big mob, with all the Warramunga kids. We was all coming into church at the Seven Mile (to the west side of that dreaming place we showed you, Diane). The mission was there before. That was when I was a little kid. We used to bring in frogs you know. We was little bit silly ones. We caught them in the swamp, and we'd take them to the missionary. 'Ah, you kids, take them back, all those things, and put them back in the water. This is a really important one. There, take it back and kneel down and pray for that thing.' That is what those missionaries would say. We'd take them back, chuck them in the water, the little lizards and all. We'd put them back in their holes; and the crabs too.

Once, I was really crazy. I brought that crab over with me. It didn't have any legs on it. We was just bringing it in. 'Oh, I want some salt, please,' I was asking. We was really stupid ones. We didn't know. 'For what? Show me what is in your bag.' I was standing with my bag behind my back. 'I want salt, please.' 'For what?' that lady one was asking. 'Show me first.' I showed that thing for her. 'Na, take that thing back in the water and you come and pray for that thing.' And we did, with no legs on, we put it back into the water. No legs ... no claws ... we put it back. We got back, and the missionary said 'come inside'. We was just kneeling down and praying for that thing with no legs.

Topsy laughed as she reached this point in her story. Glenda (Topsy's older foster-daughter, then aged ten), who was sitting wide-eyed in her swag asked, 'Will he grow another legs?' My kids had been suppressing their laughter in order to hear Topsy's tale, but they now joined in. Their explanation to Glenda of regeneration of the carapace of crabs only caused further mirth from Topsy and bewilderment for Glenda. 'Tell us more about the mission,' the kids pleaded.

Glenda (left), Topsy and Diane, July 1978 (Photograph by P. Ditton)

In the morning, we would come and eat little bread, little scones. We would still be hungry. Drink. We only would have one little drink. Cordial, like that. We'd stand up, line up. All the Warramunga, Warlpiri and Kaititj — all mixed up. He used to ask us for a song. 'Come on you kids, what song are we going to sing?' I remember one. We would kneel down and sing that one.

We was hungry, and one day I was thinking, 'I'm going to keep that frog. I'm not taking it for Mrs Cameron.' I took it to the camp, to my father's place. I cooked it and ate it; and next morning I went to Mrs Cameron. She liked me very well. She tried to take me to her place in America. This day she was asking the boys and girls, 'Did you see little Topsy?' 'I don't know. We didn't see her . . . We saw her in the creek . . . She was swimming there.'

When I got the frog, I took it to camp and I ate it all. I didn't tell the story. I told me mum. I'm going for Mrs Cameron — she's looking for me. I did. I was walking along. I saw a lot of kids. 'Come on dear,' she was saying. 'Come into my place. Where you went yesterday?' She was patting my hair. 'No, I was swimming. I went straight home. I was a bit sick.' 'Don't you tell lies,' she said. I was thinking. She took me into a little room inside and she made me sit down on the bed. 'Now, tell me the truth. What happened to you yesterday, Topsy? I saw only the other mob of kids was here.' I told her straight: 'I took the frog.' 'What did you do with that frog?' 'I ate it all.' 'I see.' She put me in a little jail, in the home, a room with just her. She was telling me a story, about Jesus and Moses. 'Don't you eat anything. Don't hurt anything. It's not made to eat. It's made for your friend.'

The first missionaries was coming to help the people. The white fellas were trying to kill all the *yapa*, and the missionary was helping us. They gave us meat, only, that's all. Plenty of rations and clothes. After that they went away. Those two, Mr and Mrs Long came and stayed. That was when the Army was happening. I was little bit big then. He was good, that Mr Long — our cousin.

That other missionary, the *yapa* one . . . he was talking to my mother and father. 'We're going to take this little girl away. She'll come back for you mob.' I had long hair then, you know. That missionary was telling my father he was going to take me away. Next time, next day, my father got away. We ran away at night into the bush. For good. We didn't return to go for that place again. We was just keep walking this way now to bush, because, you know, he was asking my mother and father for taking me away. He was going to try to make me a missionary to that America. In the night we came back to Greenwood, to the old station. We stayed there for good then. Mick [Topsy's half-brother] was a little baby then. We didn't go back to Tennant Creek. We stayed there until that Mr Long came to that old Telegraph Station. It took us about a week to walk. I was about ten, like Maureen [Topsy's mother's brother's daughter's daughter].

I remember that Army time. That Army mob was asking me, 'What's your name little boy?' I was only wearing shorts. All those Warramunga kids was saying, 'We got a new missionary.' We went back and they was telling me, 'We've got a new missionary now.' We stayed there for a long time. Mr Thomas was taking the place for Mr Long after he got away to Alice Springs.

Ted Egan [a popular Northern Territory Welfare Branch Officer during the 1960s, now a folk-singer], he used to run for us. 'You got lolly for we mob?' 'Yes, I got lolly.' He'd lift that big lid and get lollies in the tin. He was just Army bloke giving us lollies. (Now he comes and sings all around this country.) When he was really young, he was really good looking. Then he was coming back and he was saying, 'I know those greedy ones.' Everyone was really young then, and other mobs would visit us.

My father was cutting trees and making that airstrip. That white man, that Army mob, was really good. My father was just cutting trees. We used to stay at the Telegraph Station, and my father would go back into town and work for the week, from that hill the other side of the water hole.

Well, we was staying there. Mr Brown's father [an old Aboriginal man, now dead, known as 'Chicken Jack'], he was there too. In the morning one day, we was fighting for damper. The others was chasing us and saying, 'I'm going to hit you two.' And he [Chicken Jack] was throwing a stone at us. That Jungarrayi [Mr Brown] and me was up in a tree. I tried to jump over but it was little bit long way. I just let go and fell down. I broke my leg (it was a stony place). That was when we was only kids fighting for damper! They took me to the hospital in Tennant Creek and they rang up for that Mr Long. He came and prayed for us. The Army plane took me to Alice Springs. That was the first time I went in a plane. I was too sick to see anything. I stayed in Alice for a long time. I had family there. I was big when I came back. We went there, in the Army time, to the Bungalow [a government ration-depot near the Telegraph Station north of Alice Springs]. There was a big camp there. People from all different places. That *kuminjayi* [a term of respect used by Warlpiri to replace the name of a dead person] was there too, just working.

At the mission at Phillip Creek we used to stay in the dormitory. We was separate. Our parents stayed in the camp. They took the kids away from their parents.

When she showed me the camp sites of her parents and the separate dormitories at the Phillip Creek Native Settlement for male and female children of school age, Topsy's gentle reminiscence masked the grim reality of the impact of mission policy on family life. Particularly vivid in my memory is Topsy's account of how she eluded the missionaries at curfew one evening and ran away to join her parents at Tennant Creek, where her father was working. Topsy showed me the remains of the kitchen, at the rear of which had stood a large rubbish bin. By hiding in the bin, Topsy had eluded the missionaries and planned her trek through the bush at night to her family. Aboriginal children fear moving shapes in the dark and rarely wander away from camp in the evening, but Topsy had been so determined to be reunited with her parents that she had walked 30 km through the night. She was aged perhaps eleven at the time.

I was growing up at Phillip Creek, and I was working for that Mr and Mrs Ingham — only for a little while — and then we were getting ready to move to Warrabri. I was about 19 [in 1955].

I was promised to an old man, but I didn't go to him — I was too frightened. I stayed with the Inghams. Everyone was moving on the truck to the Warrabri, but I went in the car with Mrs Ingham. It was a black one with a double seat and a funny face. We went past the Warrabri and stayed in Alice Springs for a couple of weeks. They were still building at Warrabri. We lived in number six house.

Then at Warrabri, after the Inghams left, I started working for Mr Lovegrove [then Superintendent, now Director-General, Department of the Chief Minister, Northern Territory] for three straight years — cleaning, cooking lunch for him, sometimes stew, some vegetables, steak, washing clothes and ironing. Now when I stopped working for Mr Lovegrove I started working in the kitchen [a communal dining-room and kitchen for Warrabri residents]. I worked there for two years, serving up to staff when everyone used to eat in the dining-room. (It's closed now, eh?)

After the next Christmas, I started in the sewing factory with Mrs Loader. She was Nanna for all you mob. Glenda was her girl, but

Roberta was her special private girl for her when she was young. I worked there for six years. It had only just finished when you came to Warrabri, Diane. They're talking about starting it up again.

Although Topsy lived at Warrabri from 1956 until 1978, when she began spending more and more time in Tennant Creek, she had been to Darwin to undertake training courses in dressmaking in 1974. She was a widow at the time and, like several of her contemporaries, had managed to avoid entering into any permanent marital arrangements after her period of mourning (usually about two years) had concluded. Her late husband had been many years her senior; the marriage had been an arranged one. As a mature widow, Topsy had the right to choose a subsequent husband herself, and her stay in Darwin had allowed her a freedom and a widening of her circle of friends which would have been difficult to achieve at Warrabri. In the mid-1970s she was a widow who was enjoying her new-found status.

Topsy's memories of Darwin were vivid, and I had often heard her speak of her work and her friends in the 'Top End'.

In Darwin I was sewing, knitting all that patterns . . . cutting. That old lady is still there. Still asking for me. I forget her name, she's same like Mrs Loader. My hair was really long then. I had cousins and sisters there, but I missed my family. I had good friends, one girl from Yirrkala, Jenny — she used to take me out hunting and show me foods from the bush, and yams, on Saturdays and Sundays.

I came away from Darwin when that cyclone was coming, in the morning. [Cyclone Tracy devastated Darwin on Christmas morning, 1974.] I heard that news when I was back at Warrabri. I was lucky all right. I came back for a couple of days, with money for me mum and the kids. I went back again after that cyclone.

When I came back, I was working for the Cartwrights [Department of Aboriginal Affairs officers at Warrabri] too and then with you, Diane. That's all. I've got nothing now — no work. I look miserable and just sit around. If I get a job my pension money [supporting mother's benefit] will stop, and I need it for my [foster] kids, Glenda, Dion and Roberta. That Dion is still at Yirara [the residential college in Alice Springs]. They might make him a man [initiate him] this year at business time up here. That Roberta still has chest trouble. I take her straight to the hospital every time she is sick. Might be a little woman. Not like your *Nungarrayi* [my daughter Genevieve, by now aged 12], *Nakamarra* [i.e. Diane]. She's growing straight and tall, like my Glenda.

That is how Topsy wanted to tell her story that chilly September morning in 1979 in Tennant Creek as we sat warming ourselves, sheltered from the wind by her tin humpy. Her family camp was located just below the knob, known locally as Blueberry Hill. A number of Aboriginal people have camped in the area for many years. Her father, an old man aged over seventy, with whom I had travelled many miles into the country west of Tennant Creek, now lay weak and dying. His family said he had lived his life. There would be no elaborate mourning rituals for him when he died. In his prime he had been one of the knowledgeable men of the desert, but now he was beginning to pass on his authority to a younger successor. It was his close family who gathered to grieve and mourn.

Because he and Topsy had not accompanied us on our July trip to Pawurrinji, I had brought back a number of photographs for him and his family to see. This day in September had been my first opportunity to give the photographs to the family. They were passed around and discussed. Then they were held in a bundle by Topsy, who massaged her blind father's body with them while murmuring 'Pawurrinji, Pawurrinji'. He has seen it now, she told me. When he died a month later, his loss was deeply felt by those who loved him. He died, Topsy told me, knowing that his country was safe.

While her father was alive, Topsy was a dutiful daughter. She visited his camp daily, often sleeping there to be near him. When his pension money ran out, she brought gifts of food. During this taxing period Topsy refused to marry the man chosen by her deceased husband's relatives. 'I must stay near my father,' she stated simply. When she did remarry, in late 1977, it was to a man of her own choosing (a union initially much frowned upon by her own family). She then moved from Warrabri to Tennant Creek, where her new husband was working. While her parents remained at Warrabri she visited regularly, a round trip of 300 km by taxi (the only reliable means of transport). Finally, early in 1978, her family moved to Tennant Creek. Topsy then shifted from the main Blueberry Hill camp to another site, some hundred metres away, where her family had set up camp in an old tin shed. Her husband was left in their former camp to bemoan the loss of his new wife. She returned often to visit her husband, but her days and her energies were spent with her father.

In telling her story for outsiders Topsy spoke of 'her country', which included that of Pawurrinji and the country of her mother's mother where she was born. She told of her life as a child on a cattle station, a mission and a settlement, but she made little mention of her present life in a town camp at Tennant Creek.

In late 1980 she began work with the Homemakers Service of Tennant Creek, an organisation funded by the Department of Community Development, and in early 1981 she moved into a house in the town. In many ways her life changed dramatically: she is now the wage-earning head of a household. (I was able to call her on her work telephone to check details of her story.) But Topsy's life still centres on her family, and her major concern remains the maintenance of her country.

In writing of her life I found I needed contact with her country — I needed to be in Central Australia, where the smells, sounds and colours were evocative of Topsy. In Canberra it was all too remote. There are many more tales I could tell of Topsy's recent life, of our shared experience and friendship, of how our children grew together, and of how Topsy taught me to be a woman in her society and taught me to look anew at my own. I shall tell of a few of these, but in my own words.

My children and Topsy's became very close at school, at home and in the bush. They called each other 'brother' and 'sister' and had the same 'skins'. Dion made a little brush shelter to protect Morgan (then aged eight, and four years Dion's junior) one day when they had recklessly ventured too far from camp in the heat of the day. He also taught Morgan to swear, an essential for survival for an Aboriginal child. Glenda tested Genevieve's comprehension of kinship with kinship riddles and played endlessly with the dolls and 'dress-ups' at our place.

On Genevieve's tenth birthday in 1977 we decided to have a party, a novelty for her peers at school. Glenda and Roberta willingly helped me prepare 'fairy-bread' (buttered bread sprinkled with coloured 'hundreds and thousands') and chocolate crackles, but watched incredulously as I set them aside until the party was due to begin. Topsy arrived after we had eaten. She had been too busy, she said. When the girls finally settled down to play with the dolls, Topsy unwrapped her present to Genevieve — a small wooden baby-carrier, just the right size for the favourite doll, always known as Mompy.

I have seen Topsy several times since we recorded her story in 1979: once when she attended the ANZAAS Congress* in Adelaide in May 1980 and then travelled on with me to Canberra for a short holiday; and again at Warrabri during the taking of evidence in the Warlmanpa, Warlpiri, Mudbara and Waramungu (Warramunga) land-claim hearing in October and November 1980.

In early 1980, a group of women (mostly Europeans) who have long cared about Aboriginal communities began to make plans for a symposium at the Adelaide ANZAAS. Aboriginal women from the remote north, from country towns and cities, joined with these women to discuss a wide range of issues. I had arranged for Topsy and Myrtle, an older woman with whom I had worked at Warrabri, in Tennant Creek and in her new bush camp at Ngurrantiji (south-east of Tennant Creek) to attend. They flew from Tennant Creek to Alice Springs and then to Adelaide to attend the conference. Everything was new; everything noted.

During the first day of the conference, Topsy and Myrtle stayed very close. They sat in the front row of the seminar room, gave their full attention to the speakers and vigorously indicated their approval of other women's pleas for recognition of the contribution Aboriginal women made to their society. The session continued late into the afternoon, and we were all tired. Topsy had been asking about Adelaide, its history and its people, but once back at the hostel where they were staying, the tenor of our conversation changed. 'We have something to say too,' said Topsy. 'It's the same for all of us,' Myrtle added. 'I'm going to tell about my country,' Topsy insisted. 'I'll make them proud, for that old Rosie, and I'm going to tell them everything when we get back.'

After the conference we drove together from Adelaide to Canberra. We took some time to explore the Barossa Valley and to sample wines. At first neither Topsy nor Myrtle were keen to try the wines: their experience of drinking in the towns of the Northern Territory had been of flagon port. However, after the second or third vineyard, Topsy

---

* The Australian and New Zealand Association for the Advancement of Science.

became an expert on dry whites and thoroughly familiar with the vocabulary of wine buffs.

The irrigation areas of south-eastern Australia, the soil types, the variety of cultivated plants, the denseness of settlement, the lushness of the fields and the ubiquitous Murray River became the distinguishing features of 'my country' for Topsy and Myrtle. 'What I could do if I had that water,' Myrtle said thoughtfully. With her brothers and their children, Myrtle has established gardens at their new home at Ngurrantiji, a homeland centre south of Tennant Creek, but her plans are constantly thwarted by the lack of water.

Although this was the first time Topsy had visited southern cities her natural poise and scholarly curiosity sustained her. Her sense of topography and direction confounded us all. After only one day in Canberra, from the lookout on Black Mountain she confidently and correctly indicated the location of my house, the home of the friends with whom we had dined the day before and the road along which we had travelled into Canberra from Yass.

In both Adelaide and Canberra we shopped and watched a great deal of television. 'Dallas' became their favourite program. Topsy and Myrtle happily unrolled their swags in my living room, turned up the heating to create their usual semi-tropical environment, while the temperature outside dropped below freezing, then set about decoding the kinship system of these Texan tycoons. Shopping presented greater problems because we had to negotiate escalators and lifts. The latter were eventually accepted as the 'push button thing' but escalators were forsworn. We bought clothes, new blankets, chocolates, enriching face creams, and presents for all the family members left behind in Tennant Creek. We then bought cases to transport all the new purchases home. 'Canberra,' Topsy said when I asked for her impression, 'was too cold.' 'It was so cold,' she said, 'I didn't even laugh.'

After the Adelaide-Canberra trip I didn't see Topsy again until October 1980 when we both travelled to Warrabri, where a land-claim hearing was scheduled. I had come to act as a consultant to Central Land Council of Alice Springs (who were presenting the claim on behalf of the traditional owners of a tract of land south-west and north-west of Tennant Creek). Topsy came to give evidence as a claimant to the country of Pawurrinji within this claim. She explained to Mr Justice Toohey, the Aboriginal Land Commissioner, her knowledge of the land, her relatives' attachment to the country and the way in which women's *yawalyu* kept the land alive. When asked about her father, who had died in late 1978, Topsy replied:

> Yes, but he was trying to go to Pawurrinji, trying to reach his country to go back and die in his own place . . . because they like to go back to their own land, back to the place they come from and where they were born. That is why old people (some of them who are still young) want to go back in peace to their country. This is my father's family, because my grandfather was really proud of his people. He was really proud of all the people, and they were coming to his place. He never made a bad enemy from every tracks and every place. He never made

a bad enemy, never. He was really friendly, and they are his people, and they are still my father's people, and they want to go back to Pawurrinji.

Topsy explained that Warrabri was not her country, and thus her family's residence there constituted a breach of etiquette:

> This place is somebody else's sacred site, and they are buried up in someone else's sacred site tree over there. They want to go back to their own land and sacred site. All the people of Pawurrinji want to go back to Pawurrinj because a lot of old people have been passed away, and some of them young people never look back to that country and sacred site, even old people. They never look back at his own sacred site, his own important thing. They never look back, they all been pass away. They never look back at this place. That's why they are thinking and talking and crying, feeling sorry. They don't want to live any more in somebody else's land and sacred sites. This belongs to Alyawarra and their sacred site.

In speaking of Alyawarra rights in country at Warrabri, Topsy was indicating the deepest and most obvious division in the Warrabri population. Warrabri was chosen by the Northern Territory Welfare Branch as a suitable place to resettle the Warlpiri and Warramunga of Phillip Creek who were trucked there in 1955-56. Their presence gives constant offence to the traditional owners of the area, the Alyawarra and Kaititj and is a cause of shame for Warlpiri, who must celebrate their rituals in someone else's land. To minimise the tensions and to emphasise their affiliation to land the Alyawarra and Kaititj camp to the east of the settlement core of school, hospital, police station, store and offices, whereas the Warlpiri and Warramunga camp to the west. Thus each camp group is oriented towards the country of their ancestors. Even so, as Topsy stated in her evidence, the unhappiness and alienation of Warlpiri residents at Warrabri remains.

At the conclusion of their evidence, Topsy and other women requested that they be able to stage a *yawalyu* for the judge. 'We have spoken of our country; now we wish to show it', Topsy told me. As the women sat to paint their bodies with designs which encoded knowledge of ancestral activity, they sang softly of the travels and sites visited by the dreamtime heroes. I had often seen women paint for their dreamings; yet on this occasion Topsy and Rosie were wearing a design I had not seen before. Topsy confirmed she was wearing it for the first time. With tears in her eyes she said, 'Ask me later.' We were sitting very close to each other in a group of about thirty women, none of whom seemed to be aware of Topsy's distress. 'It was my father's country,' she said. 'Why did he die? Others are still alive who are older than he is.' We cried together. Still none of the assembled women appeared to take any notice.

After the women had displayed their body designs and traced out the travels of the ancestors with their dancing feet, I took Topsy home to her camp. We sat chatting for a while. 'That pattern was my father's own one,' she explained. 'Before he died he give it Engineer Jack, his *kurdungurlu*, to look after until I was ready for it. Today Engineer said it was right to use it. It's my country now. We'll go back.' Pride, defiance and determination radiated from her. With the announcement in September 1983 of the acceptance of the Commissioner's recommendation of the claim this hope has become a reality.

The critically important role of *kurdungurlu* to act as custodians of knowledge, objects and sites has been well documented in land-claim hearings in Central Australia. When a person as important and as knowledgeable as Topsy's father dies, all his property, including his ritual knowledge, is set aside for a period, sometimes forever. Ideally, his ritual partner — his *kurdungurlu* — has the responsibility for rekindling the knowledge for the remaining members of the land-maintaining group. The sharing of knowledge between the *kirda* (the patrilineal descendants of the ancestral heroes) and the *kurdungurlu* (the children of the senior women of the patriline) ensures that knowledge is spread throughout a number of families. This acts as a safeguard on the loss of knowledge.

From Topsy, I learnt much that was critical to my work: a study of women's rituals in Central Australia. From her also, I had learned much about friendship. Being in Topsy's company will always remain for me a cherished memory. It is also a hope for the future — our children will continue to be close; our paths will continue to cross. It is impossible to disentangle my personal feelings from the professional aspects of my fieldwork; indeed, to do so would be a denial of my fieldwork.

Additional reading

Bell, Diane (1978). For our families: the Kurundi walk-off and the Ngurrantji venture. *Aboriginal History 2* (1-2), 33-61

Nelson, Topsy (1980). Her evidence in the Transcripts of the Proceedings, *Aboriginal Land Rights (Northern Territory) Act 1976* re the Warlmanpa, Warlpiri, Mudbura and Warumunga Land Claim, before His Honour Mr Justice Toohey, Aboriginal Land Commissioner, Warrabri, 29 November 1980

2

Mondalmi: One of the Saltwater People

Catherine Berndt

I first met Mondalmi in 1946, when the old Methodist Mission boat *Aroetta* stayed for a couple of days at Goulburn Island on its way to north-eastern Arnhem Land. But I did not get to know her personally until I returned to Goulburn Island late in 1947. She had been working in the mission house; fortunately for me, the missionary's wife asked her to help me instead. In a motherly way she took me under her wing to teach me what she thought any educated person should know about the country and the people who lived there. The difference in age between us was almost enough for her to regard me as a daughter — but one in need of proper instruction.

Mondalmi was then only a name to me. I had learnt of her at Oenpelli, where she had relatives. Mondalmi's husband was a Gunwinggu-speaker from the mainland. She was Maung, and proud of it. She set about providing me with an account of Maung culture and people. I had begun to learn a little Gunwinggu, but knew only a few words of Maung. Mondalmi spoke Maung, Yiwadja, and also Gunbalang. She understood Gunwinggu but said she could not speak it. She felt hesitant about her ability to make long statements in grammatically correct Gunwinggu, although she could have done this at least as adequately as many other non-Gunwinggu-speakers. Her second reason, perhaps more important, was her strong sense of Maung identity.

She was 'one of the saltwater people', a person of the islands and the adjacent mainland coast. As she put it, she was not someone from the 'inside bush'. Her Gunwinggu connections were not with the truly inland people, but with those whose territories adjoined, and to some extent overlapped with, areas claimed by Yiwadja and Maung speakers, towards the coast.

People growing up in any society need to have a working knowledge of that society. They need to have an idea of its rules and ideals, what is expected of them in relation to other people — and what actually happens. There are always some people who are more articulate than others, or better informed, or both. Every member of a society is different. One person's story is never enough. But one story can give a personal slant on a larger, more complex and impersonal whole and illuminate some of the trends and changes that affect the course of social events, as well as personal lives, in a particular region.

At the time when Mondalmi and I were getting to know each other, my husband (Ronald M. Berndt) was becoming friendly with her brother, Lazarus Lamilami. Later, my husband, at Lamilami's request, got him some tapes and a recorder so that he could assemble his life-story. I

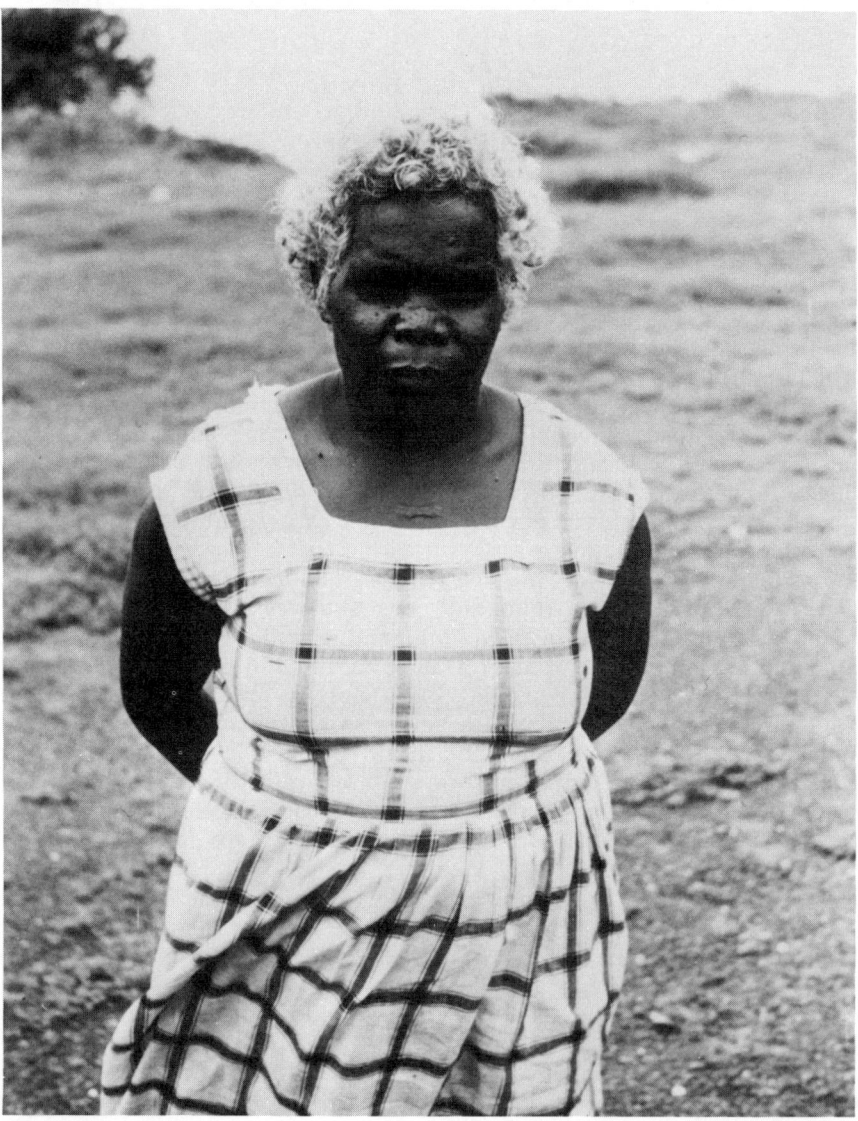

Mondalmi in 1961

helped to prepare the final version for publication. This task underlined, for me, the linkage between the personal view of an articulate commentator and the 'typicality' of life histories. Lamilami's statements about life in western Arnhem Land point up the clash of interest between traditional and introduced ways — and his efforts to reconcile these, at least to his own satisfaction. By then he was an ordained Methodist minister, the first Aboriginal person in Arnhem Land to achieve that ambition, but he did not see his ministry as leading him away from his traditional background.

Mondalmi (pronounced Mondálmi) is merely mentioned here and there in Lamilami's book, partly because of the conventional constraint between brothers and sisters, including a tabu on uttering one another's personal names. However, the convention does not indicate a lack of affection and mutual help. Lamilami and his sister were very much attached to each other, and alike in many respects. Her story complements his.

The people of western Arnhem Land, particularly those from the Goulburn Islands (about 320 km north-east of Darwin) and the adjacent mainland, suffered more severely from outside contact and over a longer period than their eastern neighbours. Even though the survivors were able to keep their own languages and something of their traditional culture, the effects were far-reaching. The remarkable thing was that people like Mondalmi and her brother were so resilient, adaptive, and good-humoured in the face of domination by outsiders.

'Macassan' traders from the Celebes used to visit the coast regularly until prohibited in the early 1900s. European military settlements were based at mainland sites west of the Goulburn Islands from 1827. The Port Essington site was abandoned in 1849, but the Cobourg Cattle Company maintained a station there. Later, there was a customs depot in Bowen Straits, and in 1883 a Chinese-labour timber-cutting camp at Mt Norris Bay, near Croker Island. From the early 1880s there were reports that the Macassans paid Aborigines largely in 'spirits' for services in the pearlshell and trepang fisheries and that Macassans were responsible for disease and prostitution. By about 1900 the same thing was being said about Europeans. A government 'Protector of Aborigines' reporting in 1908 referred to depopulation and disease at Croker Island. At South Goulburn Island he was told that 'Aborigines who worked for Europeans gathering trepang were given a daily ration of rum or square gin.'

During the last century and continuing into the 1920s, European 'explorers', traders, beachcombers and a few missionaries moved through the region or set up outposts. Until just before World War II Japanese pearling and trepanging boats frequented the coast, anchoring regularly at the mouth of the King River, a little to the south-east of the Goulburn Islands. In the mid-1930s Aborigines reportedly assembled there and became involved in 'orgies' of prostitution and liquor-drinking.

In 1916 the Methodist Overseas Mission came to South Goulburn Island, extending later to Milingimbi, Elcho Island (1921–23) and Yirrkalla (1935) in eastern Arnhem Land. Oenpelli, formerly a government cattle station, was taken over by the Church Missionary Society in 1925. In 1957 a government welfare settlement, Maningrida, was set up near the mouth of the Liverpool River, east of the Goulburn Islands.

In 1931 Arnhem Land was officially declared an Aboriginal Reserve. The fact that non-Aborigines had to obtain official permits before entering the Reserve, a provision that was tightened up following World War II, strengthened the illusion held by many Arnhem Landers that the land was still theirs.

The war itself brought renewed activity of a different sort, with military control of the Northern Territory, and Army Aboriginal settlements set up outside the reserve on the main Darwin-Alice Springs road. But it also had the effect of lessening mission and government pressure for change in Aboriginal society and keeping commercial exploitation at a low level. Mission settlements remained small and informal. Differences in living standards between Aborigines and missionaries were not as obvious then as they became later on. The full impact of liquor and mining developments did not really hit the region until the 1970s. Lamilami lived to see the beginnings of it — his sister did not.

The father of Mondalmi and Lamilami belonged to a group called Manganowal, which occupied country between Maung and Yiwadja to the west of the Goulburn Islands. After he died their mother married one of his close brothers, their 'second father', and bore two more sons. Their mother was from the Junction Bay area to the east of the Islands; her mother was Walang, from farther east but still on the coast. Lamilami emphasised his mainland birth-site, but Mondalmi located her specific 'country' at Wighu on South Goulburn Island, the point across the bay from the mission station. It was within the range of related peoples: Manganowal was more Maung than it was Yiwadja, but Maung and Yiwadja were 'company'; they belonged closely together without being identified as one.

Before Maningrida was established, Goulburn Island mission station had a core of residents, mostly Maung, supplemented by a fluctuating population of Walang and other 'eastern' people. Even today it is a small settlement of 200 to 250 people. Some paused briefly on their way to or from Darwin; others stayed longer. Contacts with 'Macassans' and other outsiders had long encouraged these people to mix with other Aborigines whose language and culture differed from their own. They sorted out their social relationships to ensure that their rights and obligations could be defined. Where they could not trace actual genealogical links, these had to be nominal, but consanguineal kinship was the basis for the closest ties.

Mondalmi identified her own mother's mother's mother and mother's mother's mother's brother, her *wulubulu,* as one basis for tracing close kinship links with a fairly wide range of people. She used this example to stress the significance of the lines of descent through females. She also used it as a starting point for teaching me about kinship, telling me what terms her own children would use for her *wulubulu,* whom they had never seen, and explaining that the terms went round in a circle: they would call her old *wulubulu* (female and male) by 'sister' and 'brother' terms.

She made it clear that paternal descent, in the 'father's line', was just as important. It was especially significant, she said, because through it people had their primary affiliation with their 'true' country. A man's sons and daughters belonged to the same named territorial unit as he did. Ideally this unit, the *namanamaidj,* was the source of personal names — all except nicknames, or 'joking names'. Getting to know Mondalmi meant getting to know that she was of the *namanamaidj* called Maiirwulidj, or Merwulidj. And the name Mondalmi came from her close *wilubilu,* father's sister. Her second name, Milimili, came from her second father's side, a more distant *wilubilu* who was Yiwadja, and whom Mondalmi had never seen. It was a Yelama name, from the *namanamaidj* of Mondalmi's second father. But that was all right, Mondalmi said, because he had married her mother and was like a real father to her and her brother. Mondalmi's nickname was Ngalwububul, abbreviated to Bubu, meaning a 'short person'.

Through her mother, Mondalmi belonged to three social categories. Every Maung person belonged by birth to one or other of the two moiety divisions, *(na)madgu* and *(na)ngaraidgu.* Each of these was again divided into two, making four semi-moieties. There were also eight subsection categories, four in each moiety. As well as these identifications traced through the mother, another kind of moiety division based on descent through the father had spread more recently from people farther east. So first, Mondalmi was *ngalmadgu* (the female form of *namadgu*). Second, she was *yarigarngurg,* a semi-moiety that has as its main symbol *obaidj* (or *wubadj*), water. Her subsection was *ngalangila.* Finally, in the moiety division introduced from eastern Arnhem Land, she was *yiridja.*

These points are crucial. Everyone in western Arnhem Land belongs to stipulated categories. Traditionally, actual kinship and nominal kinship were used in conjunction with all of these categories as a blueprint for behaviour, including correct marriage arrangements and religious ritual co-operation. Regional variations complicated the picture, but also provided identity through contrast.

The Methodist Overseas Mission in Arnhem Land tried to use a family-centred approach, and to emphasise personal relationships between missionaries and Aborigines. The rule was that in each mission community the superintendent and his wife were called 'father' and 'mother' and other missionaries and lay helpers were 'older brother' and 'older sister'. Mondalmi, therefore, at first addressed me politely as *lala,* older sister. But really that did not suit our relationship.

My first friend at Oenpelli (married to a relative of Mondalmi) was about the same age as myself. She had informally adopted me as a sister, putting me in her own subsection, *ngalngaridj.* Mondalmi belonged to the *ngalangila* subsection in the opposite moiety. In the circumstances, she could not really call me 'sister'. According to the local system, she should have called me *wilubilu,* 'auntie', 'father's sister', and I would call her *ngawinj,* 'niece'. In that system such terms did not depend on chronological age: a *wilubilu* could be much younger than her *ngawinj* and junior in status, even though the term formally signified a senior generation (a person's actual father's sisters, for instance). Mondalmi waited tactfully to see whether I would give up my *ngalngaridj* identification while I was at Goulburn Island. To her it implied too much interest in Gunwinggu (rather than Maung) concerns. When I evaded this decision, she tried not to show her disapproval. Sometimes she called me by my personal name or, if she was feeling a bit cross or impatient when I was too slow to learn something or too eager to hear Gunwinggu rather than Maung, she addressed me almost coolly as 'Mrs Berndt'. Otherwise *wilubilu* was a kind of compromise that fitted the traditional situation.

To know any Aboriginal person in western Arnhem Land in more than a superficial way, it is necessary to know something about time-honoured categories and affiliation and behavioural patterns. Mondalmi went into considerable detail in explaining not only the various categories, but how they intermeshed and contrasted, how they were used, and what was 'right' and 'wrong' in regard to betrothal and marriage arrangements. To her, and to others, these were important matters. Therefore, they are important to all who want to meet Aboriginal people on their own terms. But outsiders usually find it easier to understand the more familiar 'common human', nuclear family relationships. Of course these immediate relationships are of great concern to Aborigines too. They simply place them in a wider framework.

When she was quite small Mondalmi had been 'promised' (betrothed), to an older man, but they never married. The man who eventually became her husband was asked by one of the missionary-founders of the Goulburn Island station to come and settle there. Oenpelli people, describing him before we met, called him, in English, a 'preacher-man', someone who always spoke in the church. He brought with him his mother, two brothers and two sisters. His English name was John; his everyday Gunwinggu name was Gadawar. His mother and Mondalmi's mother belonged to the same *namanamaidj*, Murwan. Mondalmi's betrothed husband gave up his claim to her, saying he was 'too old' and therefore 'John could have her'. According to Lamilami's account, his sister 'was older than some of the girls when she got married', perhaps 'nearly twenty'. He gave her birthdate as 1906 and his own as 1908. According to the birth records kept by the mission, she bore her first child in April 1928, her second in 1930, a stillborn daughter in 1936, a living one in 1940, and another son in 1943. The next son, Bunug, born in February 1947, was often with us during those early teaching-sessions, lying asleep beside her as we sat talking.

By the early 1950s she had six sons and one daughter. Her husband (who died in 1971) did not take a second wife, and she remained with him until her death in 1969. I had spent time with her in 1961 and 1964; but in 1966 I had to by-pass Goulburn Island and went instead to Oenpelli and to Croker Island, where her brother Lamilami was living. To my great regret she was gone when I next returned to Goulburn Island.

Mondalmi told me a great deal about her own life and her experiences. She talked about her close relatives: who they were and where they lived, about their betrothals, marriages and other events, and in some cases about their deaths. She knew a wide range of other people and was a keen observer, noting and thinking about what they said and did. She told me a great deal about her children: how they got their personal names, some of their experiences, and something of her hopes for their future lives and their happiness. But this is her story, not theirs, and I am sure that they will not mind remaining in the background of what I regard as a tribute to her memory. She did not say much about her own

early childhood, except for isolated comments. I have selected r
cences that require little explanation, omitting any that seem too personal.

The early accounts she gave me, mainly in 1947, were all in her expressive local version of Aboriginal English. I have left them more ar less as I wrote them down. Over the years, other women were involved in our discussions, and we talked about their experiences and attitudes, as well as about stories and songs and local happenings. Our conversations then were mostly carried on in a mixture of Gunwinggu, Maung and English, depending on who was present.

One of my earliest questions, once we had begun to talk easily and seriously together, was 'What is the first thing you remember?'

First thing I remember . . . Well, let me see . . . I didn't notice the boat coming; I didn't look at it. (Quite small, like a whaleboat.) It was a very wet day, raining and raining, early in the morning. My proper father was away working trepang; only my half father was there. My mother and father, they keeping me away from the hut. They didn't want that *balanda,* that white man, to see me. They wouldn't go near that mission (this the time they clearing land for the mission); and anybody came, they would send me away. They frightened that white man might catch me and take me to the mission.

So I was out there sitting under a little bush, and I had a little bottle in my arms — that was my baby. And it was very wet, so I had a piece of paperbark over my head. (Over my head and shoulders, like a cape.) But it was getting very cold and I didn't like to get wet like that, so I ran to that hut. My mother didn't see me go.

That white man standing up and he saw me. (Mr Lawrence. I think Mr Watson was at the mission too, that time. His wife was there, and they had a little girl.) He asked them, 'Who that little girl? What's the name belonging to her father and her mother?' So they told him what my name, and he listening to them.

My mother looking for me now — looking and looking. My father, too. They didn't see me go away. First time they thought I must be lost. Then after while they found me sitting by the fire warming my self in that hut. Then there was a noise, and that white man came in. I very frightened. I pulled that blanket right over my head, and lying down, I wouldn't look. That white man bent his head and came right inside that hut. I was too frightened to look. His hands were all white, and I didn't like to see them. And he had boots. They looked funny. I djdn't want to look at his boots. I wouldn't look at him or talk to him. He was standing there looking at me. So after while he went away. I was very frightened. He had one umbrella — I thought it was a devil, or a spirit: all shut up when he was inside. When he went out he put it up, and I was very frightened.

Then he came back. He had some flour and sugar, but I wouldn't eat them. I didn't like to see his hands, they so white. He said to them, I want to take this little girl back to the mission. She can go to school there, and we can look after her.' That's the time my brother Lazarus was very sick.

We talking, and talking. So after while they said, 'All right, she can go.' So we went back in the little boat, my father carrying me. I said to him, 'That very nice man.' He said, 'They all right to you, but they not nice to me.'

My mother and my brother came too. First time, she didn't want him to have that medicine — only she thought, 'We better try it, might be it's all right.' Before, she been making for him some of that other medicine — you know, those green ants mixed up in water. He used to drink it for his bad cough. So she was thinking, 'Might be these white people can make him better, because we don't know much about medicine.' And she took him up to get some. True, too! After a while he got better. I forget what time, might be about two weeks my mother stopped there. After that they went away and left me at the mission.

They said, 'This little girl can go to school, and we teach her to read and write, and to sew.' So I stopped in the dormitory. I can't remember all the girls in the dormitory that time. [She named some.] Other big girls, too, only I didn't take notice of them. I can't remember their names.

There was a Sister there, her name was Miss Matthews. She showed us how to make baskets, like the people do at Point McLeay [in South Australia]. She used to talk to us about Point McLeay and the people that live there. We often thinking about Miss Matthews — we wonder if she still alive, what place she living in now.

Some boys there, too. They had a dormitory. I can't remember their names. Only that was the time just about everybody ran away; only a few of us left. Only a few old people stopping in the camp. Nearly everybody gone, and the dormitory just about empty. There was a ceremony at Malay Bay. A *gowar* ceremony — Yiwadja people, some people from the Liverpool [River], and some from Oenpelli side. The missionaries were bit wild, because nearly everybody gone from the mission that time.

Living at the mission station brought opportunities for travelling farther afield. One trip that she especially remembered was Elcho Island (Galiwin'ku). The characters mentioned are her daughter Miriam (seven-and-a-half years old in 1947), Medeg, the youngest sister of the man who became Mondalmi's husband, and two eastern Arnhem Land girls, Bali and Buraana.

When I little girl yet, smaller than Miriam, I went to Elcho on the mission boat. There was a captain, a man from Badu — I forget his name — and Mr Haymer [spelling not certain]. Mr Haymer was a white man. Medeg came too.

Sometimes when the girls were good, they used to take us for trip, for holiday, on the mission boat — sometimes to Darwin, only this time to Elcho Island. Sister used to go with us.

There was only one house at Elcho that time, and another one they just starting it. Mr Jennison [Rev. J.C. Jennison] was there, and his wife, and one little girl belonging to him. Bali was there with her mother and father. She used to come and play with us. I used to go down to the beach sometimes with that girl belonging to Mr Jennison, and we used to play in the sand and go for swim. Medeg didn't come. She didn't like to because she a big girl and had breasts. So she used to stay in room with Sister, and Bali used to come down and play with us.

When we were going away, the missionaries said that Bali ought to come with us. She could learn to read and write and sew, and then she could come back and teach the others. They asked [her father], and he said all right, she could go. So she came with us. First time, I think she was a bit lonely, because she had no countryman there. But she learning to talk Maung, and she could talk to us. And after a while Buraana came from Milingimbi and she went to school too, so there were two of them learning to talk Maung. Bali went away when they starting that mission at Milingimbi. She went to school there.

Bali lived at Milingimbi and Elcho Island, and later at Yirrkalla. When I first met Bali in 1946 she still remembered some Maung vocabulary. The mission boats going to and fro always called in for a day or so at the Goulburn Island station, and when Bali occasionally travelled to Darwin she saw Mondalmi — her special friend, as she called her. When aeroplane travel made that journey more direct, they lost touch for a time, but Mondalmi told of a chance meeting in Darwin, when someone ran up calling her name. 'First, I didn't know who she was. Then I looked at her face, and it was Bali. We cried and laughed together.'

On another occasion, possibly in 1939, Mondalmi went on the mission boat *Larrpan* to Port Essington with Mr and Mrs Charles Barrett and Rev. Wilbur Chaseling, one of the first Methodist missionaries at Yirrkalla:

We looked at that place where those white men used to be before, long, long time — nearly all broken up now. Only I saw [something] like a hill. I thinking, 'That's a funny hill.' Then I saw it was only bottles — oh, plenty of bottles! Some, they so old, like stone, and covered with oysters. We filled up our bags. One of the Barretts asked me, 'You like oysters?' 'Of course I like oysters! I'm not a bush woman from inside [inland]. My country is on the beach, and I like all those things!' Then they said, 'Who is going up to look at that old garden?' 'No, we stopping here in the shade, down on the beach. Let them go and look, themselves. We can't go!'

A different kind of journey took her inland on a mission errand, carrying a 'lot of mail' and 'plenty of cases' from Goulburn Island to Oenpelli. Her husband and two eldest sons were in the group, with Medeg and several other people, but no Europeans. At the end of the dry season, 'everything [was] very dry' and they were all thirsty. They came close to Wuragag (Tor Rock), but they didn't stop, just went straight on to the Oenpelli plain.

Medeg very thirsty, and she ran on ahead. But she didn't know the way onto the plain, couldn't see the track, so she had to wait for us. We glad to see that plain, because our feet very sore and hot from all those stones. We came to one little river, but it was all dry. 'How long we got to wait for water?' 'Oh, long way yet!' After good while, we knew that billabong [was] on in front of us. We could smell the lilies [the water lilies that grow thickly in the Oenpelli billabong]. We didn't need anyone to tell us 'You got to hurry!'. We all running to that water. We went right in. Then someone said, 'Leeches there!' so I came out.

Mondalmi remembered that the Oenpelli missionary's wife asked her to show the women there how to make baskets. Because Mondalmi could only 'hear' Gunwinggu she needed an interpreter for this — and laughed at the recollection.

There were many short trips to gather foods in the appropriate season:

Before mission, and after mission just starting, people used to go to North Goulburn when those *wunbi* plums were ready. There were plenty of turtle eggs there too. Before, no Liverpool or Gunividji or Walang people here. The old people, like those grandfathers belonging to my mother [her mother's grandfathers, and her father's too], when they saw any stranger coming, they used to spear them. Only a few Neinggu [Gunwinggu] people could come, because might be some of our people would see them at some ceremony at Sandy Creek way [on the mainland], and those Neinggu people would be friendly to them and help them. So our people would tell the others, 'These are our friends', and they could come here.

Wunbi plums made a sweet drink. The plums would be gathered each day by women, who emptied laden dillybags into big heaps onto the ground, one heap for each family group, then spread them out to dry in the sun. When they were 'nice and ready', men would make platforms for them: four posts, one at each corner of a stringybark-and- paperback 'table' spread with plums. A good, steady fire would be lit under the platforms to dry the plums properly. When they were ready the whole plum (seed and flesh and skin) would be pounded up together and shaped into little round balls 'like cakes' about the size of a saltwater turtle's egg. Then they were ready to eat.

After the plums were finished, people would go to Sandy Creek for the yams [the long 'sweet' yams, *garwulug,* and the bitter *wuli* yams that needed special treatment]. Then, after a while, we would come back here for the *mialum,* like sweet potato, they ready then. After that we might go back to Sandy Creek until those *garwulug* finished. Those red apples, *warwarang,* very good at Sandy Creek: they very large and sweet. [She showed, with her hands, a round shape a little smaller than a football]. At Wighu they big too, but not so big as at Sandy Creek, and more sour. I don't like them. But at Sandy Creek they very sweet. Those the ones we like. And the white apples too, *gabgab.*

One day Mondalmi was talking about Croker Island. It was outside Maung territory but Maung people sometimes went there. In 1941 the

Methodist Overseas Mission had started a settlement on Croker for what used to be called 'half-caste' children, but they were sent south when the Northern Territory came under military control. When they returned in 1946, 'full-blood' Aborigines were not permitted on the island except for special purposes, such as selling fish or travelling through, to or from Darwin. The official policy of assimilation held that 'half-castes' should marry each other or Europeans, and get away from their Aboriginal affiliations and identification. But people from other missions could visit with the approval of the Croker missionaries. In 1968 the children were moved to Darwin, and Croker became a settlement for Aboriginal people of the region.

Mondalmi reminisced about a beach place on the west side of Croker Island that had 'plenty turtle eggs and turtle and fish'. She described it as a Yiwadja place:

> One time, we were all there and tired of staying in one place. We went to have a look at the other side of that island. All along the beach, plenty of sugarbag [wild honey], nearly in every tree, and turtle eggs along the beach all the time. We used to get some early in the morning and have them for breakfast and dinner, and then in the afternoon we would find some tracks again and have some more for supper. Every day we used to think, 'This lot will be the last.' And then we'd come along and see the tracks, and dig up some more.

Several people were camping on the beach in one large curving windbreak of leafy branches, facing the sea. Mondalmi drew a rough plan on the

Mondalmi in 1964 recording with the author, Catherine Berndt, at left

ground to show me how their sleeping fires were arranged, and how the tide came up almost to the two end-points of the windbreak. In the last sleeping place towards one of these end-points a Maung man, Bunug, and his wife slept. ('Old Bunug' belonged to the same territorial group as Mondalmi's husband, and was therefore an appropriate person to give his own name to the baby, 'Little Bunug', curled beside her as she reminisced in 1947.)

> Bunug was lying on his blanket, and one turtle came right up the beach and started to dig a hole just by his feet. First he thought was just a dog scratching [itself]. He didn't take notice. Then he looked up, and he saw something funny there. 'Might be a devil!' No. He looked, and it was this turtle, standing up, and starting to lay those eggs.
> So he held both his hands cupped underneath her and caught the eggs as they came out, put them on one side and caught some more. 'Then that turtle finished, and starting to cover up those eggs — that's what she was thinking!' Mondalmi showed how the turtle was scraping up the sand to fill in the hole.
> And Bunug, he just tipped her over onto her back: 'No you can't get away!' They keeping her that day, and next day they killed that poor old woman — I mean, that turtle. They gave it to some poor old people that couldn't hunt, couldn't walk about and get some turtle for themselves. He said, 'You can have tucker.' They said, 'Oh just have a leg!' And he said, 'No, because we can go and get our tucker and you can't.' It didn't matter they killed that turtle. That same day there were some more tracks on that beach.
> Plenty of yams there, too. You can dig them up very easy; they not a bit hard to get. You don't finish your hunting at sundown. You away only little bit of that day, because you don't have to go far away.

Other kinds of journey had no connection with the mission or visits to Darwin and food-getting was a secondary concern. These were associated with other traditional activities still important to the Maung people and their neighbours. Initiation and religious ritual sequences were especially significant; but smaller, individually centred transactions were just as pressing.

One such journey was part of a larger complex of mortuary rites. Traditionally, after a man died his hair was cut off and arrangements were set in a train for making a *yinggoin* dilly bag, tightly meshed, and decorated with wild cotton and feathers. When Mondalmi's second father died, she said, two young men were given his hair. They called him *idji*, uncle (mother's brother, in a fairly close relationship). They took the hair to the Yiwadja side, where two women made this bag for them. When it was ready, Mondalmi and her husband went to get it. She had only two children at that time. 'We stopped there, plenty lilies and fish and yams. We didn't want to leave that camp. Only we had to go.' After that, the bag containing the hair went to Mondalmi's father's dead sister's son (who also called the dead man 'uncle'), and then to one of the dead man's father's sisters' daughters' sons. Later it was put into a newly made *wulangana* dilly bag, about 60 cm long ('big enough to carry firesticks and things like that, like we always do'). 'It supposed to go back [to] Yiwadja side . . . ' She specified the kinds of relatives who were expected to handle it there, adding, 'They had to be *yunggu'*; that is, the semi-moiety often referred to by its main symbol *yunggu*, 'fire'.

Life on the mission station gave people considerable security, but there were periods when food was scarce, when the mission stores had almost run out and everyone was waiting for the boat to bring fresh supplies. Mondalmi remembered these times as occasions when people shared and helped one another.

One episode must have occurred towards the middle of 1940 when Miriam, her daughter, was only a few months old. Magumiri was married then to Mondalmi's brother Lamilami. Magumiri's sister Gibi (short for Ngalmagibi) was married to Mondalmi's youngest brother from her second father. Namanang-manang was the father of these two young women, and brother to Mondalmi's husband John. Ngalwiyir, who also lived at Goulburn island then, was only distantly related to them. Mondalmi often referred to Ngalwiyir as a 'very good hunter'.

> One time we had no tucker in the store, and nobody had anything. Miriam only a little baby then — like Bunug (her baby son lying alongside her), but he starting to crawl about now. Miriam too small yet. We very hungry; we going for yams. We saw a big black cloud coming over, and everyone said, 'Wait till that go past.' After that we went over this way [south]. We walked and walked, I and Magumiri and Gibi. After we got little way it began to rain — *nguldjur*, black cloud. Very heavy rain coming straight down. Little Miriam very cold. I had a dress for her and we put that over her. We got underneath some lot of pandanus, very thick, and Gibi took off one of her calico for her. We looking about for paperbark, but only little bit. Then we found some bark, but it full of holes, all that rain coming through. Miriam too cold, she crying, and it was raining so hard we had water coming up and up all round. [She showed a level of about 7 cm above the ground.] So we thought we better go home. We had no yams, nothing, and we said to each other, 'Who going to give us tucker? Might be somebody!' When we got back, there was Namanang-manang, and Ngalwiyir. They had big kerosene tin full of turtle eggs — they had billycan of them for us. And after that John brought back some fish; I think three or four. And they had a big goanna for us too. So we very happy then.

In the 1940s no substantial account of Maung language and culture was available as a guide for outsiders or as a resource-aid for the people themselves, and nobody was compiling one. Local missionaries acquired a few bits of information and some odds and ends of vocabulary. For a while, the Aboriginal girls who were working in the Goulburn Island mission house had fun teaching the missionary's children a number of Maung 'swear words' which they thought would shock him and his wife. They encouraged the children to try these out while they giggled in the background. The parents suspected the words were 'naughty' but did not understand them. I was urged not to miss a moment of these exciting occasions, and to report back exactly what the missionaries said. The serious side of the message was that newcomers should at least try to understand the language normally spoken there by most of its inhabitants.

Mondalmi was pleased to have a pupil but disappointed that I would not be staying long enough to make a thorough study of Maung. She was not the only one who was eager to help with a record of traditional Maung culture, which was so obviously in danger of being lost altogether; but with her knowledge of English and her enquiring approach she was in a strategic position to influence the procedure.

The Maung and other societies of western Arnhem Land took the task of teaching their children seriously. Although Mondalmi had spent so much time in and around the mission station, she had also spent much time with her parents and other relatives. In 1947, traditional child-rearing rules and practices were not just something that lived on in the memories of old people. Some had lapsed, because of changing circumstances, but others were still important — in initiation proceedings for boys and puberty rituals for girls, and to younger people bringing up small children.

Mondalmi was an affectionate mother to her seven children. She had a placid manner and did not usually allow herself to be rattled by ordinary upsets or problems. Nevertheless, she had decided opinions. She was fondly watchful and sensitive to her children's welfare and interests throughout their childhood and early adult life. 'Caring for' and 'caring about' went hand-in-hand with teaching and guiding a child. The process was one of training children to be independent, within a co-operative context. Talking, urging, informing, helping, and providing examples of good and bad behaviour all came within that program.

She told me a story about a mythical woman who was swept out to sea when she was gathering shellfish: a 'big snake must have swallowed her up'; her baby was crying for milk, and her two older children called to her in song to tell her this. Mondalmi said her own mother had told her the story and song when she was small, and she herself had sung it a few times, but her daughter 'didn't like it', and would stop Mondalmi from singing it to her. She told about this indulgently and sympathetically.

In a different vein, she once reported having woken up with a start a few nights before, at the sound of loud noises and shouting. Her first thought was to check whether her two older sons were near her. They were, with several other boys. They told her, 'We all here. We all sound asleep, not over there!' The moon was low in the west, as one of the men in that vicinity came looking for his young daughter: she wasn't in her camp, and 'he thought she must be with someone'. Afterwards the boys assured Mondalmi again, 'It wasn't us; we were all asleep. Must have been the Devil was with her!' Mondalmi laughed as she told about this. The episode fitted in with a view she and other women had quite often expressed: that mothers worried about their sons because young men sometimes had sweetheart relationships with the 'wrong' girls and risked attacks from jealous husbands or betrothed husbands. 'Boys are more trouble than girls,' Mondalmi and the others sometimes said.

Mondalmi often talked about a girl, Y, as an example of someone who did not behave in the right way. The characters are again her daughter (then still at the seven-and-a-half-year-old stage), her two eldest sons, and her husband John.

Y, she never like to carry anything in her hand — won't carry a digging stick or dilly bag. When little girls going for tucker, we always teach them, 'Always carry a bag or a tin, you must never go without them.' Sometimes they don't want to. So we say, 'Oh, you want to be like Y, not take anything in your hands?' And they say, 'No. We don't want to be like Y.'

Even little girls like Miriam, if we went hunting for our food we would tell them, 'Now you got to get your own tucker for yourself.' And if I had any tucker, I would give it to the boys, Paulikin and Dadeinj. And might be if John had anything, he would give some to Miriam — but not I. But now we different, we look after all our children, and I would give some to Miriam too.

In other accounts, though, she and other women did make sure their daughters had enough to eat, even when they were considered old enough to be able to get some of their own food.

Mondalmi used much the same procedures to teach me as she did to teach children. She used general statements about rules and constructs. She talked of systems, patterns of relationships and behaviour, and what ought to be done in a variety of circumstances. And she gave examples and anecdotes such as the story about Y. My notes show clearly her alternation of precept and example.

For instance, she dealt with food restrictions on various occasions, with lists of the foods involved and the circumstances and duration of the tabu. There was a short diversion on boys' initiation requirements, and then we came back to the 'childbirth and after' part of the lesson. The account of 'what we do with a baby's navel cord' included a sketch on the ground of the feathered *wulangana* dilly-bag made specially for this, and how the navel cord, after being treated, was hung at one side of it. Then Mondalmi moved on to a discussion of what she planned to do about Little Bunug's cord, who, she thought, would be the best woman to make the bag, the kind of payment that was needed 'before' and 'today', and the sequence of persons the bag should go to, adding comments about what happened to the cords of the four other children she had at that time.

When she taught me about cicatrices, Mondalmi began with *ngangidar*, scars made without religious ritual overtones. They were done to 'make a girl pretty', to 'make her look nice'; they were the 'right thing to do', for women and for men. The request was always made by the person who did the scarring, and who 'paid' with a gift for being allowed to do it. She pointed out the vertical scars just below each of her own shoulders, and said that Medeg (mentioned above) had cut them with a razor blade when Mondalmi was at the stage of physical development called *mumbuli-idibdi* — just after her breasts had begun to appear. Medeg and other girls had wanted to put horizontal scars across her abdomen too, but she had said 'No, no!' and wouldn't let them.

Mondalmi also described cicatrices that resulted from women cutting themselves when a boy was initiated, the number of scars made, where, and by which relatives. She explained that this was what people did 'before', but it had not been done for a long time: she herself, for example, had no scars of that kind. This highlights another aspect of Mondalmi's teaching: she always indicated whether what she was describing was in current use, or merely remembered. Similarly, she always tried to distinguish between what was first-hand knowledge and what was hearsay. And when she did not know, or had forgotten, she said so, as with one story she originally heard long ago from her mother. She remembered it only when an old Maung woman, Munggu-munggu, told it to her. Neither she nor Munggu-munggu could remember the song that went with it. On several occasions she grumbled about 'the old people's' failure to pass on information, mainly about songs and dancing, but on a range of other subjects too. 'They should have taught us these things, so we would know what to do. We can't find out now — they all gone without telling us.'

In that mission setting of the late 1940s, her own knowledge and recall were remarkable. Her information was not mechanical or perfunctory, but thoughtfully and critically presented. When she talked about the rectangular plaited mats of bulrush-leaves that girls formerly used in the seclusion hut at first menstruation (two mats each, so they could be changed), she explained that the girl's mother or sisters used to make these, and commented that they also came 'sometimes from the [girl's] husband's side but usually too much trouble for them!'

She taught me the rules, but made sure I understood that people could circumvent some inconvenient ones. Once, we were sitting talking on the beach towards sunset, as people were beginning to head homewards. A man carrying a sawfish on a pole came past us from a patch of mangroves at the end of the beach. He drew our attention to how small the fish was. Not long afterwards two women walked towards the mangroves, each with a child astride her shoulders. When they returned, one had a large, grass-wrapped bundle under her arm. As they passed, she called out to us. Mondalmi translated. They were saying that it wasn't theirs; the man had sent them for it. Mondalmi laughed when they had gone by. 'It's very funny,' she said. If the bundle had been theirs, and they had passed us sitting alongside their track they would have been obliged to give us some of that fish. We reminded each other that the man had had one hand free and could have easily carried the bundle, and she laughed again: 'That's why he sent them up for it, or *he* would have to give us some.'

Over the years I came to know a wide range of women who helped me to understand more about Maung culture. But it was Mondalmi, my first teacher and my first and special friend at Goulburn Island, who provided the groundwork and filled in most of the details in her own inimitable style. By the early 1960s she had forgotten not only much that she had told me before, but also (in a few cases) the fact that she *had* told me about specific stories or events. Too many other things were happening, she said, too many *balanda* things — using the Arnhem Land term *balanda*, 'Hollander', to indicate a European person. She could not recall with the depth and detail that she had known so well in 1947 or, indeed much of the traditional ways of her own childhood. Not enough people were interested about talking about such things any more, she said, and younger ones had other matters to think about now.

The early mission school at Goulburn Island enabled people such as Mondalmi to learn English, and to read and write it to some extent. An adequate school was not started there until 1963. My notes are thus an important record of the knowledge possessed by women of Mondalmi's and her mother's generations, just as my husband's notes are for men.

If tape recorders and films had been available to Mondalmi and others to use, what a record of Maung culture could have been documented, even then! Her brother Lamilami was able to use a tape-recorder in the 1960s but by that time much had been forgotten. The amount of information Mondalmi gave me was formidable, on topics ranging from simple things like hand-sign vocabulary, plant medicines, kinship terms and behaviour, where personal names and nicknames came from stories, interrelationships, and, later, children's songs, to more complicated topics. If she had been supported to devote time consistently to a long-term project, the result would have made an excellent resource-archive for the Maung people themselves. Recording traditional culture would have been in keeping with Methodist Mission ideals of preserving 'the best' in that culture. But it would have been out of step with government assimilation policy and the day-to-day priorities of mundane tasks. Shortage of mission staff, and what missionaries saw as rather demanding working conditions, encouraged an emphasis on 'practical' welfare needs.

Mondalmi was a capable and conscientious domestic helper whose kindly, patient, motherly manner must have given support and reassurance to a succession of missionary households. She, her husband and their two eldest children are listed in the 1933 mission census as 'Cottage People'. They were 'mission people', not 'semi-mission' as many others are categorised in the records. They were the dependable core-population who made the missionaries feel that their endeavours were really worthwhile.

Goulburn Island, like other mission stations, was a place of refuge. It was a community where most people were known individually and all could be sure of personal concern about their health and welfare. In a world that was potentially hostile, and largely indifferent or exploitive, missionary paternalism (and maternalism) had its uses. But the mission was also part of that invading society: it was simultaneously protective and destructive. It was a filter for things, ideas and attitudes from outside, enabling people to stay close to their own country and to proceed at something approximating their own pace. It was also a source of deliberate change. Aborigines who found the mission situation too cramping made for Darwin or the buffalo plains, cattle stations and timber-cutting camps that lay outside the Arnhem Land reserve but close to home. Some came back now and then to Goulburn Island (or to Oenpelli), but others cut themselves off almost completely.

The mission that Mondalmi knew as a child was not too different from the one at Oenpelli; but the paths of the two stations diverged. The Methodists, during the 1940s, developed a policy that the Church Missionary Society failed to adopt seriously until the early 1960s — a difficult policy of 'keeping what's best in the Aboriginal culture'. The dormitory system that Mondalmi and her brother had known was abandoned: the aim was to 'work through the family unit'. Aborigines were encouraged to use their own names, languages, and marriage rules, including polygyny.

Rev. A.E. Ellemor, for several years chairman of the Methodist Overseas Mission district which included the Arnhem Land stations, told us in 1946 that he had made a mistake at Milingimbi in suggesting that men with more than one wife should 'give up' all except one. He had not been prepared for the anger of the women who suddenly found themselves unmarried in a society where marriage was taken for granted as the state of all women except elderly widows. He subsequently withdrew his suggestion, admitting that it should not be imposed from outside.

The immediate post-war period was one of restless optimism. The Army settlements closed in 1945. Some people had come home with stories of the new 'equality', amenities and skills they had found there. The Goulburn Islanders went on arranging betrothals, speaking their own languages, engaging in their traditional religious rituals and secular ceremonies. They went on being told that the missionaries were really working for them. There was a general expectation that things were going to be better, in a way that had plenty of room for Aboriginal culture and the Aboriginal past.

Mondalmi's 1947 comments reflected that optimism. There were grumbles about individual missionaries and particular incidents, but on the whole she and others felt that they had a fair measure of independence, that they could continue to lead their lives more or less as they wished and would have the best of the new world as well because the mission would continue to act as a buffer.

As time went on, life at the mission station settled back almost into the old routine, but rather less contentedly. Mondalmi's comments mirrored that mood.

In 1947 she had criticised the young men who went to Darwin, were sweethearts with one girl after another, and then came back to look for more. 'They get tired of one girl; they have to change. They don't want to stay with one woman until she gets old.' In the early 1960s she and other women were worrying more than ever about what was happening to established marriage rules. It was up to women, they said, to do something about 'wrong' marriages, and children born 'without fathers' to unmarried girls. 'If those fathers go wrong, *we* can be straight!'

By then it had become plain that the mission policy of 'keeping what's best' had always depended on individual missionaries rather than on the pronouncements of mission headquarters. During one missionary regime an edict was issued forbidding any man to take more than one wife. Existing unions were allowed to continue; but even a girl with a long-standing, traditionally correct betrothal contract could not go to a man who was already married and still continue to live at Goulburn Island.

Mondalmi's own daughter was not allowed to go to her promised husband. The issue was resolved later. Meanwhile Mondalmi made known her opinion that it was quite all right for her daughter to bear children because she was, in effect, already married in the right way. Although her own marriage was monogamous, Mondalmi recognised that according to tradition this was a matter of choice. She also knew about the Methodist policy that this particular missionary contravened.

She grew disillusioned too about the relations between Aborigines and Europeans — she now rarely used the word *balanda,* but accepted the label 'white' as the missionaries had taught her. Her view was that the two kinds of people were different, and did not have to live in exactly the same way. Not everybody could be Maung! But all people should be equal. She was too polite to say that she really thought Aboriginal people, especially Maung, were superior. This extended to appearance, including skin colour. But she was aware from her experience with Europeans that not everyone felt that way. In 1947 she described one incident in which she took her second son, quite small at the time, to a Sunday school in Darwin: he was upset, she said, by the way everyone kept staring at him, so she wouldn't let him go there again. She took him to the Sunday school at Bagot settlement, where 'all the children were the same colour, and it was all right'. What infuriated and hurt her was any suggestion of Aboriginal 'inferiority'.

Because of past contact between Aborigines and *balanda,* a number of women of the region had borne 'half-caste' children, most of whom had been taken away to institutions during the 'assimilation' era. One woman from the buffalo plains west of Darwin, who had made her home at Goulburn Island, had lost touch with her 'half-caste' daughter. She asked me from time to time whether I knew how to find the girl, how the search was going, and, if I saw her, to ask her to write to her mother. Mondalmi, listening to this once, remarked bitterly, 'Some half-caste children are like that. They don't like to think they have mothers with black skins.' She added, 'Like one girl, one half-caste girl, at the Timber Camp. They said to her, "That's your mother over there." And she said, "No! That's not my mother!".'

Yet some of the younger generation gave her hope. Mondalmi spoke proudly of 'Little Bunug' when he went to Brisbane and Darwin for further training, but sadly she did not live to see the volume of stories, *Djugurba*,* he and other young Aborigines who had completed a teacher-training course at Kormilda College compiled for publication in 1974. She was happy also that the nursing sister at the mission, Heather Hinch, was recording children's songs, as well as learning and studying the Maung language. She remained determinedly Maung. She reminded me on several occasions that her eldest son had never learnt his father's language, Gunwinggu, as her other children had, 'He never speaks anything but Maung!'

By 1964 she was less cheerful. She was not in good health and had grown too heavy to move about easily — a real hardship for someone who had been so active all her life. She was even, she said, 'ashamed' of her English — perhaps because she had more exposure to 'standard English' and was too diffident about her own fluency and ability to communicate.

Mondalmi's life-span covered a period of tremendous changes. In some of these she was directly involved: the sudden arrival of missionaries,

---

**Djugurba: Tales from the spirit time.* A.N.U. Press, Canberra, 1974.

inposing a new regime; the growing intrusion of outsiders, especially Europeans; World War II; the increased amount of interaction and intermixing among Aboriginal groups which formerly had little or nothing to do with one another — some drawn to the Goulburn Island settlement (such as Walang; but also others from farther east who 'never came here before, they stranger to us — now they come and finish up all our turtles and everything!'); — and the outward movement of Maung and their neighbours to Darwin and later to various southern cities.

When Maung people today talk about keeping their own language and culture, they do so from a very different standpoint. The range of their interests is leading them away from what was once the *totality* of Maung concerns. The effort is more self-conscious, and 'being Maung' (for instance) means something quite different. In the 1940s, to Mondalmi and her contemporaries, 'being Maung' was being in the centre of the 'real' world.

I have not discussed, here, Mondalmi's views about the roles of men and women, their status *vis-a-vis* one another, the division of labour and decision-making and authority between them, because that would require a detailed account of traditional Maung religious affairs and marriage negotiations. It is enough to say that she took her roles as wife and mother seriously. She once observed that Maung people had to have children because there were so few of them, whereas *balanda* women had a choice — there were so many *balanda,* they probably did not all need to make more. In all of her domestic and public roles as a Maung woman, she had a confident authority and assurance about her place in her world.

When I first knew her, she complained that people were ignoring the traditional rule about the *namanamaidj* as a vehicle for handing on personal names: 'Some of these people just take names because they like them, not from *namanamaidj.*' It annoyed her that there were others called Mondalmi who had, in her view, acquired their names improperly: 'like stealing!' One development in recent years would have annoyed her even more: the official use of a husband's name as surname to identify a married woman. For Mondalmi, it would have been unthinkable that a woman should take the name of her husband, a name that came ideally from *his namanamaidj* and not *hers.* This would be subsuming a woman's personal identity in a way that was not possible in traditional Maung culture. It was a further sign of the imposition of European male public authority that was so visible in the culture the Christian missionaries brought with them. Perhaps the price of the new independence that some Aborigines have lately achieved is the loss of much of the unique content of their own heritage, and more complete involvement in the contradictions, as well as the material benefits, of the wider society.

Mondalmi was shaped by her heritage, and by the times in which she lived. She was a social commentator, a reflection of the changing situation of which she was part, and in which she was an active participant. Her own story is unique, yet her experience is like that of other women at Goulburn Island. I hope that some of them will soon be telling *their* stories themselves, to help the 'younger generation' to understand their own past and its continuing significance for all the people of that region.

Additional reading

Berndt, R.M. and C.H. (1954). *Arnhem Land: Its history and its people.* Cheshire, Melbourne
────── (1970). *Man, land and myth in North Australia: The Gunwinggu People.* Ure Smith, Sydney
Lamilami, L. (1974). *Lamilami speaks: A story of the people of Goulburn Islands, North Australia.* Ure Smith, Sydney

3

A Teacher's Life

Pearl Duncan

Where does one start and what does one say? How do I write about my life without appearing to be egotistical? I have to be careful that this exercise doesn't culminate in an ego trip; conversely, I must guard against being so introspective as to appear biased and insular.

I sometimes get the feeling that there was uncanny intervention in my life and that it followed a predetermined path. My life was influenced from the start by people of strong character right down through the generations. My mother's maternal great-grandfather was an Englishman who was transported because he was found guilty of stealing a handkerchief from his brother. He came from a well-connected family, and he often told my mother he believed he was the victim of a conspiracy to rob him of his inheritance. His name was Henry Harrison, and he was born in Warwickshire. When he came to this country he married a tribal woman called Lena. He settled down and raised a family at Emmaville, New South Wales, but his wife died when the children were young, so he reared his family alone. I knew his two sons, James and Henry Harrison Jr, as old men and they highlighted our childhood with a wealth of stories about the early days. With their father they had operated a timber mill, and my mother says that many of the original houses at Emmaville were built from the timber produced at his mill.

James Harrison married Annie Munro, and their only child, Cissie, was my mother's mother. Cissie, who married James Daley, died at the birth of her tenth child, so James and Annie Harrison reared several of their grandchildren, including my mother, Pearl Daley. My mother had a lot to do with her great-grandfather, Henry Harrison, who lived to a great age — ninety-seven or so — and was the last convict in that area when he died about 1913. Recently my brother drove us to Wellingrove, where my mother showed us his headstone in the churchyard next to the little church where she was baptised. My mother had a strict Anglican upbringing, mostly supervised by her great-grandfather, who faithfully said the daily offices of Matins and Evensong and read his Bible every day. He told my mother all about life in England and taught her many English songs and poems. He also taught her to count and to say the alphabet so that she would have a head start when she began school. My mother was very bright and excelled at the Emmaville and Wellingrove State Schools. She passed the Qualifying Certificate (QC) which would enable her to become a pupil-teacher. She was very lucky to receive an education, and a good one at that, because it was not then compulsory for Aboriginal children to attend school in New South Wales and before about 1948 state schools could refuse entrance to Aboriginal children. So I was indeed fortunate that, right from the beginning, my life was influenced by learned people.

I was born at Emmaville, but my family moved to Bundarra while I was still an infant, and I received my formal education at Bundarra Central School. It is impossible to look back over the years to my childhood at Bundarra without experiencing mixed feelings — hostility, nostalgia, and thankfulness I suppose. But the feeling that pervades all my memories is a deep sadness. My hostility arises from the degradation, guilt and demoralisation I was subjected to, especially at school. Yet nostalgia envelopes me when I recall the past; and I am closely tied to the past — to people of my childhood whom I loved and who loved me. There is a wonderful feeling of tranquillity when you are secure in the nurture and love of those closest to you.

I am thankful for the unexpected kindness of people (and there were many) who set me on the right track: by believing in me, they gave me emotional support and fired me with zeal and imagination. For each insular racist I met, I also found a genuine, sensitive, concerned and true friend. I am thankful for the unhappiness I was able to endure, because in the long term I came out on top. My humiliating experiences only sharpened my wits and perception and gave me courage to face life fairly and squarely. I thank God for Henry Harrison, who was a great teacher to my mother, who in turn was a guiding star in my life.

I am always mindful of a deep sadness for the suffering — physical, mental and spiritual — that was part and parcel of an Aboriginal's life during the time of my childhood. I cannot help feeling a great sorrow for the fine Aboriginal people I knew who were incarcerated by racism, who were not given the opportunities to realise their life's fulfilment, and who could have become leaders but instead existed in a stifling sub-cultural vacuum, tacitly accepting the enormity of alienation and loss of identity. I feel anguish for my dear aunt Min when I remember her courage, her boundless charity, her selflessness and the manifold odds life stacked against her. She died unaware that the 'winds of change were sweeping the continent'; and for that I am sorry. I bitterly regret the belatedness of all the good things now happening for Aborigines.

Shortly after we settled at Bundarra, when I was about two years old, my mother and my father, Norman Duncan, separated. He belonged to a family of the Moree area. My mother returned to Emmaville, where she was well known, to work as a live-in domestic. This was the only course of action possible as the deserted wife's pension or supporting mother's benefit was unheard of then. The four of us (two boys, two girls) were left at Bundarra in the care of my mother's eldest sister, aunt Min, and her husband. My mother returned when I was in grade II at school, so she was away from us for about five years.

There was a bit of a shed made from kerosene tins flattened into sheets standing on Aunt Min's husband's property. My uncle allowed my mother to move into this shed, and she made it into comfortable cooking and eating quarters. My grandfather, James Daley, built another hut from kerosene tins and bush timber about twenty metres away from the kitchen and this became our sleeping quarters. My mother was a very independent and self-reliant woman, who never even thought of moving in with her sister. She toiled from dawn till dark at hard domestic work (there were no labour-saving devices then) for numerous people at Bundarra, at a pittance even for those days. She always described our existence as living from hand to mouth.

I feel I should digress here and mention something about my aunt Min and her husband. These two people were especially dear to me because they influenced my early childhood, having become my foster-parents for a while. Aunt Min had an extensive repertoire of anecdotes which always had a moral somewhere, and she was also quick at uttering apt proverbs to emphasise home truths. She was a remarkable woman, and I shall always remember her sayings.

Her husband, who was not Aboriginal, had a small property with a few cows and a vegetable garden. I spent a lot of time outdoors helping him milk and garden. We had to carry water in buckets from the river for the garden and for household purposes. Towards the end of my uncle's life, he was unable to control the shaking of his hands, so that I had to attend to all his business. (In retrospect, I think he was probably suffering from Parkinson's disease.) I wrote all his letters while he dictated, and I learnt a lot from him about business procedure. I still write a business letter today following the same rules he taught me. My uncle told us that he was educated at Kings School, Parramatta, and in World War I he was a captain. He came from a wealthy family but they had disowned him when he married my aunt Min. He never mentioned nor contacted his family, and when he died none of his people attended his funeral, although his funeral notice was announced over the radio. I felt sad about this because it would not have cost them much to pay their last respects. He was a wonderful person and I am glad and honoured to have known him.

My early life at Bundarra seemed to be endless summers of swimming and fishing in the old Gwydir River, and gathering blackberries along its banks. Aunt Min had a singular gift for cooking and used to bake blackberry pies and tarts that simply melted in one's mouth. My sister, two brothers and I had unwritten sovereignty over the river and the bush. We savoured a freedom that wasn't restrained by the fear experienced nowadays by people who read about the terrible things that can happen to the unwary. It makes me sad to think that my grandchildren, if I have any, will never know the kind of freedom we had. We knew every inch of the town common, which was wild bush in many places, and of the Gwydir River area and the surrounding hills within a wide radius of our home. We always knew the best places to find mushrooms, and wild flowers. Once, I found some beautiful wild violets in a little glade in the middle of the scrub on the common. We would observe birds nesting and revisit the nests and happily note the happenings from the day the eggs hatched until we found the empty nests.

During the winter months my brother and I went trapping rabbits. After school we would carry a heavy bag of traps to a selected spot, carefully set the traps and cover them. Next morning quite early, when the frost was everywhere, we would return to collect our hapless rabbits. My brother would skin and gut the rabbits; the skins were pulled over a wire-bow frame to dry. On weekends we would sell our rabbit skins to the skin-buyer. This was how we earned our pocket money to go to the pictures on Saturdays, or which we banked for the yearly show.

It never occurred to us to get into mischief while our mother was absent from home. When she was at work we were left to our own devices. Of course we had our chores, but we also had our freedom. Not once did our mother have to go before the courts with any of us. When not at school we roamed wild and free, but we knew that we couldn't commit misdeeds that would incur the wrath of the local authorities, our neighbours or our mother. This wasn't something drummed into us; rather it was an innate part of our being.

They say that I am the first Aboriginal school-teacher in Australia. I should like to qualify that by saying that perhaps I am the first who has been identified: there have been a lot of 'Johnny-come-latelys' coming out of the woodwork, so I may not hold that record.

I distinctly remember my second-grade teacher telling my mother that I was 'clever at school'. I never recognised this, and as a result I suffered a lot of discomfort when my uncles and aunts called me 'the little scholar'. I was fearful that I might be asked to demonstrate my cleverness and that everyone would discover I wasn't clever at all.

I suppose it was unusual then for a fringe-dweller to accomplish what I did with the forces working against me. We four were the only Aboriginal children at Bundarra Central School. Generally we were accepted by the white children and joined in their games. Sometimes we were even invited to play at their homes, and we all had one or two close friends at school. Nevertheless, we suffered name-calling and ostracism from time to time. I expect every Aboriginal child went through the same experience of feeling rejected, alienated and demoralised at school.

Australian history lessons were always a trial — Aborigines or blacks were always mentioned in a derogatory manner. This never failed to make me feel guilty. I remember clearly how prisoners, the insane and Aborigines were not allowed to vote; and there was a poem entitled 'I wish I were an Aborigine' that the class used to recite accusingly at me. Another thing I disliked about school was when new kids enrolled. The others would gleefully point out to the newcomers that we were black gins and lived in a blacks' camp. It didn't matter how presentable your home was — the whites always said that you lived in a blacks' camp! Mercifully the novelty wore off after a couple of days and we were part of the scenery again.

During primary-school days I especially loved to stand in front of the class and recite. When we used to sit around the fire at night my mother taught me two poems, tear-jerkers which were always popular with the class. I could not sit down until I had said both these poems. I had the expression and pauses down to a fine art.

Many fond memories came flooding back when I think back to those nights around the fire. To save kerosene, mum would read to us by the firelight, a chapter every night. Our favourite stories were *Black Beauty* and *Robinson Crusoe*. We especially used to enjoy what we called 'yarning'. Mum would tell us all about her childhood at Wellingrove, and we would never tire of hearing about those times. Sometimes we all told riddles or ghost stories. Going to bed was funny because often when we moved from the kitchen to go outside to the bedroom the breeze would blow out the lamp and we would have to feel our way in the dark. We rarely had a globe, as sooner or later there would be an accident. Sometimes we would visit our aunt Min and uncle next door. Our uncle would entertain us around the fire with stories and songs of his youth. We depended a lot on simple home entertainment. We didn't even own a radio then.

When I entered secondary school I suffered greatly at the hands of a new headmaster. He reportedly came from a school on an Aboriginal reserve, where he was accustomed to bluffing and intimidating the Aborigines. He was a despicable human being. I would have become a drop-out if he had continued. He tried to treat town children as badly as he did the kids on the 'mission' and that was his undoing. After about eighteen months his family preceded him out of town and he crept on the bus and left Bundarra for good without even saying goodbye to anyone.

But I remember with dismay how unsuccessfully he tried to break my spirit when he proceeded to place me in an 'opportunity' class, where I remained for the first year and a half of my secondary schooling. If ever he saw me playing happily with the other girls he would call them aside for a small conference, after which the girls would not rejoin me. When I asked what he had said to them, the girls would inform me that he forbade them to play with me because Aborigines were unsuitable companions. I had to be very careful not to incur his wrath; if I moved or spoke he would shout, 'Get out! Get out! I'll have you sent away to an Aboriginal girls' home.' I heard this same outburst almost every school day for a year and a half.

The next headmaster was at least impartial, and that inspired my respect. This was the turning point in my educational career. I was quickly removed from the 'opportunity' class and placed in the normal stream, and when a young male teacher joined the staff I was able to enjoy secondary school. I owe him a lot because, by simply showing an interest in me, he restored my self-respect and boosted my confidence; from then on I worked diligently at my lessons. I never looked back, even though a long illness kept me in hospital for months. I returned to school a week or so before the yearly exams, caught up on the work I had missed and gained top marks in all subjects except maths, a subject I was always unable to handle confidently because of the groundwork I had missed earlier on. Or perhaps I suffered a sort of mental block.

I used to study at 5.00 am because it was the best part of the day for me: my mind was clear and I was always able to get right down to tin-tacks. I began doing this to conserve kerosene and also because the flickering light of the lamp used to hamper my concentration. I used to run to the river for a bucket of water and light the fire. By the time the others got up, the kitchen would be warm and cosy and the kettle boiling; also the water for our ablutions would be heated. In winter, I'd also have the porridge cooked.

At the end of 1948 I sat for the intermediate certificate, an external exam at that time. We had to wait until January before we knew the results, which were published in the *Sydney Morning Herald*. The day the results came out my mother was told by every person she met that I had passed; but she brought the paper home all the same. I received telegrams of congratulations from former teachers and from my mother's former employers at Emmaville. It was a most exciting time, and I have never been so thrilled about passing any other exam. If I had wanted to continue my education — and I had wanted this desperately — it would have been necessary to go to Armidale High or Inverell High. In either case I would have to have lived in a girls' hostel, and there was absolutely no way my mother could afford to finance me — and there was no Aboriginal Secondary Grants scheme then.

But because of my good Anglican upbringing, passed on through the generations from great-great-grandfather Harrison, the local minister and the Bishop who had confirmed me took an interest, as did the wife of the local postmaster. These three people interceded on my behalf and, after a year away from school, I was accepted as a student at the House of the Epiphany in Sydney, a missionary training college controlled by the Australian Board of Missions. In 1950 I was enrolled as a private student at the Sydney Teachers' College, where I trained as a teacher. I received no special consideration and was compelled to hand in assignments and to go out practice teaching in the schools. I joined a youth group, the Comrades of Saint George, affiliated with the Australian Board of Missions, and my most memorable moment at this time was when I made my debut at the Comrades Ball at North Sydney.

I had to cope with Teachers' College and with living at the House of the Epiphany as well, and that was not easy. At the House we suffered many privations. There were many long hours in the chapel on our knees and attendance at daily Mass was compulsory. There were regular retreats and lectures and seminars guided by the most learned theologians. We were disciplined rigidly and rostered to housework, cooking and other duties such as gardening. The reason given was that such rigorous training prepared us to work effectively in the field.

This conditioning process at the House and at college made me sanctimonious and encouraged me to assimilate middle-class attitudes. I am embarrassed when I think what I must have been like. However, I must be thankful for this period of my life. I had the protection of the church, to whose precepts I dutifully adhered, and the steadying influence of sincere and genuine church people. I became very resourceful at budgeting my only source of income, £4 per month, sent to me by the vicar of Saint Mary's, Bundarra, on behalf of the Ladies' Auxiliary. Out of this I had to pay fares to and from college, clothe myself and buy the books and equipment needed for Teachers' College. Of necessity I became proficient at sewing and knitting and made all my own clothes.

To tide myself over the three-month Christmas holiday recess at the College, I used to work in the pea paddocks at Guyra, where my sister and her husband lived. On very special occasions (such as when I made my debut) my mother would make a sacrifice and send me money. Often I walked to and from college in order to save my money for a splurge in the cafeteria with my girlfriends. Once, my older brother sent me six pounds! This was like manna from heaven. I was delirious with sheer joy and gratitude.

You might think that as a young person (I was sixteen when I went to the House of the Epiphany) I had very little gaiety in my life, but that is not entirely true: I was always very serious and a lack of social life didn't bother me. At college, I made good, close friends with girls my own age; at the House, the girls were all a lot older and they more or less mothered me. The main point I want to highlight is that it was then exceedingly difficult to escape from a country town and become educated. What my generation achieved was the result of personal striving and determination. When I had to make my decision about leaving Bundarra to go to Sydney, it was abundantly clear that I should have no future if I didn't grasp the opportunity of going to the House of the Epiphany. So, being a very determined person, I became an opportunist very early in my life.

When I graduated from Teachers' College in 1951, the Australian Board of Missions sent me to Yarrabah, a mission station in northern Queensland. I worked with grades IV and V and generally assisted in the running of the school. Yarrabah was no place for the ill and inactive, yet my headmistress (I shall call her Miss P) was physically handicapped and a very sick person. I spent a lot of time running about at her bidding. She was a retired headmistress who had spent all her working life in select private schools and colleges for girls. She was insulated against the way Aborigines thought and behaved; she was the world's worst choice for Yarrabah, and for me. I was easy prey for her razor-sharp tongue, and lacked the experience to provide a comeback for her merciless harassment. As a product of the House of the Epiphany I did not condone assertiveness or disobedience and firmly believed in respect for my superiors. She stifled my imagination and initiative, humiliated me in front of *everybody* and blamed me when the running of the school did not go according to her plan. But worse still the way she treated the children was reprehensible. She ruled the school with fear. I still remember how we spent nearly the whole of one day in assembly while she ranted and raved and had the teaching assistants all searching because one frightened little boy couldn't find his pencil.

Everybody was terrified of her, so I had no one to defend me. She lived in the staff house with me and all the other staff ladies so I had no respite from her megalomania. The young girls at Yarrabah were placed in a dormitory and trained in domesticity, which included fetching and carrying for us. They were trained by a white woman known by all of us as 'Matron'. Miss P. ruled the girls and Matron with a rod of iron, and there was nothing I could do to alleviate their wretched subjection.

Yarrabah is the most beautiful place in the world, and life there could have been idyllic. My present soul-searchings and yearnings always take me back, for I think part of me stayed behind when I left Yarrabah. We

Pearl Duncan's début photo, 1951, at age 18
(Photograph courtesy of the Duncan family collection)

were employed by the diocese of North Queensland on a teeny-tiny allowance plus our board and keep. I never considered myself poor; it was a joy to teach the children, but nowadays it makes me a little envious when I see Aborigines receiving top salaries for helping their own people. Some of them never even identified as Aborigines when I worked at Yarrabah for almost nothing.

After two years at Yarrabah I returned to the House of the Epiphany to do a year's course at Sydney University. The Bishop of North Queensland wrote entreating me to stay at Yarrabah, saying that a further two years should be considered as vital for my further training. However, I stuck to my guns — I had simply reached saturation point with Miss P.

At Sydney University in 1954 I did a crash course in anthropology; linguistics, tropical medicine and genetics were thrown in for good measure. There were about thirty doing the course, which was especially designed for people going out into the field in Papua New Guinea, British Solomons, Polynesia or Melanesia as teachers, nurses, planters or government employees. For example, there was a husband-and-wife team, both pilots, going to New Guinea as pilots for the Anglican bishop.

The lecturers were Dr Capell and Professor Elkin. We did three years of anthropology in one year; I had assignments, a lot to read, and huge essays to write. I remember a long essay on the Dobuans and another on the Ellice Islands. It was only then that I began to realise what a wonderful people the Aborigines are. Professor Elkin was a marvellous lecturer. I had not known about the kinship system and what a complicated thing it is; nor about the languages. Dr Capell lectured on languages and beliefs; these were fascinating.

Soon after the annual examination Dr Capell gave a little talk to the children at the Sunday school where I taught. Afterwards, while driving me home, he said, 'You've done very well; you've topped the section in your examination.' I couldn't believe it.

In 1955 the Australian Board of Missions appointed me as a teacher at Saint Paul's Mission, Moa Island, in the Torres Strait. I was told that a headmaster or headmistress would be taking up duties, but in the three years I was there I had to run the school myself with the help of community teachers. Saint Paul's was entirely different from Yarrabah: the white staff had their say in island matters only when consulted, and there was no dormitory system, so there were no house girls to fetch and carry for us.

The Saint Paul's people were not of Torres Strait Islands descent — they were descendants of the 'Kanakas' who were 'blackbirded' from Polynesia to work in the canefields of Queensland. Most of the family names designated which Polynesian island the original parent came from. It was all very interesting. These people had far more self-esteem and self-determination than the Aboriginal people at Yarrabah. They were sturdy and upstanding, and running their own affairs. However, I am pleased to say that when I re-visited Yarrabah in 1974 it was completely different. The old colonial way of life had disappeared, and it was a thriving community of confident, happy people all working to make a better, more forceful Yarrabah.

At Saint Paul's I lived quite close to the school in a little palm cottage, a veritable haven for grass and carpet snakes. There were no venomous snakes, but I was always terrified. Once, a severe electrical storm punished my little cottage, and I was badly shaken and frightened. It was my first really bad tropical storm. When the Priest-Director of the Torres Strait left with his family, I went to live in the mission house, which was the best building on the island. It had big bay windows which looked out over the reef and the lagoon, and a magnificent view of the nearby islands. I never got tired of looking at the view, with all its changes of sea colours and moods.

Apart from school-teaching I had to do the medical work, which entailed being on call any time and mainly consisted of first-aid. When we had serious cases, we had to contact Thursday Island Hospital by radio, and the doctor on duty would ask us to describe the symptoms; then he prescribed medication to be found in our clinic. I was thankful that women due to have babies were sent to Thursday Island before the event. One major medical case I haven't forgotten was when a spear-fisherman was stung by a stone-fish while out on the reef at low tide. He came to me, a huge man in dreadful agony, with a swollen foot of shocking dimensions. I had to inject a pain-killing drug. Both he and I were nervous and scared about that injection.

Sometimes, if all members of the staff were absent, as happened during Synod, I had to manage on my own. One of my duties then was to man the radio morning and afternoon. I often think that my weather reports must have been quite perplexing. Another of my duties during two years as the only female staff member was to act as hostess for various visiting dignitaries. I met some very interesting people: film crews, authors, artists, a Fulbright scholar from the U.S. doing research in marine biology (the reef was a marvellous place), bishops from other dioceses, master pearlers and the captains from the island boats.

Saint Paul's school was a happy place and I had sole control. The children were especially endearing, always ready to entertain me with island songs and dances. Impromptu concerts were quite the order of the day during craft and sewing lessons. There was much freedom from the classrooms; we had our art classes outdoors, down on the beach or inland, where it was quite a jungle under the mango trees or the wild almond trees, which the children called *meccae* trees. Our nature rambles were a joy as there was such a wealth of natural material at our fintertips. When the tide was way out there was a wonderland of exposed reef, but there it was more a case of the children teaching the teacher. During the school holidays I often visited the other islands of the Torres Strait by lugger. I always liked to visit Darnley, where I had friends, the Government school-teacher and his family.

When I left Moa Island the people gave me the *wongai* fruit to eat. It is a belief in the islands that if you eat the *wongai* fruit you will always return to the Torres Strait. I earnestly hope that I shall.

I am told that it is now possible to make inter-island visits by helicopter — a far cry from the days of the pearling luggers. I remember most vividly what a magnificent sight it was when the pearling luggers came into Saint Paul's. With their snow-white sails billowing against the bright, blue sky and green, tropical sea, they were like resplendent white birds gliding into the bay. Sometimes the divers would bring home a turtle or a dugong, which meant fresh meat for everybody instead of canned meat. That night the food *(kai-kai)* would be cooked island style, which was exceedingly tasty, and there would be dancing and singing until dawn. But occasionally a lugger would mournfully negotiate the channel into the bay with its flag at half-mast, and we knew that somebody, probably a diver, had lost his life. I hope that when I return to the Torres Strait I am able to take my son so that he can see an alternative life-style to the grasping competitiveness of western culture.

I spent three happy, memorable years in the Torres Strait, but the isolation began to affect me. Although I am serious by nature I am also a gregarious person. I had a very dear, close friend in Sydney who helped me resettle there and to apply to the New South Wales Education Department for a teaching position. She was non-Aboriginal and did a lot of voluntary social work among the Aborigines at La Perouse, Sydney. My first appointment was at La Perouse State School. (This school was probably the only one with a curriculum geared to foster integration; the Aboriginal and non-Aboriginal children mixed well together; the teachers were well-selected; and the Minister for Education took a special interest in the school.)

When I first came south I missed the gaiety of the classroom at Saint Paul's and the closeness of the island children as we discovered and learnt together. It was a long time before I became accustomed to children who appeared to be insipid and colourless, too inhibited and regimented for my liking. We could not suddenly go off to examine natural phenomena without disturbing the whole school, and the necessary permission notes from parents negated the spontaneity of the exercise. For a long time after leaving Saint Paul's it seemed strange to enter a classroom with no hibiscus or frangipani strewn on desks or in dark curly tresses.

I taught in many New South Wales schools, particularly in the Sydney suburbs, and also in two country towns. During the early years in Sydney I was employed full-time as a teacher. In those days teachers had a heavy workload in large classes, a lot of book work, and in my case extra duties. I was the sports-mistress, and this meant that I spent a lot of my free time coaching the girls, especially in basketball. Inspections in those days were always traumatic experiences for everybody. Apart from all this, I had to attend Fort Street Evening College, where I passed the Leaving Certificate and afterwards a series of exams to qualify for the award of a Teaching Certificate. Where were the Aboriginal Study Grants then?

My first country school was Glen Innes, where I was never made to feel different from the other staff members and where I made many friends; but my second country school, Inverell, where I was appointed as teacher-librarian, was a disaster. I didn't really have my own class and so none of the children felt loyal to me. The children were openly outraged at my being Aboriginal, and the headmaster, angry with me for not staying in the city, mishandled the situation. Children called me 'black gin' and yelled at me from school buses as I walked to and from school. It was unnerving, and as I did not have any close friends in Inverell to support me, I cracked up and went to the school inspector in a flood of tears. I was quickly transferred from Inverell and remained in the Sydney metropolitan area until early 1973.

My son and I then went to New Zealand, where I taught at a primary school at Otara, Auckland. I was amazed to see such a large proportion of Maori teachers in the schools, where Maori culture was taught and

Pearl as a teacher in the 1960s
(Photograph courtesy of the Duncan family collection)

respected. In my class the European children could dance and sing Maori songs just as well as, if not better than, their Maori counterparts. The Maoris seemed to have their land-rights well and truly sorted out and to me the presence of Maoris in shops, banks and public life was a real tourist attraction. When people go to New Zealand they expect to see Maoris and their culture. All this made me realise what a long, hard road the Aboriginal in Australia had to go, and I was filled with righteous indignation.

We returned to Australia late in 1973 and a year later found ourselves in, of all places, Inverell. What a strange turn of events! While teaching in Sydney I had purchased a little cottage at Bundarra for my mother. She lived in it for over ten years, but prior to my going to New Zealand I sold the house and settled her in a pensioner's unit at Inverell. There were none at Bundarra, and mum had wanted to stay in that area. So it was that we returned to Inverell almost penniless. We had a difficult time finding housing but we persevered and finally found someone who was

Three generations: Pearl, her mother and son
(Photograph courtesy of the Duncan family collection)

willing to rent a flat to Aborigines. I could write a book about some of the degrading experiences we had when trying to find accommodation; it was indeed a rude awakening after New Zealand. We were eventually allocated a Housing Commission home, and my mother left her pensioner's unit to live with my son and me.

Things really upset me at Inverell and I became fired with exuberance and zeal in tackling the stark and glaring racism there. As a result I upset both black and white complacency. The whites were incensed at being accused of racism, and claimed they were not racist because they did not discriminate against all Aborigines. As Kevin Gilbert says in his book *Living Black,* discrimination is seldom directed against well-educated and articulate Aborigines, but against those who show by their demeanour that they are products of past mistreatment. The Aboriginal people did not like me because I tried to get them to recognise the subtleties of the various forms of racism. But I succeeded only in disturbing their blissful ignorance, and for this I am sorry. I should have left well enough alone, as I only alienated myself from both black and white. I became an island and, as the saying goes, 'no man is an island'.

Now that I have served on the National Aboriginal Education Committee I am able to see things in a different perspective and have a broader concept of Aboriginalisation on the national level. I am thankful that not all Aboriginal communities are as apathetic as Inverell, where the local organisation is white-oriented and white-dominated. Nowadays I keep a very low profile on Aboriginal affairs at home. I am glad that I was made a member of the National Aboriginal Education Committee, for I was able to discover for myself that there are many flourishing Aboriginal organisations functioning well at local level. After my disappointment in Inverell my faith has been somewhat restored.

I am convinced that the National Aboriginal Education Committee has a major role to play in Aboriginalisation and will go from strength to strength as the reformation in Aboriginal education begins at the national level and filters down through the state consultative groups, to the regional groups, then to the grass-roots level — the Aboriginal communities themselves.

The situation as I see it (and I can really only speak about the urban Aborigines, or the contemporary Aborigines of the eastern Australian states) is that people with an essentially Aboriginal background are suspended between the two worlds of black and white and are suffering in one way or another from 'loss of self'. In order to understand this assertion and the Aborigine who has no tribal background, it is necessary to study the past, because we are all products of our past. We all know that the Aborigines were basically proud and dignified, identifying with the earth, the seasons, and natural phenomena. Their myths and legends were all connected with survival and self-preservation. However, their rich and powerful social structure was effectively destroyed by the white settlers of this country; thus, the Aborigines had to 'assimilate' in order to survive. That assimilation had to be accomplished against enormous odds, and those who made it were few indeed. Those unable to assimilate became the outcasts of white society and generally lived in gross degradation, so that many 'part' Aborigines did not identify as Aboriginal.

What does an Aborigine do when his whole life-style has been destroyed? He takes the line of least resistance, thus becoming an object of scorn and derision for the very persons responsible for his situation.

Loss of self starts at school, where Aboriginal children can only be described as outsiders. They do not belong to a peer group, and they are unable to influence the value systems of the school or relate to its dominant pressures. They are in a state of alienation. Articulate, ambitious, middle-class, white parents are able to manipulate the ideology of the school and intercede successfully on their children's behalf. The Aboriginal children's state of alienation progressively consolidates as they pass through the school system. This loss of self, in all its forms, is impoverishment of the soul of the worst kind.

It is time, too, for many white Australians to buck against a system that stifles initiative and represses instinctive feeling and spontaneity and which, for them also, begins a loss of identity. I am confident that this phase is passing for the Aborigine. Now Aborigines are riding on the crest of the wave towards self-knowledge and self-esteem. 'Blacks long ago felt their deprivation of identity' and potential for life; but is it a prophetic statement that white 'soul' and 'blues' are just beginning?

Additional reading

Gilbert, K. (1977). *Living black.* Penguin, Melbourne
Long, J.P.M. (1970). *Aboriginal settlements.* Australian National University Press, Canberra

4

Utopian Women

Jenny Green

Emily Kame Kngwarraye pads along the road in her worn out sandshoes, chatting amiably to me in language that is a mixture of her own and English. She is a woman of strength, humour and wisdom. Her name Kame means the seed of the *atnulare* plant, a yam that grows on the land belonging to her clan (i.e. the land-holding group). This plant is significant in the clan's dreaming stories and song cycles. Her pierced nose symbolises a natural arch or rock formation that is one of the important places on her traditional country.

Although she is over seventy, Emily is full of energy and enthusiasm. She spent her childhood living in the country belonging to the Alalkere clan (her father's clan), and talks of the days before Europeans began to influence the lives of Aborigines. She now lives on one of the outstations that have recently been established on the Utopia Station lease. She is one of the many women that I grew to love and admire during the time I lived there.*

Utopia is the name given to a pastoral lease of about 1800 sq. km, situated 240 km north-east of Alice Springs. It has been cattle country since two pioneer pastoralists, Sonny and Trott Kunoth, settled there at the end of World War I. The property changed hands several times before the lease was purchased in February 1976 by the Aboriginal people living there, who formed the Angkarape cattle company to direct cattle operations and to maintain the property.

Early in 1977, after a series of experiments, they sacked the cattle-management consultant firm they had hired, appointed a book-keeper to maintain the financial and clerical side of the company's affairs, and ran the rest of the place themselves. What followed at Utopia was a process of decentralisation. Particular clans moved to establish outstation communities at Atnarare and Ngkwelaye, on their traditional land.

---

*This chapter was written in 1979 and there have been some changes since then.

After initial conflicts about the distribution of power and the cattle company's assets, equitable arrangements were achieved. The cattle business was focussed on a series of smaller outstation groups, and the company was financially independent of government funding after only two years of operation under Aboriginal ownership. The outstation movement is one of the most important things to have happened to Utopia in recent times. It signifies an affirmation of cultural independence.

Most of the younger women at Utopia grew up in the vicinity of Utopia Station, but the older women remember the time before the cattle were introduced when they lived on their own land. It was the pollution by cattle of local water supplies and the lure of tea, sugar and tobacco that prompted the Aborigines to move closer to the station homesteads. However, even after the ration system was introduced after World War II many people remained in the bush, and women walked for several days every week to collect their allocation of flour and sugar from the station. During the 1950s people gradually drifted in from the bush and established camps closer to the homesteads.

The women and girls worked for the pastoralists, and were paid in kind: brown sugar mixed with tea, flour, jam, bullock meat and a portion of plug tobacco ('niki'). They were employed in station kitchens washing dishes, clothes and floors. They looked after the station-owner's children and tended fowls and goat herds. Some women worked in stock camps. There is also evidence of Aboriginal women living as 'wives' and mistresses of European pastoralists. At that time (the 1950s) inter-marriage was illegal, and any 'mixed-blood' children could be taken and placed in special institutions far away from their parents. As Aboriginal people in Utopia say: 'Those whitefellas were hungry for *kwiye wangke'* (Anmatyerre for young woman with firm or budding breasts).

After the introduction between 1965 and 1968 of legislation granting equal pay for Aboriginal and non-Aboriginal workers in the cattle industry, many of the positions held by Aboriginal men and women lapsed. Aboriginal people remained on the fringes of stations, becoming increasingly dependent on the meagre benefits they received there. Station homesteads became the focal points for the distribution of their rations. Later, pensions and other services such as those offered by the Health and Education Departments were also dispensed from these centres.

The women now live on the five outstations that have been established on Utopia. These communities are generally small, 40-150 people, comprising several extended family groups belonging to the clan that owns the country on which the outstation has been established. Considerable mobility exists, since people travel to visit relatives, for ceremonies, hunting and shopping.

Groups of women and children spend much time together; for example, during batik and literacy classes. These gatherings serve as a forum for the rehearsal of women's song and dance rituals, they form the basis of hunting and gathering trips, and also provide an opportunity for the exchange of information and community news. In this atmosphere children are cared for and basic knowledge about child-care is handed on to the younger girls.

Women's literacy classes; Emily and Ruby in foreground

Until recently, Aboriginal women's ritual and ceremony has been relatively neglected by anthropologists. More detailed and insightful investigation of women's business is now being undertaken in some communities, but the general view that Aboriginal women play only a minor role is still prevalent, though Aboriginal women themselves have never doubted the significance of their functions in all aspects of community life.

The anthropological literature indicates that the assessment of the women's position in Aboriginal society reflects the way women were viewed in the observer's society at that time. In this way it has been possible to view Aboriginal women's ceremonial life as unimportant.

Women have an intimate knowledge of the country which is traditionally theirs, either by patrilineal association or through the ties of conception affiliation. Women also inherit rights and responsibilities for country from their mother's clan. Women have *kwertengerle* relationships to this country, and this creates links in the pattern of land ownership and religious responsibility between clans. A *kwertengerle* relationship to land can be loosely defined as a managerial role as distinct from one of ownership. As one woman at Utopia said, 'Women are the main ones for country; men just look after it.'

Women's ceremonies are called *awelye*. Women say that they perform *awelye* 'to make ourselves happy'. Their purpose can be to promote the health and well-being of the community, to instigate success in matters of love, to limit conception, or to celebrate some notable event. They are also a means of familiarising the younger women with the songs and dances that demonstrate their intense spiritual ties with traditional land,

and thus draw upon and renew the power left in the country by *altyerre* or dreamtime beings.

I was fortunate enough to observe many of the women's ceremonies, and to participate in some. One was a cycle of ceremonies associated with the country belonging to Emily's mother's clan, the Arlperre. The country was revealed to me through the performance of elaborate song cycles and dances. Every afternoon the women congregated and prepared for the *awelye*. They smeared their bodies with animal fat and traced the ceremonial designs on their breasts, arms and thighs, using brushes called *tyepale* (made from flat sticks padded with cotton). These were dipped in powders ground from charcoal, ash, and red and yellow ochre. The paintwork was appraised critically by everyone and mistakes or omissions of detail corrected. The women sang as each took her turn to be 'painted up'.

The singing continued for hours, interspersed with dance. Several women who had been painted danced together, led on many occasions by Emily, the most senior woman of the Alalkere clan. She carried the ceremonial painted stick (*kwertere*). Meanwhile the other women beat the rhythm with their hands, and sang the songs relevant to the dreaming story. These depict the travels of the dreamtime ancestors through Alalkere country, including the mountain devil (*angkerrthe*), the emu (*angkerre*) and the kangaroo (*aherre*), and other totemic plants, animals and natural forces.

The knowledge of songs is shared by many women, including those from different clans. The women are keen to record their songs on tape, and these cassettes are often produced when groups of women are together. There is often much joking and commenting about the quality of the recording, and frequency of interruptions, coughing, extraneous dialogue and the barking of dogs during the performance.

Contrary to popular belief, women play a vital role in ceremonies for the initiation of boys into manhood. These ceremonies last several weeks, and the women who are classificatory mothers for the initiates and those who are the mothers of the boys' future wives play a special role. The dancing associated with the ceremony is enjoyed by everyone. People laugh at each other's mistakes or peculiarities of style. Young girls and sometimes even small boys join with the women, and toddlers look on and clap their hands. If some fall asleep during the long night everyone is woken at dawn for the excitement of viewing the boys adorned with ochre and feathers.

Women's ceremonial life and their knowledge and attachment to their country is a key issue in the documentation of land claims. In late 1978 a group of women from Utopia and surrounding stations were asked to give evidence before the Land Commissioner, Mr Justice Toohey, in support of their claim for an area of vacant Crown land just north of Utopia that contained country belonging to several clans.

The women told of their traditional affiliations with their country and demonstrated their knowledge of family and relationship structures, of the song cycles and of important places in the country. They talked about hunting trips, and the older women told of the times when they had lived there. However, many of the women were intimidated by the court procedures because they had little experience of European meetings, these mostly being attended by men. Moreover, the women were inadequately prepared for the Utopia claims, and their evidence was treated very much as an afterthought. There was no effective interpreting service available, and the women of all clan groups were jumbled together. In addition, evidence was heard at the end of the claim hearings when time was short. During the cross-examination of the women the emphasis was clearly on the verification of genealogical information, the implication being that women have no more profound knowledge of their country than that of immediate family structures. This is not so.

After the formal part of the hearing the women suggested that they show the judge some of the song and dance cycles of their country. This provided eloquent evidence confirming their knowledge of, and attachment to, the land.

Fortunately this land claim was granted, and preparations were made for groups of the owners to move to their country and establish outstations there.

In 1979 a claim for the Utopia pastoral lease by the traditional owners was heard. (Note that a lease does not give ownership.) Then the women played a more significant role. Both women's and men's evidence was heard separately for each area of clan country, and the women performed several ceremonies for the judge. The Utopia claim was also successful, so that now Utopia people have freehold title to at least some of their country.

The environment at Utopia has been altered since the establishment of the pastoral industry there. In spite of this, following the rains in the Centre over the past few years, an abundance of plants (food and medicinal) and animals is available. As the women have a detailed knowledge of the seasonal availability and locations of these foods, much of their time is spent in collecting them. The women thus provide a valuable contribution to the diet of people living in bush communities.

Hunting trips are enjoyed by all. As many people as possible cram themselves into vehicles, together with their crowbars, axes, guns and billycans, and supplies of tea, sugar and flour to enhance the picnic afterwards.

The edible and medicinal plants collected by the women include varieties of bush potato or yam (*anatye alatyiye*), solanums or bush tomatoes (*ilperrantyiye, maynyeme, akatyerre*), wild orange (*atwakiye*), wild fig (*utyerrke*), wild banana (*alangkwe*), conkleberries (*anwekwetye*), and also the edible seeds of some acacias. Wild honey, commonly known as 'sugar bag' (*arwengarlkere*), is found in the limbs of corkwood and coolibah trees. It is scraped from the hollow, sticky centre of the tree trunks. Pitjuri (*ngkwerlpe*), a nicotine-containing plant that is mixed with fine white ash and chewed, is also collected on bush trips. The women collect plants when they are most abundant. If large quantities of a particular fruit are collected, the excess is spread on canvas roofs to dry in the sun.

Small game are also targets of the women's hunting trips. These include witchetty grubs (*tyape atnyemayte*), honey ants (*yerrampe*), and various lizards, such as the goanna (*lewatyerre*) and perentie (*ilkwete* and *amwelye*). Occasionally echidnas (*inape*) are found.

The women's skill and persistence in collecting these foods is impressive. Presented with a crowbar of my own, I had ample opportunity to attempt to emulate my teachers in the art of digging for yams, witchetty grubs and honey ants. Hunting is hard work, and after many clumsy attempts, I was usually left with an aching body and very little food; hence I have nothing but admiration for these women, who could locate the hiding place of a witchetty grub with such surety, and then prize it from its hole with a few accurate strokes of the crowbar.

One afternoon Kathleen Pitjara located echidna (*inape*) tracks in the rocky foothills and traced two of them to a low cave. Sensing danger, the two echidnas retreated to the furthest corner of their hole, just out of reach. As their hiding place was surrounded by immense rocks, it appeared that the echidnas were beyond reach, and that any further assault on their privacy would be impossible. The only way to reach them was to move a huge boulder that obstructed the entrance to the cave. After spending some hours digging around the rock with crowbars, and then using a tree trunk as a lever, the women finally dislodged the boulder and sent it crashing to the bottom of the hill, where it shattered into fragments. With the path to the cave now cleared, it was easy to pull the echidnas from their hole.

To cook echidnas the hair and quills are singed in the flames, and the quills are then removed one by one, using the teeth or pliers. Once naked, the echidna resembles a smooth round football with legs and snout. It is then buried in the coals of the fire and left to cook. Its carcass consists of a thin layer of muscle and huge swathes of fat. Most of the smaller animals, such as lizards and grubs, are also cooked in the ashes of the fire.

On bush trips I frequently lost my way. Once, to my dismay, I realised that I had left my new, black Akubra cowboy hat somewhere. Surveying those endless vistas of witchetty bush and mulga, I had no idea where I might find it. When I told Emily of my loss, she disappeared into the scrub for only a few minutes and returned with my hat.

The preparation and distribution of bush foods follows strict conventions, and to depart from these is to risk retribution from the individuals in the community who are custodians of the dreamings or totems of particular plants and animals. I once transgressed these sanctions when I decided to bake an *anwekwetye* pie. *Anwekwetye* look and taste a little like blackcurrants. I cooked the pie then moved proudly over to a group of women, imagining they might like some too. I put down the pie and left. The women threw the pie away and sent an envoy over to explain to me that *anwekwetye* is not to be cooked, but is to be eaten fresh. The women were fearful of the consequences of breaching this law relating to the preparation of food, but fortunately nothing happened, and I was excused because of my ignorance.

Bush foods provide a nutritionally valuable complement to the diet of people living in communities where hunting and gathering is still feasible. The improvement in the health of people living in outstations can be partly attributed to the increased availability of bush foods, and their lessened dependence on such foods as flour and sugar.

In 1976 the Institute for Aboriginal Development, an organisation based in Alice Springs, held literacy and numeracy courses at Utopia which lasted for several weeks. The women were motivated to learn more, and for a time afterwards the primary school teacher continued classes for the women after school. At this time I came to live at Utopia, to work with the women as a part-time instructor employed by the Department of Education. The women said that they wanted to continue learning about reading, writing and counting, and also to acquire sewing skills, to which they had been introduced while working for station owners.

I was confronted with the task of catering for the educational needs of a large and diverse group of women, ranging in age from 15 to 70 years. Some of the young women had spent several years in the primary school on the station, and so could already read and write, but others were illiterate. The classes were attended by about thirty women each day, with literacy being taught in the mornings and sewing in the afternoons. Later, one of the literate women was employed as a part-time instructor to assist the others.

We soon abandoned the idea of trying to teach everybody to read and write English, and began to concentrate on functional literacy in their own language. However, the languages spoken at Utopia, Anmatyerre and Alyawarra have had insufficient linguistic analysis to provide a basis for a bilingual literacy program. I therefore had to spend much of my spare time attempting to learn to speak the local languages myself.

I concentrated on teaching those skills which were needed in the women's everyday lives. These included the handling of money, signing

Emily and Lilly untying string from tie-dyed material
(Photograph courtesy of Toly Sawenko)

of names, reading money values, weighing and measuring. Classes inevitably expanded to include discussions about social issues such as the eligibility of women for unemployment benefits, pensions and child endowment money, voting in state and federal elections, and the functioning of government departments and other organisations.

Sewing and craft classes were extremely popular. The women learnt to do tie-dyeing and to print from woodblocks. The blocks were made by sawing cross-sections of wood, sandpapering them till smooth, then burning patterns into the wood with a piece of bent fencing wire heated red-hot in a fire. This technique of patterning wood is similar to that used to decorate traditional wooden artefacts such as dishes and carved animals.

Batik remains the most popular method of dyeing material used by the Utopia women. It has the advantage of requiring little technology, yet it is an exciting and flexible method of creating designs on cloth. It is a technique that can be well adapted to bush camp or outstation communities. The wax can be heated in metal pots or in old hub caps, over open fires, and the material can be supported either on cardboard cartons or on frames made of branches. The women apply the hot wax using brushes or Indonesian *tjantings*. After several applications of wax and dipping in different coloured dye baths, the wax is removed from the finished article by boiling, using flour drums on a fire.

Julia Murray was employed for a time as a part-time instructor by the Aboriginal Study Grants Scheme to work with the women, and she and I used to travel around the outstations, camping a few days in each and carrying sufficient material and dyes and literacy materials for our stay. The women built bough shelters — low shades of branches and leaves — to accommodate the batik and literacy workshops. We improvised sewing-machine tables out of 44-gallon drums and sheets of iron, and our chairs were flour drums resting on old tyres to give extra height.

The standard of the batik work has improved dramatically since the first tentative 'pretty flowers'. Increasingly the women are incorporating bush plants and animals into their batik designs. Some of the more elaborate pieces are like poetic and symbolic maps of the country belonging to the artist. Emily has created some beautiful silk batiks which show stories from her country, Alalkere, and contain symbols of the emu (*angkerre*) and bush tomatoes (*akatyerre*). Some of the batiks take several days of intensive waxing to complete.

At first most of the articles produced by the women were used for themselves or relatives. We then began to look for markets for batik shirts, skirts, scarves and lengths of material and devised a 'Handcrafted at Utopia' label. The women have been selling garments to shops in Alice Springs as well as privately to individuals. Although the money obtained from these sales is small in terms of the hours of work involved, the women persist because they use the money to supplement their low incomes, and clearly because they enjoy doing batik. An exhibition of the Utopia women's batik in Alice Springs almost sold out in the first week, and possibilities then opened up for interstate and overseas markets for their work.

The opportunities for employment in bush communities are limited. Although some women are employed as health workers, or in the school as teachers' aides, cooks and cleaners, most have no income, apart from that derived from child endowment, widow, old-age or invalid pensions. The incursions into Aboriginal land by the pastoral industry, and more recently by the mining industry, have in most places caused a decline in traditional hunting and gathering. Aboriginal people have now entered the cash economy, and the possibility of their becoming economically independent is crucial. The sale of batik at least has the potential for providing the women with some measure of economic independence.

From the beginning of the women's programs at Utopia there was great difficulty in obtaining from the Education Department adequate funds and materials to keep the programs going. It was necessary for us to raise our own money to purchase materials, dyes, sewing machines and all other items. The women ran hot-dog and cool-drink stalls on picture night, and sold second-hand clothes in order to raise money for the purchase of supplies. Fortunately, the women now receive an allowance from the Aboriginal Study Grants Scheme which they pool to purchase these things.

It is hoped that the batik venture will eventually become independent, but in the meantime the women need assistance and tuition in the ordering of materials, the sale of articles, distribution of profits from sales, and banking. It is crucial at this stage that the women's programs receive serious support rather than the sporadic funding offered so far.

When the Aborigines first took over Utopia, only one or two women at Utopia knew how to drive, but many were keen to learn. We started these lessons by having the women drive slowly around the airstrip in low gear, in an old Toyota with unreliable brakes and an overheating problem. In the afternoon groups of learner drivers used to pile into the truck to be taken to the airstrip, where they waited until it was their turn to have a lesson in changing gears and so on. Unfortunately, my instructions in Anmatyerre were often inadequately delivered. Emily was particularly enthusiastic, and we had some hysterical moments careering through the scrub with me grappling to extricate her foot from the accelerator, which she had frozen flat to the floor, while she, laughing in panic, let go of the wheel and clutched me. Fortunately the airstrip is treeless, lone bullocks being the only hazard for inexperienced drivers.

Funds were available through the Aboriginal Benefits Trust Fund for community projects, and the women applied for money to purchase a vehicle. Such a truck would be used for a variety of purposes: in the first place it would be used to continue the women's driving lessons. Women who knew how to drive would teach the others. It would also be used for hunting. Previously the women had been limited to either hunting within walking distance of their camps, or accompanying the men on their expeditions. When women join men's trips the results are often unsatisfactory for them, as the places chosen by the men for the pursuit of large game such as kangaroo or bush turkey rarely coincide with those places preferred by the women. The country surrounding communities that have been occupied for some time contains little game, plant foods or firewood. In contrast, the environs of the newly established outstations are more bountiful. There is a noticeable increase in the frequency of foot-walking hunting parties in these communities. However, the acquisition of motor vehicles allows the women to hunt wherever they like.

In late 1978 the application for vehicle funds was approved, and two Toyota Hilux half-tonne utilities were purchased. One was to be used by the Atnarare community and the other shared by the Three Bores and 'Homestead' communities. These trucks are used constantly, and many women can now drive. They, in turn are teaching others, especially those working as health-workers, who need a vehicle to get about more easily.

The trucks are used frequently for hunting trips, and for collecting women for ceremonies and meetings at neighbouring communities, for transporting women and children to visit the female *ngengkere* (traditional healer), for the collection of water, firewood and bush materials for modifying camps, as well as for shopping trips to neighbouring stations. Some of the older women, who had previously been camp-bound because of their age and frailty, are now taken hunting. On several occasions the women collected Julia and me for batik workshops when our own vehicles broke down.

Many women are now competent bush mechanics, and they fix vehicles that Europeans would consider unmendable with minimal equipment and a great deal of ingenuity. They are proficient at changing and patching tyres, and identifying the sources of mechanical problems.

It is important that the women maintain their independence and mobility through control of their own vehicles. There are not many communities where Aboriginal women have had the opportunity to do this, as the

Two Lillys inspecting the engine of the Atnarare women's truck
(Photograph courtesy of Julia Murray)

emphasis in government funding has usually been on the purchase of assets to be controlled by men. Some people were also very sceptical about the Aboriginal women's ability to maintain control of vehicles. However, after almost two years the truck belonging to women of the Atnarare outstation was still going and used regularly.

However the health of a community is assessed, whether by using the absence of physical illness as a gauge, or by accepting the broader definition that encompasses the mental, physical and cultural well-being of a community, there is no doubt that the impact of white contact on Aboriginal health has been devastating. The effects of an inferior European diet, insanitary living conditions and the enforced co-habitation of incompatible groups of people have led to chronic health problems. The physical and mental health of Aboriginal people has declined, with despair, distrust, alcoholism and vandalism becoming commonplace. The ceremonial and religious life of communities has been disrupted, and in many cases the ties to the land have been weakened or lost.

In the context of what is happening to Aboriginal people in most parts of Australia, the people at Utopia are in a relatively fortunate position. They have some land and are less susceptible to the destructive pressures of Europeanisation. Compared to many other communities, Utopia has few problems with alcohol, vandalism or the neglect of children. People living in outstations feel that they have more control over excessive drinking. Access to alcohol has also been clearly limited by the closure of the take-away licence at the closest hotel, 160 km away. This move was especially welcomed by the women.

In 1976-77, through the initiatives of Dr Trevor Cutter and the Central Australian Aboriginal Congress, negotiations took place with the people of Utopia regarding the establishment of a local health service. A submission was prepared and funding approved through the Department of Aboriginal Affairs. At the end of 1977 Dr Helen Tom went out to Utopia to initiate the project.

The health service is directed by the Urapuntja Council, an organisation incorporated specifically for this purpose. For the council, men and women are chosen by each community as representatives. The council regulates the employment of staff and the spending of funds allocated to the health service, and makes decisions about matters of policy. A doctor, two sisters, an administrator and nine health workers are employed by the medical service.

A crucial role in this process is played by the nine Aboriginal health workers living in the communities at Irreltye, Ammaroo, Three Bores, Utopia, Atnarare and Ngkwelaye. Most of the health workers are women. They are chosen by their communities because of their experience in midwifery, their literacy or for their general social standing. During the relatively short time that the training program has been in operation these women have made excellent progress, learning many new skills, and taking an increasing role in the provision of primary health care and community health education. They are responsible for the treatment of eye, chest, ear and gastric infections, skin wounds and infections, the administering of daily eye drops for children with trachoma, and attending daily to cleaning the children's ears and syringing them when necessary. They also provide first-aid treatment for snakebites, fractures and burns, and give advice on nutrition, antenatal care and hygiene.

The health workers also have a role in educating their communities about the proper uses of western pharmaceuticals. The Aboriginal people living at Utopia recognise a distinction between western medicines and their own. They also recognise the need for western medicines to cope with diseases introduced by white people.

The *ngengkere,* or traditional doctors, are seen as the regulators of the physical and emotional health of a community and are consulted in times of major illness or sorcery. They are men and women of unique power and training, and are recognised by reputation. Hence, people will travel long distances to visit a particular *ngengkere,* even in some instances crossing language barriers to do so. Often *ngengkere* are consulted first in the case of illness, and the advice of white doctors sought only if this fails. There is much knowledge shared by the community about the treatment of everyday health problems. Bleeding, massage and the medicinal use of native plants are practised.

On one occasion I returned from a bush trip with a raging fever and sore throat. As I lay miserable in bed, Emily appeared, suggesting that she look after me, and cursing the wind and the general unhealthiness of the place where I had become sick. Then she massaged my neck, head and arms, frequently stopping to put her hands under her armpits and wiping them across her face to moisten them with sweat. I have seen this technique used by a *ngengkere* in the treatment of snakebite.

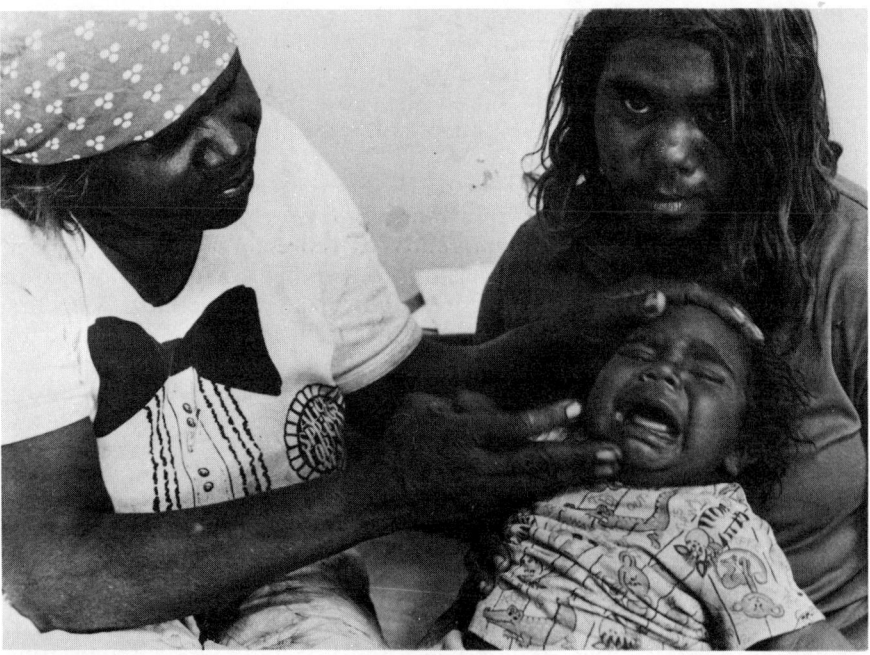

Lena and Abie, health workers, looking at a sick child
(Photograph courtesy of Toly Sawenko)

Fresh blood is used as a sterile fluid for bathing wounds and sore eyes. Many of the women have rows of fine scars on their arms, the result of cutting themselves to provide blood for the treatment of sick children. The drinking of kangaroo blood is also recognised as a strength-giving elixir.

The people have a pragmatic view of western medicines, which have now become readily available. However, medicinal plants are still collected and used. Often when on bush trips with the women we have made diversions to collect particular plants endowed with healing properties. Many of these plants are crushed with fat and used as compresses, or boiled and used for the treatment of pain, itching, scabies or bad colds.

Many of the women are respected as knowledgeable and competent midwives. Although some of the younger girls go to the hospital in Alice Springs for their first baby, for subsequent births they often place themselves in the capable hands of the older women in their communities. These women have considerable knowledge of pre-natal care, for example the identification and turning of babies that are 'lying the wrong way'. Gloria Ngale, who is identified as 'number one baby doctor', is currently training the white sister as her apprentice, and all births at the Utopia clinic are under Gloria's supervision, and thus follow Aboriginal ways.

The Urapuntja health service is achieving significant improvements in some of the health problems of the communities. It is operating successfully within the context of the outstation movement, and with the bulk of the work being carried out by Aboriginal people, particularly the women.

The Aboriginal women at Utopia are coping well with the pressures and changes in contemporary Aboriginal society. Within this changing society they represent a powerful and energetic force, in spite of the fact that their role has generally been ignored or devalued in the process of European interactions with Aboriginal communities. Utopia, at least, is alive and well.

Additional reading

Toohey, Mr Justice. *Anmatjirra and Alyawarra Land Claim to Utopia Pastoral Lease.* Report by the Aboriginal Land Commissioner to the Minister for Aboriginal Affairs and to the Administrator of the Northern Territory

5

Eileen McKenzie

Luise Hercus

Every time one of the Adnjamathanha people die, they have to go through a narrow gap and they [the dead people] grab that person and jump in the sea [Spencers Gulf] and they hit the sea so hard, that's why there's that cool change. You notice every time any of the mission people — Adnjamathanha people — die you see that cool change come with little clouds. We call cloud *vulgaṉa*. When anyone pass away they say he *vulgaṉaṉa*.

This is what Angus McKenzie, Eileen's husband explained to Sally White* and me in 1971. Similar beliefs are known from other areas, but his statement nevertheless symbolised to me the idea that there is something special about Adnjamathanha people and their country, the Northern Flinders Ranges of South Australia. The Adnjamathanha — 'the Hills People' — have some European ancestors because of the presence for over a century of European settlers, mainly from Scotland. Yet even in appearance, the Adnjamathanha stand out. As Eileen McKenzie put it:

You can always recognise us Adnjamathanha; we're heavier and have stronger and thicker legs than any of those other people. Must come from walking about on all those hills.

On another occasion it was pointed out that the 'thicker legs' could result from the Scottish ancestry of the Aboriginal population.

The Adnjamathanha stand out in other respects. All the surrounding Aboriginal languages (Guyani, Banggala, Nuguna, Yadliyawara, Biladaba and Ngadjuri) are extinct, and Dirari is reduced to a single speaker. But older Adnjamathanha people still retain their ancient traditions and the knowledge of their language and their country although many of them live and work in a European environment. Eileen McKenzie possessed

---

* Isobel White is often called Sally.

this deep knowledge of Aboriginal traditions, and the elders' anxiety that they should not be lost for future generations. She, like the late May Wilton of Beltana, helped Sally White and me to understand the women's view of their complex system of kinship terminology, which is reflected in ten different series of personal pronouns. She unravelled for us some of the intricacies of the Adnjamathanha language. Eileen was a widow when I recorded her story, but until her death she remained active and could cook and sew for herself.

Eileen McKenzie
(Photograph courtesy of the McKenzie family collection)

Like virtually all the Adnjamathanha of her generation Eileen had come to terms with her changed environment. Her life in the pastoral industry was like that of the wives of European station hands, one of hard work. But it was enriched by her Aboriginal knowledge and her sense of 'belonging' to the Adnjamathanha people and to Adnjamathanha country. Eileen herself occasionally talked about various periods of her life:

> Mum and Dad were at Wertaloona Station when I was born in 1909. I'm *unaga* [third child, girl]. My brother, Steve Coulthard, he was *widiya* [first child, boy]. He's passed away now. Then there was Wally Coulthard, *warriya* [second child, boy] in between me and Steve. Joycie is *munaga* [fifth child, girl]; *wanga* [sixth child, boy] is Sandy; Dan, Clara's husband, is *yara* [seventh child, boy]; Rosie is *ngalaga* [ninth child, girl]. *Milara* [eighth child, boy] died, and some more passed away before the names finished [i.e. the fourth and the tenth child]. Rachel's got no name [she was born when the ten Adnjamathanha birth order names had 'run out'], and then there was Mona, the last one. I'm *unaga*. Yes, Mum had a lot of babies. That was when Dad was working on the coppermine. That was a good coppermine — they called it Donald's Castle — not far out from Wooltana.
>
> We had three donkeys, and we used them to cart water from a good soak that we had there. We used to get about two 40-gallon drums,

Mr Ted Coulthard, his wife and four of their daughters. Eileen is on the left (Photograph courtesy of the McKenzie family collection)

or something like that, which we could cart with the dray. There was one donkey in the shaft and two in the lead and we used to walk and take the water back.

We were kids and Dad used to work on the mine: we were smart girls. Mum would take their dinner — there was one old white man there, Old Jack McPhail he used to be. He used to help us. Dad and Jack McPhail would dig copper and bag 'em up, and Mum used to sew the tops with a big bag needle. We used to just pick copper from the dump with little billy cans: we used to get jam tins or golden syrup tins or something like that. Then we would cut them out [on top], and when we had finished with them we'd make a little wire handle on it and then we'd go all around the dump and fill all of it and take it back to Mum to clean it. Mum might brush it, or some of us got to clean it up, and then we put it in a bag and sew it up, until we got a wagon load, and then we took it into Copley. They used to call it Leigh's Creek — that was before the coal-field. Blackfellows had a history there; it was their first business [i.e. first stage of initiation].

Rachel Brady, one of Eileen's younger sisters
(Photograph courtesy of the McKenzie family collection)

Everybody could go to this first business, (they called it *Malgara*), but not the *Yandawada* [final stage of initiation]. Women were not allowed to go to, nor young boys. From Copley we used to go back again to the mine with our stores. We never got the government ration in those days. We used to buy our stuff, but the old people — there were old people everywhere and particularly at Mount Serle — they used to get the ration: a little bit of flour, sugar, tea, rice, sago and a tin of condensed milk, and matches they used to get.

In the end the coppermine just finished. I was about nine or eight then. You know, we were sitting around Ram Paddock then. *Minarauda* they called it, because there were a lot of bullock bushes [*Heterodendron* species] there. We were sitting there and at Mount Serle, and all the time there we were getting the government ration. We were just sitting there getting rabbits — skin the rabbits and soak the skins. Then we used to wait for money. We used to get good money with the rabbits. Everybody used to do rabbiting — my grandfather and grandmother too. We all talked Adnjamathanha. Only white people talk English.

Then we were working on different stations, and we did contracting, carting wood and loads [of wool] for the stations. We had two donkey

Mr and Mrs Ted Coulthard, parents of Eileen McKenzie. Mr Coulthard used to make walking-sticks, boomerangs and fighting weapons, and his wife used to carve emu eggs. That is how they made their living, since in those days there were no pensions nor unemployment benefits for Aborigines. When he was young, Mr Coulthard used to cart wool with a donkey team from Wertaloona and other places to Copley (Photograph courtesy of the McKenzie family collection)

teams — a lot of donkeys. There were about twenty-four. We used to go with Dad, and Mum used to cook for the family. Dad would get the load of wool, and my brothers and I used to help him. My brother Wally and I would get the donkeys in the morning while Dad was having breakfast. We got them together and then we'd be ready to start. We used to take the load from Wertaloona, from Wooltana, Balcanoona and Mooloowatna, at shearing time. We used to take the wool down to Copley, and then come back with the stores. We were on the move all the time. I could have gone to school at Copley — there was a bit of a school. Mum said I could stay with someone; the de Mels used to be there, Ernie's parents. [Eileen's father and Ernie de Mel's father were first cousins.] You know, I was frightened; I didn't want to stay. I might do the wrong thing. I might get a hiding. So I'm going back with Mum.

A lot of people were camping at Mount Serle in those days, and Mum used to go back there and stay until a baby was born. One day when they know it's coming close she'd go there and wait for the baby. When a little girl is born, when they cut the cord, the grandmother will say, 'That's going to be his wife' (and she would name someone). 'I want them two to get married'. That's what happened to me, I didn't have any say in it. But we liked one another because we used to live there, at Wertaloona Station. The old McKenzies were at Wertaloona Station, and we used to take the load there and were waiting for the wool or something like that, or work around there. We were all growing up together. Everybody grew up like that. And he [Angus] was working then at Wertaloona, at Balcanoona and Wooltana. [Eileen did not refer to Angus by name; she used indirect ways of referring to him.]

I was married the blackfellow way, with a fire-stick. [A fire-stick was given to a couple as a symbol of marriage.] 'You look after your wife.' 'That's your husband and you cook for him, wash clothes and all that, and when he comes back from work you have everything ready for him.' It was my grandfather and my husband's grandfather, them two old chaps. Sydney Ryan was my grandfather, and Frome Charlie was his. He was the one with the fire-stick. And then there were those two old ladies, Mrs Ryan and Frome Charlie's wife, Lucy. She lived a long time and died at the mission. That's how I got married.

I had the two girls then. Thelma is *arranji* [oldest child, girl] and Myra is *warriga* [second child, girl]. That terrible depression was on then: you can't get a job. So we sat down at Ram Paddock and we used to get rations, a pannikin of flour and a pannikin of sugar for each. We used to get that every Friday. That would have to last us till the next Friday. I made little Johnny cakes and I used to be very careful. Get a rabbit, or get a little kangaroo-meat and fry it up with the flour. That's like a damper. You must never waste something like that. You've just got to have meat and tea. Going out and getting kangaroos with the dogs and catching some rabbits with traps was all we used to do. We used to do kangarooing a long time ago. That's when you got to make a living for money. We never do it now.

Then, after, we *did* get a job. That's when they were doing the crutching at Wertaloona. They would be going out for the crutching for maybe a fortnight, and I would just be waiting there, catching rabbits. Or we might get a bit of meat from the station, a quarter between us.

Ram Paddock was a real Aboriginal place, and the white people shouldn't have hunted them from there. That's real Adnjamathanha history place, and so is Mount Serle and that special little spring down from Mount Serle — Adu-wathanha they call 'im. The squatters there used to be nice people, but then another lot came at Mount Serle, Ram Paddock, Patsy Spring and Mount Finniss, and these new whites made everybody go. There's been a missionary there for a while before, and it was all right then. People used to camp around the houses at Mount Serle and everywhere, but when the missionary came [to settle permanently], those whites didn't want the mission close to their houses so everybody who was still at Mount Serle had to shift first to Ram Paddock. After that, Mr Thomas from Balcanoona gave them the land at Nepabunna: we Adnjamathanha had a big waterhole there — Niba-awi — and a big rock — Niba-bana. Those white people didn't want the mission near their house. They reckoned it would spoil their kids. That must have been in 1931 because we were the first to move out from Ram Paddock before they all got hunted from there and we camped at Niba-awi for over a month before the mission went there: my boy Eric was the first child born at the mission. They were real good people that first lot of missionaries, Mr Eaton and them. They had a good shop there too.

We'd had an old Tin Lizzie [model T Ford] to get around and work, but then it didn't go properly any more. And then in the depression we can't get the petrol. You see, you can't buy it, you might just get a gallon. So we left the car in an old dray shed at Wertaloona and we made a bun-cart [the chassis and wheels of an old car made into a horse-drawn vehicle] from the old buggy. And later on we got some more donkeys. Well, my brother got them when he was working on Murnpeowie Station (that's the brother that passed away), and he sent us a letter and said, 'If you come over here' (because he'd joined the army then), 'you come here and bring the kids, I get some donkeys here for 'em and a cart'. They were pleased too. And we got to go there. 'Oh, Uncle,' they said, 'give us a donkey!' He said, 'There's three donkeys and a cart. You can take that and a goat. He gives us *two* goats — and the little kiddies! So we managed to get the dray back, and the cart and donkeys. And now it was *our* donkeys. And we took the new cart and left the old cart with Mum and them at Nepabunna so that they could cart wood for the people there. We got another donkey, and we used to go round working with the bun-cart with four donkeys to drag it.

And that brother, Steve, he was in the army, and he died there. He had the measles and he was cooking. He was cooking up dampers for the soldiers. He got pneumonia, and it was too late to take him to the doctor. And he died.

We got an old blitz wagon [a rough and tough, World War II truck] later. It was all right. We went to Wertaloona to make a big yard for cattle, and then we used to go up to Mooloowatna fencing. And I got very sick (that was before Barry was born), and my husband took me 'in the blitz' all the way to Broken Hill to the hospital. And I had to have treatment there for a long time for that sickness. Then we sold the 'blitz' and got a little Ford; and then a Ford V8. In the end we had a Landrover. We were travelling around working everywhere. We were really living at Nepabunna, but I used to go out with him [Angus] when he was working all the time and Myra and Thelma [Angus and Eileen's daughters] were stopping there at Nepabunna with Mum. That's why Myra and Thelma can talk Adnjamathanha right through — they stopped with their grandmother. And when they were big enough to cook for themselves they had Mark and Eric [their brothers] with them. They went to school at the mission, and they can read and write and send for parcels and that.

Lately there was some work on the highway. [Angus] worked until the last. He got the sickness when he was working on the highway up there. He got very sick then. He can't work any more, the doctor told him, and he's got to come closer to the doctor. So we were living in that house in Hawker where you've seen us. [Angus] used to come down here [Port Augusta] to see the doctor. The doctor said, 'You've got to come and get a place here.' And so we got this house. [Angus] had very high blood pressure and he got worse, you see. [Eileen never again pronounced his name and used indirect ways of referring to him.]

We go to Hawker and to Nepabunna when it's something special — like when my cousin passed away.

It's a good place here and we like it. Myra is not working now, she's got to look after me now. She's with me all the time now, and her little boy.

I was sad when I heard in January 1981 that my friend Eileen McKenzie had died.

Additional reading

Hercus, L.A. and White, I.M. (1973). Perception of kinship structure reflected in the Adnjamathanha pronouns. *Papers in Australian Linguistics No. 6,* Department of Linguistics, Research School of Pacific Studies, Australian National University

Schebeck, B. (1974). The Adnjamathanha pronoun and the 'Wailpi kinship system'. *Papers in Australian Linguistics No. 6,* Department of Linguistics, Research School of Pacific Studies, Australian National University

────── (1974). *Texts on the social system of the Atynyamatana people with grammatical notes* (Pacific Linguistics, Series D, No. 21). Department of Linguistics, Research School of Pacific Studies, Australian National University

6

I Was a Drover Once Myself: Amy Laurie of Kununurra

Amy Laurie and Ann McGrath

Amy Laurie was about sixty-nine years of age when I recorded her experiences. She lives in a Housing Commission home in Kununurra which serves as a meeting place for her numerous relatives, some of whom spend most of the dry season on the surrounding Kimberley cattle stations. As Amy explains, 'You should see when they all come in together. This yard is going to be full.' Much of her time these days is taken up looking after the youngest of her twenty-one grandchildren. Possessing an excellent rapport with the teenagers, she listens attentively to their viewpoints, taking an active interest in land rights and other vital issues affecting Aboriginal people. She is astutely aware of the dilemmas and difficulties facing the younger generation, but despite the absence of ultimate solutions, she remains positive. Amy is eager to share her past experiences with 'the kids', telling them a 'good yarn' about 'early day black-fellers' or a 'bullock rush', and teaching them pride in their culture.

I first met Amy Laurie through Helen Sheehan and Sylvia Hurse, partners in a female-staffed hawking business serving north-west stations and settlements. When I told them of my research interests in Aboriginal women's work in the Northern Territory before World War II, they recommended that I should visit Kununurra and meet Amy. When I did visit there in 1978, Sylvia drove me to collect Amy and bring her back to Sylvia's house. Before getting out of the car, Amy had already launched into her life story. Young people today did not believe she was a horseman and drover, she explained, with obvious pride in her achievements. She narrated her first experiences with horses and in stock-camps with a vibrant sense of immediacy and humour. Sometimes her jokes eluded me because of my unfamiliarity with her rapid and often excited speech, but I found myself irresistibly joining in with her laughter.

I was a drover once myself 77

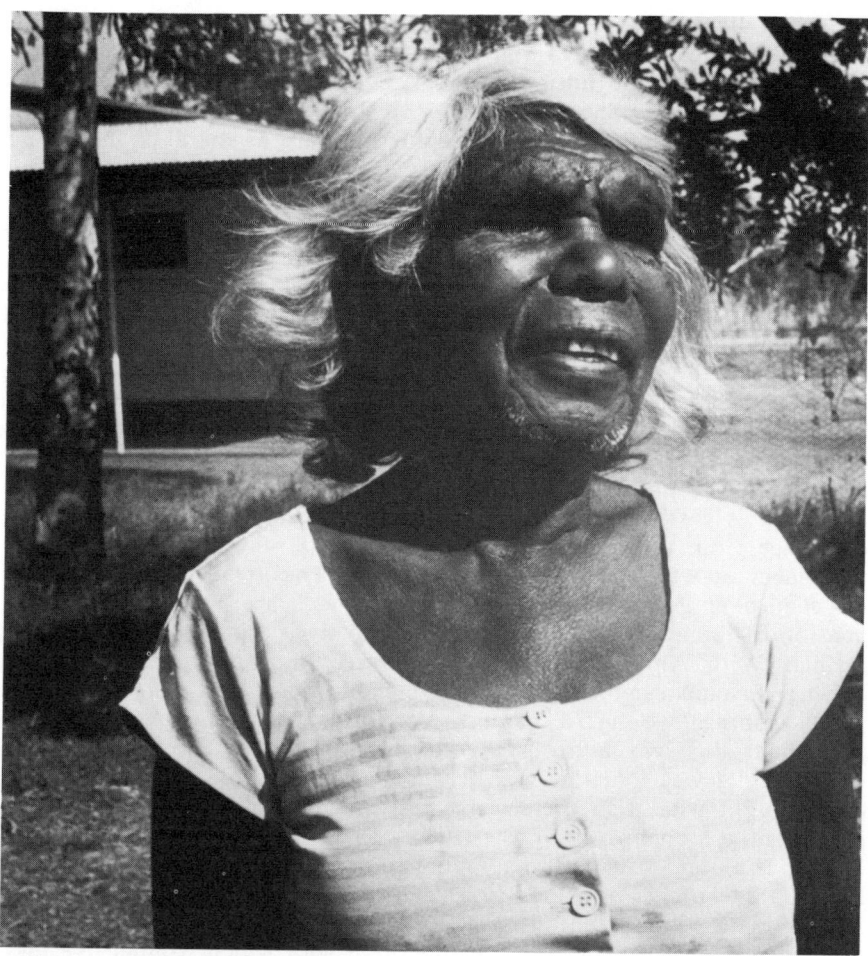

Amy Laurie (Photograph by Bruce Shaw)

After a few taping sessions, we made a video together so the school children could hear the 'early day stories'. Amy ran the show, even prodding me to ask leading questions so she would have the opportunity to repeat her favourite yarns. We sat on blankets in her front yard, under the shade of her special gum tree — 'my countryman tree' — while young children scurried past the camera hoping to get on film, and one of her grandchildren thrust his small body on to her lap. Once, a group of small children started a grassfire in her yard in the middle of one of Amy's fascinating narratives. First she yelled out at them to throw sand on the fire, but then changed the instructions, telling them to keep it going so the long grass, which she considered untidy, would be burnt off.

It was sad saying goodbye to Amy, and I felt something of a traitor to be returning to the south after just beginning the friendship, like so many Europeans have done over the years. Amy said she would miss my visits. Only a few whites in the town have anything to do with Aborigines, and Amy likes to have friends of 'different colours' and ages. In July 1979 I drove to Kununurra and eventually caught up with her again. She did not recognise me until I was very close, as her eyes were clouded over with cataracts. She looked older, a little worn out, and was having money problems and difficulties keeping her yard as she liked it. 'I'd like a bit of a block so I could have a garden; I'm too old to dig one myself, but I'm gonna ask that welfare mob to dig up the dirt so I can plant some flowers.' Amy has a knack for getting things done. She persisted, and on later visits I found her with a nice garden plot.

She managed to secure some time away from her baby-sitting tasks to take me and a friend fishing on the Ord River. On the journey her vision improved; she was able to distinguish intricate details of the landscape, pointing out the routes she took on droving expeditions, and describing the whereabouts of almost hidden waterholes where they used to herd the bullocks. She told us about the country now flooded beneath the massive lake Argyle and recollected that some of the Miriwong people cried for it when it was immersed by the dam waters. Amy's knowledge of the landscape is vast; she described in detail the lands lying behind what we could see from the road. She also told dozens of yarns associated with the places at which she had once camped. The great distances drovers travelled over this rugged country on horseback are beyond the comprehension of the average Australian, and droving is a lifestyle now virtually extinct. With Amy as guide we traversed the countryside, eventually driving through car-high grass to find magnificent and peaceful waters. While fishing, we heard strange piercing shrieks, but Amy was not perturbed: this was a brolga protecting its young. The fish were not biting, and I was told this was because it was the cold time of the year. Amy caught what fish there were, resisting returning to town until the last possible moment.

Amy is a good friend, and sometimes, probably because of our relative ages, I think of her as a grand parent. Like my own grandmother, she is imbued with vitality, enthusiasm, and the ability to throw herself into life. Earthy and realistic, the positive drive with which women like these conducted their lives left them little time for bitterness or anger, though there are some regrets. Amy always wanted to learn to read and write, and admits it may now be too difficult because of her failing eyesight.

Determined to survive in the white-dominated frontier, Amy adapted to her environment. Though some of her grandchildren may criticise the compromises she made, they maintain a special respect and love for her. Despite the extremely racist nature of the Kimberley frontier, Amy bravely maintained her self-confidence and pride. Strong women like Amy and my grandmother have laid solid foundations for a less-accommodating younger generation. Amy Laurie has contributed lessons of simple dignity and resolute courage. Fragments are revealed in this story which we so enjoyed sharing.

Earlier, Amy had sketched the outline of her life for an article by J. Gardiner in the *Kununurra News*. A summary will make her own yarn easier to understand.

Amy's maternal grandmother, whose European name was Lucy, was a Gurindji woman who was married first to an Aboriginal man, by whom she had a son Jack and a daughter Alice (Amy's mother). Lucy and her two children were taken from her husband by Jim McDonald, of Scottish origin, at that time the owner of Kirkimbie Station in the Northern Territory. Jim married Lucy and they had several more children. Lucy's daughter, Alice Yarwar, when old enough, was 'given' by Jim McDonald, to be the wife of Mulga Jim, one of the station stockmen, an Aranda man from Hermannsburg. Amy was their eldest daughter.

She grew up around the station quarters rather than the Aboriginal camps. When she was about twelve, McDonald sold Kirkimbie and they moved to Salt Pan. After a major flood they went to Palm Springs, near Halls Creek, and later to Spring Creek. When Amy reached twenty, her father, Mulga Jim, arranged her marriage to Alec Smith, the son of an Aboriginal woman and a European drover from Queensland. Amy and Alec joined a droving team and worked at many pastoral stations in the East Kimberleys. She was widowed within a year or so when Alec died of fever.

Amy's second husband was George Ah Kim, a man of Chinese and Aboriginal descent. Their daughter Phyllis was newborn when he was accidentally killed. Amy feared that her daughter would be seized by police, who had power to place 'half-caste' children at Forrest River Mission. Her wedding to Don 'Darkie' Green, the son of an Afghan camel driver and an Aboriginal woman, enabled her to keep Phyllis. With their other two children, Pearl and Tex, they lived for a while at Rosewood Station, where Amy worked as a domestic. Eventually, after the war, Darkie left Amy and secured a divorce. She then married Bill Laurie,

Taken at Palm Springs in 1923. Jim McDonald (standing beside the car), Amy Laurie (standing immediately behind the car), holding her young brother Sammy, and Amy's mother (standing next to Amy)
(Photograph courtesy of the Australian Investment Agency)

who was also of Aboriginal descent. Bill and Amy and their children Martha and Reggie lived at Kildurk, and later at Lissadell. They separated because of Amy's drinking problem, but she would not divorce him. Later, she met Leo Thomas, a Queenslander of Aboriginal ancestry. They moved to Kununurra when work on the diversion dam was beginning, around the early 1960s. For many years now Amy has lived as a single woman at Kununurra, earlier at various camps and more recently in a home in town.

> I've never been in school. My experience was on the bullock. That's why I sit down and think all the time that I'm getting old now, that nobody knows my home, my friends. We had many years of travelling; they're all gone. Since I left the grog, over two years ago, I started thinking then, and now all my memories have come back to me. That's why I like to tell the story and everything like that of what I knew when I was a kid. All my memory came back to me of what my great-grandfather, great-grandmother told me. That's how I came to think about old time stories.
>
> My grandmother was Gurindji, a dark girl. My mother was Djaru from Ord River. She married to colour — a black-feller, Aranda from Hermannsburg — and he was a good black-feller too, with his own horses and things like that. He came from Darwin my [other] old grandfather. And this white bloke, a Scotsman — old Jim McDonald — that's the grandfather who grew me up. My grannie fell in love with old man McDonald and that's why he had six sons [she had six children] — one in Queensland, Alec ['Sandy'] McDonald, Duncan McDonald. My mother and my uncle, they're black, but the others were half-castes.
>
> We all came to that quiet country you know [the area now 'pacified', when the first violence was over], but before that the black people didn't know the white man, didn't know horses. My great-great-grandmother and grandfather didn't know anything [about white things]. When they saw the [first] white man coming with the wagons through Inverway Station down to Sturt Creek, they reckoned, 'That's the Mamu — devil-devil.' . . . My great-grandmother told me when I was a good size girl — not real tall . . . The first horses they saw they killed them for meat; they cut them on the front — brisket part — and left the rest . . . My great-grandfather and mother used to tell me about that first white man . . . They tried to run away, running around in a little bit of bush and scrub and singing with the boomerang. 'That's the white devil-devil riding 'nother devil-devil,' they used to say. 'Yes, that's the devil coming. Look out!' And the white man kept riding closer. Then they started singing the devil. They were killing with the boomerang, singing 'k-i-l-l-i-n-g the boomerang' like that, and these two came right up. The black-fellers got up and ran away. That was Leichhardt [possibly Lake Hall, as there is no evidence that Leichhardt reached the Kimberleys] travelling with the wagon team to Inverway and down to Ord River. He started shooting them. . .
>
> The old native people used to have a camp there, at a lily pond straight down from the junction of the Ord River and the big Ord

River. They were fishing all along the river, [using a technique of] rolling up the spinifex grass to get the fish. They never did anything to the bloke; just fishing. The white man was coming up — all in white, and the first Aborigine who looked at him was afraid and ran away . . . and you know what they [the white men] did next? Shot the lot! But two young boys got away. They were underneath the grass that they rolled the fish in, and they put those lily roots on top of their heads . . . Two old fellers who were sitting up making the big fire for fish on top of the bank . . . thought the noise was the stones cracking in the fire . . . The two boys went up to Turner to tell the other mob there was some sort of a people in this country who kills you. 'They had something long on one finger [hand], and when it points and coughs, people die. A big mob are dead in the water like fish,' they were telling this mob. 'Don't wait when you see them. There's some sort of an animal they ride bigger than kangaroo' . . . that's the horse. After that they didn't start to fight because they had nothing to fight with — only boomerangs and a few spears. They went over to the other side of the hill then, near Turkey Creek, and went up in the hills and stayed around there, never coming down to the river.

Later that bloke [probably Buchanan] came up with the wagon and started mustering all the black-fellers, and quietening them all down. This is how they started Ord River Station. My grannie was a young girl then camping at the creek where the Racecourse is now . . . The white man came there and made the camp. They had tents everywhere, and were quietening down all the bush black-fellers. They'd get all the young girls and young boys for the work . . . and they didn't want to fight. The mob from Dunham River down to Wyndham and over at Gordon Downs were cheeky. They used to spear the whites, but not around this way . . . They thought he was a devil all the time until my father came. He had a bit of a language and he'd say, 'This a different mob of people. They're black and we're white; that's gotta be our company in this world.'

Before that, people would come into the station for their kids, because they took all the women and some young boys, and taught them to talk English and kept them on the stations . . . Men about twenty-one or thirty, they shot them down. One thing, they never killed all the kids — only the big men who might be strong, some married men and single boys, but not all the young teenage boys . . . They quietened them down like the horses. The white blokes told them, 'We don't want to kill you.' My father knew the language, and talked — 'Not kill, because we wanta be mate longa white man. Muster the horses, the bullock and everything, and learn you English and all that.'

My father, Mulga Jim, went right to Kalumburu quietening all the people, you know. He used to tell them not to run away but stand up. They had nothing on, and didn't know who the stockmen were. There was not a station or anything, just tents, donkey wagons, bullock wagons. That bloke Leichhardt [or Lake Hall] from Queensland, he came right up to the Ord River, and that's where he finished up. The blokes who quietened down the people started on young girls — pretty dark ladies — and that's where the half-castes come from. All the young white men chased the dark woman and the half-castes were bred from this. The dark girls used to be frightened of the white man, but later they were getting married to them all around . . . The old men told the white bloke, 'All right, you wantim this young girl, you can havim, you can live with him.' They'd say, 'Yes, I'm too old now, you can take him.' ['him' here means 'her']. They used to grow them up. The blokes gave them everything — blankets, clothes, things like that; they didn't know how to use them. The white men taught them how to make a bed and cover himself up, and flour . . . they started making paint to paint themselves for the corroboree. They were wasting the flour! . . . All the time people like my great-grandfather and mother used to tell us, 'We didn't know horses. We didn't know white man. We didn't know everything! From Ord River right up to Mistake Creek, right up to Flora Valley, down to here — they didn't know anything. Poor feller, I reckon. What they want to shoot him like that for?

On the stations it worked like this: your [European] father would quieten my father, who'd quieten down my mother and everybody else like my brother, and explain why the man came from the station looking for them. My father, who'd been a schoolboy, was very good to tell the white man not to attack the black-fellers, to leave the young boys and young girls for work, and their mothers. He used to tell them, 'You must leave mother and father to keep them happy.' My father went to a big court down at Perth as a witness over killings by policemen who were shooting people right down to Kalumburu. [This was related to the Forrest River massacres 1926-27.] They shot people because they were wild and fought back to the policemen . . . When all the policemen and policeboys had gone a long way away, the black-fellers would sneak up. They'd creep up to the camp shelters, and sneak up and spear them, but all the men came up from outside and shot them. The black-fellers also used to plant themselves — some in a tree, some in a big rock — and everyone was hiding like that . . .

Around 1912 they started having that Forrest River Mission. That's the old Noble missionary — my father's [adopted] countryman who came from Queensland. My father started telling policemen, 'What about we save the kids? Save the small ones and you can do what you like with the big ones that are cheeky.' He told those policemen to stop shooting from temper, told them to stop because they might be in big trouble afterwards. That missionary wanted all the blacks from this country down right through to Wyndham.

The evidence given by Amy's father, Mulga Jim, to the 1927 Royal Commission on police behaviour in the East Kimberleys declared that police had not ill-treated or murdered Aborigines near the Forrest River mission. It included some biographical details:

I came from Alice Springs, SA. I have been in this country a long time working as a stock-boy and drover. I came to Wyndham with Jack Salmon with bullocks and Constable Regan told me about the murder of Harry and asked me to help him catch the murderer. Regan and some other white men went out with Sulieman, Frank, Charlie and myself . . .

Amy herself remembers something of her father's association with Forrest River:

My father and Noble talked together in their language. At the mission they looked after a big mob of kids . . . they're all my brothers, because my father adopted them and left them there at the mission. He said they were his, and when he got married, he might come and pick them up, and that's how we came to be relations with black people so those people couldn't go against us. They all think about me from the mission — everyone looks out for me — sisters and others, because my father was good to them, though he's from a different tribe — Aranda from Alice Springs. This way is Warlpiri on this side, Gurindji and Mudbura people. All of them are together now.

When I was a little baby, when I was born, I was at Kirkimbie Station, Northern Territory. We had a bit of a cattle station there, but they left it after all the stockmen had a row . . . I was reared up in Western Australia because my father moved away from the Territory to find another job. He used to get paid, but he was the most sensible out of that big mob who worked on the station mustering bullocks and things like that when I was a little one. He came to Saltpan with old man McDonald, Duncan, Sandy and somewhere about three or four hundred horses. I can just remember shifting from Kirkimbie Station to Salt Pan. We used to work on that salt — it grows really big — and there was a spring running through it, and lots of stone heaps. You wash it with the water and next morning you just get something like a big spoon to scoop up all the salt. Very good place. We used to cart the salt by donkey wagon to Ord River Station. That was around 1922. It flooded then — Ord River Station, Turner, Flora Valley, Mistake Creek. They were all flooded, and we nearly got drowned except that we were on a little island.

That's why my grandfather shifted from there and we went to Palm Springs, near Halls Creek. This place had a big garden and grew bananas, dates and vegetables. We couldn't stop there long, and they didn't make a living because the kids ate all the fruit. Jack Skeehan, David Skeehan's father, had that place. That's where grandfather [Jim McDonald] died. Duncan was a teenage boy, Sandy was a good size boy, and I was a middle aged 'boy'. Skeehan sold all the horses to my father; they could pick out whichever horse they wanted . . . 'I want that horse.' 'All right you can take this one now' — like that. But my two uncles said, 'No, we don't want any horses.' My father took six, seven, maybe eight horses with saddles and everything, just for the family. Timor ponies — a good lot of horses. He sold all of them. That's why we came down this way then. My father came down to Spring Creek [a Vestey's Station in northern Western Australia], and we started work. I was only a girl then — somewhere about nineteen — riding horses. From when I was young, I worked the bullock the same as the boys . . . Women used to like it you know, like to be alone, droving all the time. Some friends and I, we all liked it. Riding horses and working in the stock camp — that was my experience . . . I first started when I was about ten.

When I was a little one, you know what those stockmen used to do? Chuck me over! Pick me up from my bed. They'd say, 'You wanta sleep all the time?' Bang! — and down in the water. There was a big mob of girls and boys; they did it to all of them . . . We'd be coming back wet, cold . . . sometimes about six o'clock in the morning, before sunrise, we had to go on the horses. 'No go out!' 'Oh, really?' When I got up to twenty-one I was married — tribal law you know — and left the place with my husband, and that year he died, droving. He was a boy from Queensland named Alec Smith. He had taught me to ride when I was younger. He used to make me get on the horses and when I fell down from the horse he gotta belt me — give me a whipping. 'You gotta stick to the saddle', he'd say . . . I liked riding, but it's a long job. You get tired riding such a long, long way. A hard life but I used to like it.

I was working with a bloke called Nugget Quinlan, who also came from Queensland. He had a droving station, and we stopped and worked for him there at Nine Mile Station [near Wyndham]. My father, my mother and some others were with me. They've all died now, but each would work . . . walking the cattle to No. 3 Bore, Gordon Downs and Sturt Creek, then go to No. 4, call in at No. 7, and more. We used to meet them cattle. And I on a horse. We'd go to Wyndham, to the dock there, to the aerodrome which they cut all the trees down to make. That's where the road was for the bullock; it was a clear tunnel which met up with the river at the base of Coolibah Pocket. We'd go to Colorado boundary, from there to Maxwell Plain at Carlton Reach — the Racecourse now. We used to call it Lily Creek when we were droving. Sometimes we'd camp up at a place called Four Mile. That bloke Terry [Brahn] has a place that used to be our camping area for the bullocks, and a stockyard belonging to Ivanhoe Station was right where the PWD [Public Works Department] yard is now. This country had no houses of any sort. It was just a wild country — a big jungle. They just cut all the trees down.

Those droving days were good. I used to do cooking and horsetailing. I'd pack up all those packs on the horses, on all the roads, make the camp-places where the bullock can lay and cook by myself. We'd camp all the way from Waterloo right to here, the Kununurra racecourse. Some boys came up from Wyndham and I had a holiday. We were short-handed man — only five of us — three men and two women. All those other mates have now died . . . I reckon I had my best days because of cattle work. Droving is the best. These young people, when they say 'I can't ride a horse', they can't. Day and night I watched the bullocks. Might be horsetailing from eight in the night up to ten at night, then another man or woman would come in and watch when you're asleep . . . all the way like that, we'd watch the bullocks. Sometimes there'd be a big rush — you've got to be on a horse. They used to be really wild bullocks. We had one rush down there at Four

Mile on that road to Cockatoo. You know where Bubba Darey lives at Golden Gate? We came through that way with all Victoria River bullocks — really big ones that carry trees and all. They had another rush with lots of bullocks. We were camping up near here and another mob was at the racecourse. That night the two of us — that mob and this mob — got mixed up. We didn't know what bullocks belonged to who but for earmarks. The Rosewood mob went back to Rosewood, the Victoria mob back to Victoria River Downs. Oh, we had a lot of rough times. You can't put that cattle through the gorge. You've got to jump off your horses, leave your horses sitting down. Some of the mob has got to be in front and another mob cuts the other mob off; and, half-'n'-half, you've got to put them through the gorge. When that big rain came one time we were at No. 3 Bore. No trees there, just a plain. They call it Munga Plain — this side of Dirrindudu. Oh, you can't hold the cattle there. They got this way and that way, and make the ground very dry. You've got to move them all along. Big work there. I could've been a millionaire if I'd known — if they would have paid me! I keep thinking about that. I left droving because I had a kid, though for a while I carried the kid in the saddle. When I was about twenty-two, I started having a baby. I wasn't like these young girls today: I didn't play with the young boys like these girls. The first baby I had was to a Chinese half-caste, George Ah Kim, who I was living with before Darkie Green picked me up. He was born in Australia to a black mother, and his father had a garden at Muggs Lagoon. He was well-educated — come back from China. I only had him for one year, and soon as the baby was born, he had an accident on Rosewood Station. A horse fell on top of him and he died. Might be wild horse, quiet horse, the drovers they were always changing horses — fresh horse every day. I remember the last time I went down droving through Cockatoo Lagoon up to Coolibah, right down to Wyndham and back. That took a long time. After that I thought well I can't ride horses, can't put kids on them, so I told my boss, 'I can't ride a horse anymore 'cause I got a family now, coming.' When I was young I never had none.

In those days we never got nothing — no wages. You know that day [in those days] coloured people can't get paid or something like that. Some blokes, the white man, got paid. But I never got no money out of it. Old Quinlan started thinking about the pay like the Queensland award, and one time he said like, 'All right, you are a very good woman. I'll give you six horses.' He gave me saddles, bridles, packs and things, and I started selling those horses. He gave me clothes, and we used to eat tucker all right, but all the rest of the time we were working for him we were never paid anything but tucker and clothes, and anything we wanted from the store. Anything you wanted you got because we didn't know money. Some people came in from working on Ord River and Mistake Creek Stations. They said, 'What's the matter this one don't pay you?' 'You know money?' 'No . . .' After that Quinlan was telling us, 'Now, I'm gonna pay you next year like . . .' Oh, we were there for nearly two years droving with him . . . and this New Year of another year came and I started getting forty dollar a month like that, and I recognised the money. It was £2 or a £3 note — pounds before, not the dollar.

I used to give the money to my husband. I had this Darkie Green then, and he'd buy all the things, because he had his schooling and his friends and things like that, not me. He was a coloured man. You know a long time ago Afghans were in this country, with camel wagons, donkey wagons, travelling on the road. His mother was running around with the Afghan, so he had a bit of colour in him. Oh, they're all different — different nations you know — some Chinaman, some Afghan; there's got to be some Japanese at Halls Creek. They're coming on these young girls.

When I was a younger woman with kids I saw everybody chasing after white men for husbands, but I didn't think about all that. A lot of blokes asked me and I said, 'I don't know, not right thing. Might be for some people . . . I got too many of my own relations, and my parents.' A *lot* of blokes asked me you know. I said 'I can't' and how I felt. If I was on my own, with no family to think about, like my uncle, and all the others, my parents' relations, then maybe. But I was afraid they'd say 'Oh, we don't want to go to that woman now — she married to the [white] bloke' . . .

When they bombed Wyndham [March 1942], in that Second War — Japanese war — I was with Darkie Green, and I had two daughters, Phyllis and Pearly — one four and one a baby. We were camping near Wyndham and that night the bomb fell. We walked away that night — all night with the two kids . . . We broke all the green grass and put it all over the truck to cover it up. We had a big truck with a load, and we were frightened. We travelled right back to Rosewood and worked there then. On our way we went camping and all the black-fellers were everywhere. They didn't know about the bombs. All the 'sensible' boys and girls talked to them. They were still myalls. We travelled all night telling the folk to look out for bombs, but those other people couldn't understand, and today you can't put any sense into them yet.

After I left old Bill Laurie because he was drunk and belting me too much, I had a bloke from Queensland called Leo Thomas. We used to work for George Wilson, a contractor for Kununurra fencing. We'd go down to Wyndham to get the cement in a big truck; then we'd cart all the cement up to the hill and start making the fence for that tower on top of Kelly's Knob. That pub wasn't there; they had a canteen over there and everybody used to go and have a feed and a drink [around 1959-61]. There were no bottles or cans, but they'd pour grog into a big tank like a petrol tank and fill billy-cans up with grog. This Kununurra was nothing. All our children used to go to school at KRS [Kimberley Research Station], and they shifted Ivanhoe at the Crossing because down there it was too low and the water spilled over. After that they built a toilet — right where the Camer-Pesci pub is now — and everybody went there to have a bath. And that PWD building was the office where we used to get that dole. And they started making the houses all the way along. No hospital . . . the first hospital was straight up from the Co-op building. That's where my daughter Martha got married in the church to Johnny Nixon. And all them Yankees they started putting up a school, and me and the boy I was living with worked there. I used to clean up toilets, louvres, and all the rubbish. After it was finished, clean up, wash all the house inside, clear away rubbish, put it together and cart it away. Kununurra started to be a town then . . . I used to work helping carpenters. Those days cheap — clothes and things weren't dear. I didn't know what to do with the money. I used to get good pay. That's the first time I saw the money then, and I gave it to the bloke I was living with who came from Queensland. He used to buy me something but I was never interested . . . The old people at the Reserve tell me there was a Dreaming (like Adam and Eve — black-fellers calls it Dreaming) near that hill across from my camp. All the dogs used to take all the whores [female dogs] down to the water to breed puppies [i.e. a Dog Dreaming site]. . . . That was a long time ago — before Kununurra. I didn't think that I could still live to see Kununurra growing like now. And how many grandchildren you reckon I have now? Twenty-one! All big ones, and some of them are married now. One of them is married to a policeman in Perth; one boy is on a station. You should see when they all come in together. This yard is going to be full!

Looking at my boys [grandchildren], I tell them, 'You wanta be good boys, and maybe one day they might put you longa Gurindji side, longa my countryside. But you've gotta put up with that strict law.' In my country, Gurindji, they don't like wrong people married. You've got to be straight skin [have a proper marriage; "skin" means sub-section], and that's why I ran away from my country and I wouldn't go back. This way they've got none: like a white man, they don't know what the Law is. Maybe two or three old people know, but there were too many people working at Lake Nash Station, Ivanhoe Station, and maybe Carlton Station. They never could get up with any sort of Law these days. The Texas Downs mob, the Turkey Creek mob came up here and the Gurindji mob came here last year and started talking about tribal law . . .

The Gurindji mob say that now the tribal Law is the better. You have to keep all the young boys away from their mothers, and they aren't allowed to talk to young girls. They treat the boys rough. A silly boy is left out in the bush for about a year and not allowed to see his parents. I reckon jail is better, but jail is no good to them, because they can't learn. They do the same thing, and go to jail more and more.

In a way I don't like the tribal Law, because it's too hard for the kids. I sit down and preach to my grandchildren at night-time, and talk to them. Kenny was a good boy all the way, and Garry, he was a bad boy, but they listen to me what I tell them. They wouldn't listen to old Pearly, their mother. They say, 'We'd sooner listen to good yarn old grandma got.' They don't want to talk to young girls in front of grandma. I tell them not to walk around at night: 'Make your bed, play the music and go to sleep'. They take notice of grandma because they're right up with the grandma and they love grandma and I love them too. All them kids, I like kids. I don't go hard on them; I belt them when they do the wrong thing, but only when I catch them at the right time, not for nothing. I told them they should take notice of their mother: 'I'm just grandmother to take care of you that way'. I reared nearly all of them up — all the Haywood family boys, Johnson family, a few others round here in this town. They're big boys now. These women around Kununurra don't teach their daughters how to do housework. I see young girls running around after school. They want to run for grog or boys. I used to make them work. One worked at Kildurk for the Duracks and the other at the Wyndham pub. Now they are married they tell me 'You're not boss anymore'. Martha tells me that.

I used to get really *mad* on the grog, but not now. I don't think of it, and I've no patience for grog now. They sit around me drinking and I don't like the smell of him no more. When I go to the pub, I just sit down and maybe have a couple of bottles of cool drink and bring some cans home. I don't like the women sitting near me if I can smell that breath with grog on it.

When I was a drunken woman the police got me for drunk-an'-run-around, and that's why I left the grog. I used to end up in jail all the time — three months. They didn't think about me, an old woman, but I spent three months down Broome. Five times I went there. Oh, I used to have a good ride too — down and back! I reckon jail is all right. They feed you really well, and *pay* you, so you come back with your own money when you work around. They used to ask me, 'How come you come back in jail again?' 'Why? Because you have everything here.' They used to cut off some time off my three months — maybe two and a half months I'd be there — because I was a good worker. Oh, I don't like it now. I reckon people drink because of mates. They make you drink. If you don't they say you're crazy. They think I'm crazy now because I gave up drink. They say I'm a Christian. If they don't have any grog in them they won't speak up for themselves; once they got grog, you can't stop them.

Today you can't put any sense into people yet. Maybe they've got no mind or they're thinking about things like they were before, and not this year or next year or what's going to come. You go down and preach to them now, and they wouldn't understand what you mean and what you're trying to be. At the reserve, they say, 'You think you're *gadia*' — meaning white man. 'You think you're something bigger than everybody.' I said, 'Oh, I'm tellin' you for your own good. You wanta work your brains. One day you'll be like that puppy dog if you don't understand any English.' They say, 'What that for? We've got a government look after us.' See? All right, I just leave them alone.

That's why every time they want to go to a meeting now, like a land meeting, they all sit down and say, 'What this meeting is? What for?' I try to tell them, 'We've gotta help. We gotta be black and white in this country — *our* country — but we'll have a more chance to fight back to keep our country because we have nothing like white man.' No, they can't understand that meeting — nothing. 'If you go to the meeting you'll see something what you gotta see, or you wanta be *myall* all your life?' I dunno. I go round to every house and tell them they've got to go tomorrow. Those girls don't go. I don't know why, maybe they're frightened, maybe ashamed. They don't have to talk; they can sit down there, sit around, and can ask you what you think about it.

Some white man is our relation now we're together. That's why they call them uncle, brother and so on, because they're living together. One time ago we walked from Wave Hill Station carrying our swags. A big man came up and took us back to Wattie Creek, and we were asked to sit down there. He gave us everything he had. He was like a father, uncle, all them country people. White man call them uncle, like old man black-fellers. They're all right; they understand them. Some people don't like colour, but better to be mixed like the birds and the flowers mixed. They look very nice all the colours mixed in the flowers.

I reckon they had a good mind these people round here, my countrymen; not like the cheeky mob — cheeky yet. I hear young people like my grandchildren say, 'We bin really silly bugger.' 'What for?' I ask them. 'Well, they never did anything to white man, who kicked him, knocked him out — everything. No nothing — no fight.' Old man black-fellers say, 'You know why we bin let 'em shoot we. Why? We frightened? No, we never gotim rifle.' And we didn't care, they reckon . . . 'We can die in our own country.'

Additional reading

Shaw, B. and McDonald, S. (1978). They did it themselves: reminiscences of seventy years. *Aboriginal History 2* (1), 122-39

7

Lorna Dixon

Janet Mathews

One evening in December 1976 I received a telephone call from Pastor Bill Reid in Bourke, New South Wales. He told me of the sudden death of Mrs Lorna Rose Dixon, who had lived in Bourke for more than thirty years. I had become very fond of Lorna during the six years we worked together. My field research in country areas of New South Wales has involved collecting Aboriginal music, languages and stories of the past. We first met in 1970 after a strenuous and rather frustrating day. Rain was pouring down and I had visited many Aborigines who either knew nothing or were out. Someone said, 'Lorna Dixon might know something. She's moved a lot amongst the dark people.' When my car slithered to a halt in front of Lorna's house, she answered the door. After a brief explanation, she happily came into the car for a chat, saying, 'I heard you were in town and I *did* want you to come and see me.' It was obvious that this warm and enthusiastic woman had great knowledge of her Wonggumara language and the past.

Lorna was waiting for me next morning as arranged and we drove to a secluded place where we were free from interruptions by children or family problems. Recording with Lorna was never dull. In addition to her Wonggumara language, the memories of tribal customs, beliefs and stories told by elderly relatives came back into her mind. We recorded more than sixty tapes of one and a half hours each. At times she asked me to turn off the recorder because she had things to say for my ears only.

During the years that I knew Lorna her character emerged clearly. Although she was a very fat woman, she was far from lacking in energy. She had a wonderful sense of humour and enjoyment when life was kind to her. Some days when recording, although I knew she was deeply worried about family problems, I would hear her voice almost choking as she whispered in my ear, 'Turn the thing off, Janet, would you? I *must* have a good laugh!' Having done that and mopped her eyes, she would struggle to make her naturally smiling face solemn and say, 'I'll be all right for a while now if we can only be serious.'

Very few around Bourke knew that Lorna could speak her language fluently and was familiar with many traditions. In her mid-twenties there had been dramatic changes in her life and all speech in her language had ceased abruptly. When alone, especially in bed at night, she had translated her thoughts into Wonggumara for years. She had been told legendary stories and customs in this language and, in her mind, recited what she had learnt in her youth. During this period, Lorna had corresponded with a cousin in Broken Hill. When young they had always spoken in Wonggumara, and Lorna devised a method of spelling it for their letters because they felt their feelings were better expressed. My interest was aroused when she corrected my mispronunciation of Wonggumara words by spelling them in an Anglicised style. Unfortunately, Lorna did not refer to many members of her family by name. She used a kinship term when talking about them.

Lorna was born about 1911, and her maiden name was Ebsworth. Her maternal grandmother was a Wonggumara woman whose husband was George Dutton. Dutton's reminiscences (published by Jeremy Beckett) complement Lorna's story. Dutton's own mother, Lorna's great-grandmother, had also been Wonggumara. Lorna's father, Albert Ebsworth, had strong loyalties to the Wonggumara. His mother came from that language group and his father was an Irish station owner. Both his mother's parents were Wonggumara; Lorna remembered these old people clearly and much of her traditional knowledge had come from them. Various calculations of her paternal great-grandmother's birth date, in relation to her memories of the Burke and Wills expedition camping near Cooper's Creek, suggest that she could have been as old as 105 when she died in 1936. Her husband, who died in 1926, is reputed to have been a centenarian also.

During Lorna's early childhood her father apparently worked on Naryilco Station in the south-western corner of Queensland. Lorna said that 'many Aborigines were employed there and most of them were fullbloods'. The Ebsworth family lived somewhere near the homestead, and there were apparently several older children at that stage. The mother and grandparents of Lorna's father appeared and disappeared frequently. Wonggumara associations drew the Ebsworths, including Albert, to the Tibooburra district several times a year. When Lorna was still young, Tibooburra became their headquarters and the four generations spent a large part of the year coming and going from their rented house in an old settlement along Thompsons Creek, south of the town. Lorna said, 'Dad was known as a good drover and the whites liked his station work too. He could always get a job, and took time off if he wanted to camp somewhere or visit the Cooper. Usually we all went together, but sometimes he just took us children. Dad's meat [totem] was carpet snake and mine was goanna.'

Lorna recalled that life in Tibooburra 'suited us, but we did need to escape and get back to the real country sometimes. In Tibooburra we had everything, were comfortable enough, well fed and loved by the old ones. Dad often went off on his own and we knew it was for some sacred or secret Aboriginal gathering.' Lorna did acknowledge that they had little money and few material possessions of real value. She went to school, and the name of her teacher was Mrs Gaiter. Lorna progressed to sixth grade, and her comments on those years were:

> Except when doing lessons I was free, and so were all of us. Being a large family, we didn't bother with other people much and they didn't bother us. We always behaved decently and kept ourselves cleaner than most. Whether amongst the dark people at Cooper's Creek or near the whites in Tibooburra we obeyed the strict Wonggumara rules of behaviour and these seemed OK with the whites. Most of dad's money went in rent for the house and for years we still fed ourselves from the bush. Sometimes we went out before school, but it was better in the afternoon. Mum, granny and great-granny took us kids to help gathering food. They had their yamsticks and dad had made smaller ones for us. We caught small animals, like possums and echidna; if we were lucky we got lots of grubs too. The bush vegetables were beautiful to eat and much better than the stuff from the shops. Some were from roots and others, like wild spinach, were from leaves. Thistles were great to eat and there was lots of wild fruit such as oranges and bananas. When dad was working on stations near Tibooburra he killed meat and brought it home to us. I didn't know how people could suffer until I was a lot older. Maybe we did keep to ourselves, but we never felt like outcasts. That's a word I learnt much later, and it hurt. If we'd only been able to carry on in this way I'm sure we'd have been happier and had less illness and sadness.

Most of the family frequently travelled the 200 km track from Tibooburra to Cooper's Creek because both areas were of great importance to the Wonggumara. Lorna's great-grandparents had their hunting grounds near Cooper's Creek and claimed to have helped the Burke and Wills expedition in 1861. Lorna recounted what she had been told:

> Great-granny and great-grandad were amongst a lot of Aborigines who tried to help the explorers. When food was short they made a sort of nardoo damper up there. The white men weren't too keen on it and said it upset their tummies, but later ate quite a lot of it and did some of their own grinding. The whites said they liked fish better, but our people had to feed themselves and couldn't give them fish often. Some of the Aborigines did not like having these white men around and would have speared them, given the chance. They were the mob from the other side of the river, and they kept coming back to have a go at the whites. My old people were amongst the fellers who tried to protect the men. They were pretty harmless, the whites. Our mob dug a couple of holes in the ground and kept leafy branches beside them. When the wild chaps turned up, the explorers jumped into the holes and our lot chucked the branches on top of them. Then they just sat around as if nothing was happening.
>
> A lot of pituri grew near the Cooper and most of our people often chewed it. They said they felt sort of relaxed and cheerful. I tried it

once but it was bitter and tasted horrible. They did give the whites some to chew, but that wasn't a good idea. It just made them rip-roaring drunk and as silly as rabbits!

Lorna felt that her great-grandfather had been honoured when the white people made him 'king' of the Wonggumara and presented him with a plate that he often wore. (Howard Creamer reports he was King Toogali.) The amount of time Lorna spent near Cooper's Creek is uncertain, but there is no doubt that she knew the country well. They seem to have used her father's camp equipment, as she talked about 'dad's gear' being useful.

Another Wonggumara speaker, George Harrison, of Bourke, whom Lorna called 'uncle', has recorded many tapes with me and has been a wonderful Wonggumara informant. They were both absolutely definite that Tibooburra was in their territory and said, 'This was the place where everything began for the Wonggumara and our sacred memories radiated from there.'

At Mount Poole, south of Tibooburra, stood a rock that the Wonggumara believed had been created for them in the Dreaming. This was the White Lady, or Cuba Walga.

Howard Creamer (Aboriginal Sites Survey Officer, NSW National Parks and Wildlife Service), who visited the site with Lorna in 1973, reports that:

> Lorna Dixon said the boulder was actually the body of the White Lady. The significance of the White Lady to the Wonggumara is best explained by cross-cultural comparison with the teaching of the Christian Church:

Lorna Dixon (left), Mrs Brown, her grandson and Howard Creamer
(Photograph courtesy of Howard Creamer)

she is their equivalent of Mary the Mother of Christ. The Wonggumara even call her Ngamadja (mother), but a more personal name seems to have been Canji. In the words of Lorna Dixon: 'She was the Queen of the tribe, the head of the tribe on the women's side. She had to be a maiden to be a Queen. She was the Mother of everyone and yet she was a virgin. If someone was very sick and the doctor said there was a chance of them dying, all the mothers, aunties, sisters, the cousins, they'd all paint up in black and white, like you see them dressed in black after a death. Then they would go in rotation to the White Lady and pray to her. They would say: 'My Mother, my child is sick. Would you make him better.' Next morning, that child would be running around.'

Lorna's faith in the Roman Catholic Church could have influenced her thoughts about the White Lady. Lorna told me, 'She was carved from white rock and had well shaped breasts; her head was made from gleaming gold.' With the advent of white people, Aborigines feared for the safety of all shining stones and their custom was to hide or bury them, so the golden head was buried in a dry creek bed. Until the mid-1930s many Aborigines, including Lorna, visited this site regularly to add dirt or branches and ensure that their secret was safely hidden.

Lorna told a Wonggumara legend relating to the White Lady:

Way back, a great 'medicine man' lived near the Cooper and came to Tibooburra with his 'man'. His 'man' was a spirit servant and did anything his master told him — even changed his shape. This time he was told to turn into a pelican and (rain had fallen) to drink all the water lying near the White Lady's feet. Then he said to the bird: 'When you spread your wings and start to fly, all that water in the pouch under your beak will soon turn into gold. Take it back to Cooper's Creek for me.'

Well, the bird crossed the Queensland border, but the water was heavy and made him tired so he needed to stop flying and have a rest sometimes. The first time he came down some Aborigines threw spears at him; one pierced his pouch and another hit his body. The pelican flew away while drips of his blood and the water fell on the ground. As soon as the water touched the ground it turned into gold and his blood became opal. The poor, wounded pelican went as far as he could, but toppled over and died on the crest of a hill before he reached Cooper's Creek. His blood flowed down one slope and left a gleaming mass of opal and the water ran down the other side and turned into gold. We, of the Wonggumara, call this hill Cabranara Cali (Pelican Hill) but the whites call it Bald Hill. Although not very far from Cooper's Creek, it's closer to Durham Downs.

Lorna finished this story by telling how, as a child, she accompanied her parents, paternal grandmother and geat-grandparents when they decided to follow the trail of the pelican:

When we set off we got into a cart pulled by a couple of dad's horses. The ground got too rough for them and dad left the horses and gear with friends. Then we walked quite a long way until dad borrowed some camels and we rode these. Little patches of gold and opal were sprinkled along the route and we could see where the pelican had rested because there was more of both. Sometimes we had to dig around to find it under bushes or sand. Having seen it, we knew it was our duty to cover it up if the gold and opal were not hidden. There was lots more of both when we reached Cabranara Cali.

Their house on the outskirts of Tibooburra was comfortable enough for their large family, but not a mansion. Although living like Europeans, they strictly observed many of their traditional customs. If these were not carried out they believed that both the old and the young would suffer. In addition, most of their ailments were treated and cured by the accepted Wonggumara bush remedies. Lorna's knowledge of this type of medical treatment was impressive.

Until the time of her death, Lorna still had strong beliefs that she would not change:

If I'm going to sleep I'm just miserable if my head doesn't point towards the sunrise. Any Wonggumara people who slept or were buried another way were believed to be offering their body as a home for a bad spirit. We buried our dead with their heads towards the rising sun. I'm still scared of that roving spirit of the dead, and he causes awful sadness in our minds after someone has died. There's only one cure. I've used it all my life, and I'd do it again if someone close to me died. A cousin we loved died a few years ago and we were all upset, especially Paul who was only a kid. I gathered a bundle of green dogwood [*Myoporum deserti*] leaves and set them alight so they smoked a lot. Paul was asleep, but I stood near him and let the smoke blow over both of us. Then I wandered around the house and let the smoke drift about. We all felt better next day.

She continued:

I still know when people are sending me messages from far away. Birds and animals tell me. Just one curlew singing close to the house at night means I'd better get ready for bad news. If I see a goanna, my 'meat', near my feet I know he's telling me about something important. More often good than bad.

One day when we were recording in the car Lorna became very restless and agitated because she was sure that a Willie wagtail was telling her, by its behaviour, to expect bad news. She kept worrying about her young son, who was at school. Then she thought that her husband and another son could be in trouble while fishing some distance from Bourke. Discreetly, I moved the car some distance but a wagtail appeared again. This happened several times and she was in a bad state of anxiety. At lunch time we went to the school and checked that Paul was all right. Her husband and son arrived home late having had some trouble with the car and the roads.

During Lorna's many wanderings through Wonggumara country she grew aware of sad events. There was one place near Cooper's Creek where many Aborigines had been killed by troopers. Both Lorna and George Harrison described the bones spread over a large sandhill; in many of the skulls there was a small hole. They said that the size of the skulls indicated that most belonged to women and children. On one visit her father had showed her some children's skulls that had obviously been crushed. The family considered it a duty to keep the bones hidden and always covered them with sand before leaving the area.

The descriptions of massacres given by Lorna, George Harrison, George Dutton and Jimmie Barker were similar. Their districts were not very far apart. Lorna's paternal grandmother had suffered tragedies; one of her children was burnt to death near Cooper's Creek and another was shot by a European, possibly a trooper. 'Grannie had deep scars on her head where she had hit herself in mourning for her children.'

Another of Lorna's memories was of the last known 'medicine man' in north-western New South Wales, Narandindi (Davey Ryan), who died at Bourke. Lorna had admired his skill when he cured her sister Jean of an unpleasant illness during childhood.

Lorna's mother had recounted some details of her initiation at the age of fourteen or fifteen:

> Mum with other girls was taken into the bush by some old women for about eight weeks. They ate what they could find for themselves in the bush, but they couldn't eat everything; there were taboos I think you call them. Mum said she learnt how to behave according to our rules and to respect the men's sacred duties and to help them in the correct way. They told her how to look after her man, their kids and camp. Then there was some sort of a ceremony and they made a scar, and after that she was a woman.

Lorna's father had long scars down his back and a solid square scar on his chest. Lorna said, 'There were a few others as well, and I think these could have been according to Wonggumara and Galali rites.' She was fascinated by the scars of her great-grandfather King Toogali:

> I've never seen anything like his head, it was just like a galvanised iron roof on top of his body. There were ridges and hollows all over it. Hair didn't have any chance of growing, except for one little tuft that managed all right. I was very fond of the old man, but it was curiosity that made me keep stroking his head. The skin was tough and horny, especially in the deep grooves. He had scars all over his arms and body and I had no idea which were symbolic. He got into this awful mess when he was young because he was always in fights.

Lorna was probably in her teens when her father, Albert Ebsworth, received a message that a large tribal gathering was to take place at Innamincka:

> Yes, Dad was working on a station somewhere in Queensland, when a man arrived with a message stick. For something like this they still

used message sticks because then we knew the whites had nothing to do with it. He thought this Innamincka gathering could be one of the last of its kind and decided to take three months off work. There was going to be a beaut corroboree and some young fellows were being brought in from the bush for the final part of their initiation. One of these chaps was a Wonggumara and related to Mum. Later he was well known in Bourke as George McDermott.

Dad decided to take us all with him. We had a cart and horses — just piled into it and took off. Aborigines came from everywhere! Durham Downs, Nocundra, Nockatunga, Tibooburra, the Northern Territory and farther down the Cooper. We were a mixed lot. Most of them knew the ways of white people but, like our family, had old ones with them who wanted it to be like the days of the past. The camping was a sort of mixture of old and new. When we reached the place there was no squabbling about where we'd camp. You know the sort of business: 'I want to be under this tree, near water or away from those blokes.' The corroboree ground was large and had a claypan in the middle. This was the centre and we were arranged around it in the same sort of pattern as our own territory when at home. The old men knew just where to go. In the Wonggumara there were our two lots, the Calbera and Dhinewa. They had always lived on opposite banks of the Cooper, but kept apart except for marriages and special things. Like on the Cooper, we were next to one another, but no Calbera could camp with a Dhinewa. Hundreds of people were there, and I don't remember anything about women's rites, but think something went on amongst the old women. I loved the singing and dancing, but there were so many unknown people I got a bit muddled about who was who.

Lorna's tremendous enthusiasm and enjoyment of special occasions led to a certain exaggeration sometimes, but her story of this initiation never varied.

In the middle of the claypan the men put up the trunk of a *laba:nja* tree. This was about the height of a telephone pole. As no limbs grow out of the trunk it was quite straight and just had a few bushy leaves on top. The claypan was clear ground and all sticks or rubbish had been brushed away. Around the edge of the large corroboree ground were lots of large, red sandhills where tea-tree grew. All the elders, wise men and important people were closer to the tree than me, but I had a good view and was about 100 feet away from the pole.

Then the young men came in. I can't remember how many, perhaps about twenty. They were decorated with coloured feathers, and if they weren't full-bloods their skins were painted black. They wore a *mandera* [brief pubic cover made of emu feathers] and headbands made from skin. If their own 'meat' was a goanna, possum or kangaroo that had a skin, this had to be worn. They walked across the claypan in single file and couldn't look up at the crowd. No one could smile, laugh or talk. We hardly wanted to breathe — everything was dead quiet. The bark had been taken off the tree, and I think it'd been rubbed with emu or goanna fat because it was very slippery. One of the elders told the blokes that this was their final test before reaching manhood and they had to climb the tree trunk; when they reached the top, they had to stay there until he said to come down. They had to hang on with hands and feet for about five minutes. It didn't look easy. George McDermott was the first to climb, and they all did it perfectly. He wasn't very young, maybe about thirty. In those days initiation didn't happen often and they just had to grab the chance. George had done that.

With all their paint and feathers they looked marvellous. After the climb they were told to go to the river and swim. They marched off and came back later in the sort of clothes they usually wore. Many wore white men's clothes because I think most of them were station workers. They had been told that they were now free to marry, and some marriages had been arranged according to the old rules.

Lorna said there was no tooth avulsion in the Wonggumara initiation:

I don't know much about what went on in the bush before the final ceremony that I saw. I do know that there was no contact with homes or families and there was lots of food they couldn't eat. They couldn't eat any fat, nor large fish. Small fish were allowed and any parts of emu, kangaroo or goanna that had no fat. They were taught to fight and protect themselves in the Aboriginal way. When we were at school we had to be obedient and behave well whatever went on around us. Sounded something like that when they were in the bush. But, sort of scary too.

They returned to Tibooburra and their normal way of life. During part of Lorna's school years and for a year or so afterwards, she was mainly living with her grandmother and great-grandparents. Visits from her parents were frequent, but intermittent. Her father was working on Yandama Station, not far from Tibooburra, and her mother was the cook. After leaving school, Lorna worked in the hospital for a number of years.

Lorna was definite in her statements that they suffered no discrimination while living in Tibooburra, but they must have been fortunate. In 1938 there was still a solid family group whose headquarters were the Tibooburra house. Lorna had her job at the hospital and her four brothers, Alf, Arnold, Albie and Cecil, were usually employed in station work. Her brother Albie was working at Naryilco Station, just over the border in Queensland. Lorna did not say which brother was at home on the day that disaster struck them in the form of Mr Smithers from the Aborigines Protection Board arriving on their doorstep:

He told us we were to be removed immediately to the Mission at Brewarrina. We mustn't argue, and he'd use force if he had to. He couldn't contact three brothers who were well out of town but he was jolly well going to get hold of Dad. He did that by radio to Yandama Station and collected other men that way too. We had a few hours to pack, but were only allowed a small swag each. Dad came home and we just had to get ready. From our house they took Mum, Dad, my six sisters and me, one brother, Granny and my step-great-grandfather. That made twelve of us. Later, Albie had to make his own way across from Naryilco to Brewarrina. It was quite a while before he knew we'd gone.

Dad had horses, dogs and gear for work; he just had to leave them — the same with our fowls near the house. I suppose people just grabbed them all after we'd disappeared. We didn't know why this had happened: we were well, had no eye troubles, why did they move us? We never had a sensible explanation. About 4 pm they loaded us and our swags into the trucks. I think there were about sixty of us. Mum's father, George Dutton, and lots of aunts and uncles had been grabbed too. We got to Wanaaring that night and were told to sleep or stay awake in the open near the trucks. Most of us had been crying all the way, and we just kept on crying for days.

Next morning we were piled into the trucks again and arrived at the Mission at about 10 pm. We were told to get out at the schoolhouse. We were scared stiff and shivering with fright. The place looked eerie and weird. People were everywhere as we dragged our swags with us. A white man was barking out orders; he was carrying a rifle and had a revolver on his hip. For a long time we thought he had the power to shoot us if he wanted to. Out in the darkness people were peering at us by the light of hurricane lanterns. They thought we'd been plucked from the bush and were in our natural, wild state. They were the wild ones. Before then, none of us — not even Dad — knew anything about swearing or drinking. From that first night onwards we had to listen to people using shocking language and fighting between themselves.

All the women were told to sleep on the schoolhouse floor and the men on the verandah. The white man, the manager, wandered around with his rifle for ages. The days followed and we were always frightened, but the nights were shocking. Granny died very soon after we got there, and a bit later our step-great-grandfather died, as well as lots of other old people. They just couldn't stand it, and we lived in or near the schoolhouse for several months. We were given some rations, but they never lasted the full week. We cooked on open fires near the schoolhouse and our food was terrible. The bread was flat and hard because we had no baking powder and no fat or jam to spread on it. There was something between six and ten chops weekly for all our family. Drinking water came from the Barwon and was muddy and nasty.

Lots of Mission people caught fish in the river, but we felt safer just huddling together and doing what we were told. Even when we felt less scared we couldn't gather food from the bush there. Cattle and sheep had grazed around the Mission and natural bush was too far away. After all the deaths, there were still about forty of us sleeping on the schoolhouse floor at night and squatting on the grass each day. The place was full of kids in school hours and there wasn't much shelter on bad days. Sandflies, mosquitoes and flies plagued us.

From the first day we kept asking the manager if we could leave, but he said he had orders to keep us there.

Not many did leave the Mission and the only reason given by Lorna was their fear of the consequences if they disobeyed the manager, who was always armed.

We all kept asking if we could leave and the answer was always the same. Dad, Mum, my brother, me and a couple of my older sisters all wanted to work and kept on asking. The manager said that we couldn't unless he gave permission and recommended us.

After about three or four months some huts were built for the new residents.

We were still scared, but it was better. Our shack had two rooms, a small kitchen and tiny verandah, but we managed to squeeze into it. The manager wanted three of my sisters to go to the dormitory for unmarried girls, but we told him we wanted to be together. Never once were we allowed to go into Brewarrina to see a film or shop. We hadn't much money, but some bit of an outing would have helped. People were sometimes given lifts in the Mission truck, but never one of us. A dark woman, Mrs Hardy, ran a small store on the Mission but everything cost a lot. Mr Salter, a hawker, came out once a week and everybody bought what they could afford from him.

School hours were fairly regular, but they didn't learn much. My two young sisters went, and Jimmie Barker took the lessons when the manager was busy. That was a relief, because the manager often let fly with his stockwhip at the kids. There was some sort of a dark nurse if we were sick, but she mainly worked on their bung eyes and their shocking sores on the skin and in the hair.

We didn't get many of these, but perhaps we kept ourselves cleaner than most of them. After six months we were given dark grey flannel to make dresses and calico for underclothes. Both were stiff, hot and prickly and never softened after washing. It was just as bad for the men and boys; nobody was ever issued with thin clothes. We always suffered from sore and chafed skin, and the thick clothes in summer were dreadful.

Tragedy struck the Ebsworths soon after they moved into the shack. Lorna's sister was pregnant when they were removed from Tibooburra. When labour began she was taken to Brewarrina Hospital, where she was in a section for Aborigines only. When her family visited her next day, she was obviously very ill, but nobody seemed to be doing anything about it. 'Her baby girl had arrived safely, but my sister died soon after we'd gone back to the Mission. She was young and healthy, and we just couldn't believe it.'

The baby was brought back to their shack at the Mission and Lorna recollected, 'We were not allowed to get in touch with the doctor or hospital and never knew what caused her death. Dad was very upset and pleaded to see the Catholic priest, but, as usual, the manager said no and that was that.'

The details about when the Ebsworths were converted to Catholicism are doubtful. From Lorna's remarks, it must have been soon after or just before her birth. She was a very devout Catholic and said this religion had given great comfort to her parents and herself. 'Mum and Dad taught me all about the Wonggumara religion. Like me, they believed in them both. Somehow, they fitted in together.'

Their four years at the Mission passed slowly. When they had gained sufficient confidence, they supplemented their rations with fish or mussels from the river and occasionally caught birds.

> Then a new manager arrived and Dad asked if we could leave. We were really staggered because he just said, 'If you want to go, there's nothing to stop you.' The other fellow had made us sweat it out through the years, and a prison sentence couldn't have been worse. We couldn't see what we'd done wrong. It hurt, because we felt we'd been made to suffer because of the colour of our skins.

They packed up quickly and moved to Bourke. In the little Mission burial ground Lorna's sister, grandmother and step-great-grandfather remained. Lorna felt that the poor conditions had taken years off the lives of her parents.

> Mum was very weak when we got to Bourke and just faded away and died in a year or so. Something had gone wrong with Dad's eyes while we were at the Mission. It wasn't trachoma, but he was nearly blind when we moved. They got pensions in Bourke and, although they were both dead in a couple of years, they seemed happy enough there.

Lorna settled into a house in Bourke with her husband, Eric Dixon, who came from Walgett. She had twelve children, and when I saw her in 1976, about fifty grandchildren.

There was little the Ebsworths could do when told by the Mission manager, 'Your Aboriginal language is dirty and English must be spoken at all times. I don't want to hear any of your filthy lingo and if I do, you'll suffer.' Thus young people were brought up to scorn their native language. This was why so few people knew that Lorna's Wonggumara was locked away until I appeared with my tape recorder.

Having unlocked the door to the past, everything poured out. Lorna intended that her children and grandchildren would remember. She used to say, 'Now that I know its important I'm telling them everything I know — over and over again. Like the way I learnt from my old people; I want them to hear and remember too.' When I visited Bourke, Lorna even made sure that she had dispensation from Mass 'because my friend is in town and I can't miss a minute.'

Howard Creamer tells of flying Lorna from Bourke to Tibooburra in November 1973:

> Across the Warrego at Goombalie, over the Paroo at Wanaaring and on across an incredible remoteness. Lorna's excitement at rediscovering

Tibooburra had clearly won in the battle with her misgivings about flying, this being her first flight. She was indeed a help with the navigation, pointing out landmarks such as the flooded Bulloo River overflow and seeing Tibooburra from far away. While I was placing all my faith in a constant compass heading to get us there, Lorna knew exactly where we were going!

The morning after our arrival Lorna took us to the old settlement along Thompson's Creek . . . Lorna and a Tibooburra friend began to dig into the dry creek bed. 'You wouldn't think there's water here, would you?' she asked as we watched in amazement. Soon a pool, brackish but drinkable, appeared at the bottom of the hole. 'It's a wonderful thing, that,' said Lorna with obvious satisfaction.

Lorna guided Howard to several sacred sites, and a comment she made to him gave me pleasure because it showed her pride in talking about her people and her country: 'I'll follow my rules until the day I die. That's one thing I'll swear to do, and if I can teach my children, I will. I want to spread it out so that they and my grandchildren may take to it one day.'

In May 1974 Lorna Dixon was elected to membership of the Australian Institute of Aboriginal Studies. She thoroughly enjoyed her changing world when she realised that her knowledge was of great interest to research workers. Her whole horizon widened, and those undeserved feelings of shame were forgotten. She was an adventurer at heart and her first aeroplane flights and the completely different surroundings were just taken in her enthusiastic stride. Many times she had said to me that 'these things are all tremendous fun'.

Lorna Dixon (left), Peter Ucko (Principal, AIAS), Jacquie Lambert, Petharie Bani and Ephraim Bani in a Canberra restaurant (Photograph courtesy of AIAS)

Lorna's first visit to Canberra was in August 1974 when she attended a special function to welcome twelve new members, most of whom were Aborigines or Torres Strait Islanders. Jacquie Lambert, Administrative Officer of the Australian Institute of Aboriginal Studies, described Lorna's visits for me:

> It was on this first occasion that I got to know Lorna and to appreciate her tremendous warmth, and sense of humour and adventure. This visit coincided with an air strike, and to pass a long weekend the Institute organised a bus trip to Perisher Valley, a nearby snow resort. Once we reached the snowfields Lorna, despite her somewhat excessive weight and being in her early sixties, expressed great enthusiasm in taking a ride to the top of Back Perisher Mountain in a chairlift. This was the kind one had to jump into and out of while still moving, and it is doubtful if she would have fitted anyway. It took me some considerable time to persuade her that jumping into and out of moving chairlifts was *not* the easiest thing in the world to do.
>
> On another occasion the Institute sent Lorna a telegram requesting her attendance at its Biennial Meeting. Planes do not fly every day from Bourke to Canberra. Lorna, anxious to arrive in time for the Meeting, and despite having a sprained ankle, within the hour jumped on a plane for Canberra. Although she arrived a week early for the meeting, we enjoyed her unexpected company.

In 1976 I visited Bourke and was distressed to hear that Lorna was in hospital. On arrival there I learnt that her blood pressure had reached a dangerous level. She was on a strict diet and some medication, but the doctor thought the outings with me would be good for her. Apart from

Taken at Kosciusko in 1974. (Left to right) Mr Frank Gurrmanamana, Dr Les Hiatt, Mr D. Burramara, Dr John Howard, Dr Betty Meehan and Lorna Dixon (Photograph courtesy of Betty Meehan)

a slightly later start in the morning, longer lunch break and earlier return to the hospital, our routine was much the same. Sometimes George Harrison joined us, and we recorded for many hours while sitting on the banks of the Darling River.

One day Lorna told me a very sad story about how she had been longing to visit Lake Lauradale for thirty years and no one would take her. For many hours she kept returning to the subject. This was the gist of her remarks:

> Yes, I must get someone to take me there when I get out of hospital. It's only ten miles from Bourke and the road is very good. The plains teem with kangaroos and emus, but I like the birds best. There are lots of unusual ones — the ones I tell you about, you know. The lake's covered with birds and is always blue. Oh well, I must try and get there some day.

The following morning I was due to collect 'Uncle George' and then go to the hospital for Lorna. When they were both in the car I told them that, their work with me having been so concentrated for years, we were going to take an hour off and drive to Lake Lauradale. Lorna's face was radiant. She clapped her hands and said, 'I wondered if I could talk you into it in that way'.

The visit was quite memorable, although the distance seemed closer to 50 miles (80 km) and the road was appalling. They both showed me plants, birds and animals that could well have been hidden to others. Emus are notoriously inquisitive birds and their curiosity is aroused by the colour red. They demonstrated this when they say a large flock near the curved horizon of bare plains. George whistled, and waved my old red cardigan, and Lorna flapped her bright red dressing gown. In a very short time the emus were within a few metres of the car, where I was poised with my camera.

George told me that the water in Lake Lauradale is salty and undrinkable in the summer months and fresh during winter; although surrounded by dry, flat plains the water comes from a spring in the centre. The level appeared to have dropped during our visit in late autumn. There was a crusty salt deposit on the mud a couple of metres from the water's edge. The birds were there in thousands, both sailing and soaring. Lorna showed me many varieties that she had described, but which I had never seen. On the plains she had identified many groups of cocklerinas [Major Mitchell cockatoos], whose feathers had special associations for the Wonggumara. They were treasured so that they could be worn on ceremonial occasions. I know that Lorna's and George's enjoyment of the visit was as great as mine.

After another day of recording, Lorna and I kissed and said goodbye for the last time. Later she was released from hospital and wrote telling me that she felt much better. She must have been reasonably well during the next few months when Howard Creamer describes another visit to Bourke:

I arrived, without warning, at Lorna's home at Bourke in September 1976. She was sweeping the yard in front of her house as I drove up, said hello and asked how she had been keeping. I inquired how she was getting on in her 'V.I.P.' role as Member of the Institute and how Wonggumara research was progressing with Janet Mathews and others. She answered the questions, but really admitted that she had not recognised me when she said, 'I'm still waiting for that young man to come back and go to Tibooburra again. Do you know the one I mean? He's about your age.' Our mutual delight was obvious when I explained that I was the young man and the beard, which I hadn't had in 1973, had caused her confusion.

The next day Lorna came with us to visit the cave painting site at Mount Gunderbooka. Although I could tell that her heart was with the Wonggumara sites over 200 miles to the west, she entered into the expedition with her usual cheerfulness and involvement. She pointed to the wild orange trees, the hop bush used for curing sores and the dogwood trees, the leaves of which were burnt to ward off bad spirits, as we drove to the site. Apart from some information about old Granny Moisey dancing the shaky-leg corroboree at Mount Gunderbooka, Lorna was not familiar with the site. Its main value for her lay in the contribution that such a site could make towards educating young Aboriginal people. Lorna remained convinced that they would come to realise the importance of their heritage one day.

Lorna's fatal heart attack occurred in December. It was impossible for me to reach Bourke in time to attend her funeral. My small tribute to her memory was her obituary published in the Australian Institute of Aboriginal Studies *Newsletter*.

Lorna was a remarkable woman. Her life had not been easy, but she had contributed a lot to her family and those around her. Her vast knowledge of the Wonggumara language and their traditions has been a great gift to our Australian history. I shall always remember Lorna Dixon with the deepest affection.

Acknowledgments

I should like to thank the following people for having given me additional information about Lorna Dixon and her family: Mr H. Creamer, Mrs Bobbie Hardy, Ms Nancy Hughes, Dr Max Kamien, Ms Jacquie Lambert.

Additional reading

Beckett, J. (1978). George Dutton's country: portrait of an Aboriginal drover. *Aboriginal History 2* (1), 3-31
Creamer, H. (1974). Investigation of Aboriginal sites in the Tibooburra area of New South Wales (typescript)
Mathews, J. (1977). *The two worlds of Jimmie Barker: The life of an Australian Aboriginal, 1900-1972.* Australian Institute of Aboriginal Studies, Canberra
────── (1977). Lorna Rose Dixon. Obituary. *AIAS Newsletter* (new series) No. 7. Australian Institute of Aboriginal Studies, Canberra

8

Emily Margaret Horneville of the Muruwari

Lynette Oates

When I first met Emily Margaret Horneville (1882?-1979), known to the locals as Mrs Oinable or Mrs Ornable, she was lying bedridden in her tiny corrugated-iron house on the outskirts of the Goodooga Aboriginal Reserve. That was in July 1972, when I was on a field trip with Janet Mathews. Janet had previously recorded Emily and had come especially to introduce me to her since she was practically the sole surviving speaker of Muruwari, a language I had been commissioned by the Australian Institute of Aboriginal Studies to salvage. Janet had warned me that Mrs Horneville's reception of us could be unpredictable, stimulating, even vitriolic, as she was of uncertain temper. Should we arrive on a day when, for her, the sun was not shining, we were likely to be told to depart in no uncertain terms. But all was well, she received us happily. After Janet had recorded, I commenced my first session of 'sitting at her feet' to be taught the language. In actual fact, I sat perched on the end of her bed. The tape recorder was balanced precariously on an upturned oil drum on the uneven dirt floor, and I handled my note pad and pencil on my lap with whatever dexterity I could muster.

Over the next six years I visited her once or twice annually. When she was feeling well and happy she produced a fund of linguistic information. At such times, her quickness of mind, powers of concentration and physical stamina amazed me; she could work for a two-hour stretch without tiring. This was all the more remarkable because her deafness meant that she had to strain forward to hear properly. Sometimes though, a question would annoy her. She would say such things as, 'What are you always asking me about that moon for?' This referred to a legend about the moon. Then she would continue, 'That's silly. I'm sick of that!', or 'Ask me something else, I don't like this talk.' Possibly her dislike may have stemmed from her inability to remember the language at that point. On her co-operative days she would admit to ignorance; when unco-operative, she would not.

There were days when she recalled personal incidents, grave or comical, serious or trivial, each recounted in its right context of names, times and places. On such occasions I could not help feeling that she was momentarily

Emily Margaret Horneville

re-living the experience. The details had been indelibly etched upon her active and retentive mind. At other times the thoughts strayed to bush creatures and bush lore. These were, to her, an unending source of wonder, and all things natural were observed in fine and accurate detail. People she had known, both Aborigines and others, were remembered with the same sharpness. She always spoke of people in the context of their nuclear or extended families, giving details of their spouses, children, and anything of importance about them. On several occasions she named in birth order each child of a large family; the largest had sixteen children. She seemed to see each one in her mind's eye as the name was recalled.

Emily's dynamic interest in life ensured that conversation did not flag. Many were the laughs we shared together, and many were the hours that sped by in satisfying dialogue. 'I ought to get a medal for that talking, I ought,' she once remarked. Where possible, I would interrupt the flow of Emily's conversation and ask how she would say the same thing in Muruwari. If she were particularly absorbed in the story, she might ignore the request, or fling me a sentence in Muruwari in the same breath as she continued with her English story. Her speech was often difficult to understand because of the speed with which she spoke both languages. It was her habit to slur Muruwari utterances into English ones, and vice versa, so that often it was impossible to detect where one language finished and the other began.

Slowly, however, the picture of her life emerged. When a life spans almost a century, precise biographical details are difficult to piece together, particularly when my research was not specifically aimed at obtaining her life history. But accuracy of detail is relatively unimportant; it is the quality of Emily's life that captures the imagination.

Her birth occurred in the traditional manner about the year 1882, or a little earlier, at Milroy Station on the banks of the Culgoa River in north-western New South Wales. The place was a secluded part of the large sandhill on which the station stood, and was studded with scrubby little wattle trees. In after years her mother teasingly pointed it out to her while handling the stones that were strewn in the area. When warmed they were placed in the small of the back or on the stomach of the woman in labour, and this induced a more comfortable birth.

Emily was the fourth of six children; two brothers and a sister preceded her, and two brothers were younger. She described her mother as a full-blood woman of the Muruwari language group. She bore the characteristic cicatrices of her people. Emily admiringly recalled these 'pretty little marks made with a possum's tooth. My, they were neat.' On her mother's side Emily's roots were deeply in Muruwari tradition. She was related to Bill Campbell, one of the last Muruwari speakers, who recorded his language for the Australian Institute of Aboriginal Studies. Their mothers were sisters and, like her, he was born at Milroy. Emily's father may have been of Muruwari descent, or he might have been an itinerant European who formed a brief liaison with her mother before he melted into the blue. She never mentioned any link with her European heritage. Although she did occasionally talk about her 'father', her more frequent references were to her 'old step-father', who was undoubtedly of Aboriginal descent.

Her childhood was a happy one. The period of massacres and threats of extermination during the black-white conflict were now mercifully over, and those who had survived the earlier ravages lived without fear of violence. (The time when government authorities insisted on children settling on reserves where they could be 'educated' had not arrived.) Thus, Emily grew to womanhood in the security of a small group of her own people on a station where Aborigines were accepted. Milroy Station, 60 km north of Brewarrina on the Culgoa River, was always home to Emily. Mrs Armstrong, the boss's wife, was referred to with much affection: 'She was like a mother to me.'

Most of Emily's childhood was spent in the Aboriginal camp on the station. Both her parents worked there, as she did herself later on. She was married at the station, but left it after the death of her mother (maintaining the tradition of leaving the place where someone has died). Journeys were made up and down the Culgoa to Weilmoringle Station, 50 km upstream, where most of her relatives lived, or to Dennawan, about 20 km further north. It was here that a sizeable community of Muruwari people lived in relatively stable conditions. Trips were also made to call on relatives and friends on many of the surrounding stations and, until she was about eight years old, visits were made to a small group of Baranbinya people living on the north bank of the Darling River downstream from Brewarrina. It was at this formative age that she learned Baranbinya, and it was a wonderful feat of memory that she could remember so much of this language in her old age. All Baranbinya-speaking people appear to have died or been removed elsewhere during Emily's childhood, so that her recall of this language spanned a period of almost ninety years.

Childhood activities centred largely on the traditional life of an Aboriginal camp. The camp, she explained, was never dirty. It was swept clean daily, yard and all, so that it was as bare as a claypan. Many activities took place on the river: all day could be spent fishing with a pole (a dead tree branch with string and bait attached), swimming, or canoeing in boats made by Emily's step-father from the readily accessible river gums (*garawa*). Emily became a champion swimmer (she claimed she was never beaten), and an equally champion tree-climber. Swinging on the supple limb of a tree was another occupation that kept her happy for hours. 'I was a terror for that,' she remarked. 'I could swing there all day.'

Sometimes Emily accompanied the women to the swamp to gather nardoo seed (*dhawinjdhawinj*). It was later ground on a big stone by a smaller one called a *warul*. Occasionally she went with the family when they were hunting in the moonlight for possums and other nocturnal animals. A favourite winter pastime was goanna hunting far out in the bush where the goannas were in hibernation. A yamstick would prod the ground seeking the hole where the goanna might be sleeping. When one was found the animal was dug out. She remarked: 'They're so fat, you know, when you get them out, and there's nothing in their gut; it's quite clear inside. And oh, lovely to eat!'

She learnt the way of all wild things: how to tell the tree where the native bee hid its honey; where emus' nests were hidden; when the quandong were ripe in the bush; how to predict climatic changes from the behaviour of ants and insects or by the pattern of clouds in the heavens. She remarked to me one day: 'There were schools around, but I didn't attend any. Mumma took me to the bush. I learnt my ABC, but that's all. I wouldn't have that schooling. I went to *my* sort of school — in the bush!' That proved to be a rich schooling indeed.

At night, she would lie near the camp-fire and listen to Aboriginal legends being told by her 'aunty' or one of the other women. Her mother disapproved of the legends, probably because so many of them had sexual allusions. In consequence, in her old age Emily was extremely reticent in talking about legends; indeed, it was a very long time before she would admit that she knew any. 'Mumma used to say they were only lies,' she would comment.

She spoke with delight of moonlight buggy rides and of her prowess on a horse.

> I was a great one for the horse. I used to borrow a horse from my uncle who looked after the mail exchange.
> 'Don't you knock the horses about,' he'd say to me.
> 'Righto,' I'd say.
> Then I'd saddle up and go for a ride — way to blazes!

Much of Emily's fun-loving nature remained until her old age, so it is easy to imagine what a 'torment' she was when young. She used to tease the camp children till they cried. Then her mother would spank her. 'Not roughly,' she reminisced. 'But Mumma wouldn't stand for any nonsense.' Sometimes Emily used to tease me. One day when I told her how I couldn't find the cigarettes I'd put away for her old cousin, Robin Campbell, she said, 'You're going! You're going properly! You mightn't find your home. You mightn't find your kids! You might go right past the place!'

Mumma was undoubtedly the strongest influence in Emily's life. Her mother was always there in the background, to admonish, protect and instruct. From her mother she learned the Muruwari standards of behaviour, rules of conduct and kinship obligations. These meant much to her through life. She lamented the complete breakdown of the Aboriginal marriage system, remarking, 'Today people live like dogs. Don't go the old ways now. Wicked, isn't it?' Emily followed her mother also in complete abstention from alcohol and in her very strict moral code. How deeply she felt is revealed by an incident towards the latter part of her life. She was placed in a hospital ward with a woman whose head was shaven. Although her hip was broken, Emily was so shocked at being placed in the same room as a man (so she believed), that she decided to throw herself out of bed and crawl out of the room. Fortunately, the woman moved and revealed a breast, much to Emily's relief.

Emily's mother sought to protect her children from the potentially harmful incidents of camp life, particularly fights. Emily recalled:

> By gee, I've seen some fights with sticks; and with boomerangs and nulla nullas too. Mumma wouldn't let me see the fights. She used to

hunt me away with the two little boys — brothers. We used to go away and 'plant' [hide]. Wouldn't come back till everything was quietened down.

She was full of admiration for her mother's sister, 'me old aunty', whom she described as the 'gamest woman going'. 'When they were fighting, pushing the sticks, she'd walk across to block it. My, she was game! Never got stabbed, though.'

If not in camp, Emily was up at the station homestead, playing with the white children or doing little odd jobs. 'I used to pick up papers; I used to sweep the verandah or toilet, and do a little weeding. Not hard work, you know.'

When Emily was ten years old Mrs Armstrong suggested to her mother that she seek employment so that Emily could learn to work. The position was found at Bunari Station, out from Warrawina Station, many kilometres from Milroy. Emily was employed with another girl. They were accommodated in one side of 'a sort of stable', sharing it with the dray and buggy that stood on the opposite side.

Memories of her stay at Bunari were particularly vivid, possibly because she was away from home for the first time. Also, her mistress was the only European person whom she recalls ever 'abused' (swore at) her. Although Emily praised her mistress's cooking and said they were well fed, she hated her for the beatings she received. 'She was rough. She used to hit us with a whip. My, she was horrible.'

In retaliation, the high-spirited Emily named her 'The Piebald-Faced One' because of her many freckles. Emily 'got up to a lot of silly mischief'. On one occasion when the station owners went to Bourke, they left behind instructions that Emily was 'to be a good girl and look after the fowls and the geese'. She told what happened.

I got dressed up in the boss's pyjamas and I was parading up and down, up and down, when I seen the buggy. Well, run! I ran right down to where we used to sleep. But she saw me running. She came marching down to the shed. 'You been a good girl? Where are Mr French's pyjamas?' My, she gave me a belting for that.

On another occasion she was asked to take water to some geese sitting on a nest out in the swamp. That morning she had received another beating from her mistress. So, instead of putting the water in the dish by the nest, she poured it *into* the nest, thereby of course, killing all the maturing chicks. 'Cruel, eh?' was her comment as she related the episode. Her mistress carefully counted the days to when the chicks were due to hatch. Then she and a friend, Dolly, and Emily went out to inspect the anticipated hatching. Her mistress's comment was 'Oh look, Dolly. See what she did — tipped the water in her own nest.' Emily's comment when reliving the memory retained some of its original note of gloating triumph: 'It wasn't 'er at all! It was me!'

That Christmas, Mrs Armstrong's daughter, 'Miss Mabel', made Emily some clothes as a Christmas present — a dress and a garment that Emily quaintly described as 'a little pants with a tail board'. When the parcel arrived her mistress refused to give it to her, but made out that Santa Claus had brought it. 'Isn't Santa good to bring these?' she asked Emily. 'No, Miss Mabel made them for me,' was the spirited reply.

There was one moment of glory for Emily during this apprenticeship period — the day she was selected to pit her swimming prowess against that of a noted swimming champion from Sydney, Miss Sybil King, who was visiting the station. Emily described the preparations for the event:

> All the men went down. Had a day putting up a big bough shed on the river bank. Oh, beautiful and green, you know. Low grass — on the Culgoa — down from Milroy Bridge.

Then she described the manner in which all the people assembled, how Mrs Armstrong and her daughters, Miss Mabel and Miss Edith, came to see her swim and the way Miss King was there 'jumping about with her costume on'. Emily herself was embarrassed by all the attention given to her, and said, 'All the men were calling out "Come on Bunari!" That's what they used to call me. "Come on, Em. You gotta beat Miss King!" ' She continued:

> I was cryin'. But I put my costume on. Oh, Culgoa was a banker — level to the banks.
> 'When you hear the gun go off, you go and leave Miss King. Don't wait for her!'
> Never answered, you know. I was frightened. Gun went off. I left her! She couldn't catch up with me!
> 'Come on Bunari! Come on Bunari!'
> She was used to heavy water in the sea, but in running water I got away from her. They ran to the bank, lifted me out, carried me on top. Poor thing. They used to torment her often after that! But they made a fuss of me. 'Oh, Emily won a big match!'

Mrs Darcy was a Muruwari relative who worked at Milroy. Some time after the race a brother of hers came to Bunari to see how Emily was faring.

> 'How you going, sister?'
> 'Oh, no good. They're knocking me about, brother.'
> 'E went 'ome and told Mrs Armstrong. She didn't like it. She said to fetch me 'ome. They took me ten miles to Mrs Grogan's place. Next day I said I'd walk 'ome to Milroy. Got me little swag, few clothes, bottle of water. They put me across the river in a boat. 'Now you follow that little pad,' they said. And I began walkin' the ten miles 'ome. Oh, she was a wicked brute! One of the toffs. I couldn't take my part — only small — just aged ten, you know.

Great was the rejoicing of the Milroy camp when the small figure of their returning member was spied some distance before she reached home.

Emily's resourceful and independent spirit is revealed in another youthful adventure. In her late childhood, when she was what she termed 'a great lump of a girl', her sister left her in a camp near Brewarrina in the care of an elderly woman. This woman took Emily to catch crayfish in the river so that she could sell them in town and purchase alcohol with the money. She left Emily in a Brewarrina street to mind a dilly bag of provisions while she went to the hotel. Emily recalled that it was a brilliant moonlit night, so, weary of waiting, she took a loaf of bread and some meat and, in her words:

> I off down the bank, across the river — was only ankle deep — back to camp. I cooked myself meat in a little quart [billy]. Had a good feed. Laid meself down to sleep. When the old woman came back long time after, I roused on her for leavin' me. Said I would tell me sister. She was a bit techy then — frightened — might tell the *kandjabal* [constable]. When my sister come home she blew hell out of the old woman.

For the remainder of her youth, until her marriage, Emily moved about and was employed in a number of places. Apart from Milroy, her happiest memories were of Yuri Point Station, 25 km further downstream, owned by Mr and Mrs English. She was treated by them more like a daughter than a servant, and every reference to them was concluded with the comment 'They were a lovely couple'. Two skills of Mrs English remained clearly in Emily's memory — her piano playing ('She could make the piano talk!'), and her ability to pack oranges.

> Good gracious, Mrs English could pack oranges.
> I said, 'I will help you, Mrs English.'
> 'No you can't do it like I can.'
> But she let me pack them right a-c-r-o-s-s, a-c-r-o-s-s, like that. Couldn't get to Mrs English's number! The old boss used to laugh at me.
> 'You pack it in, Mr English,' I said.
> 'No, I can't do it. I tried.'

One spring Emily was anxious to know whether the quandongs out in the bush were already ripe.

> I asked Mr English, 'Any quandong?'
> 'No, no quandong. Don't ask a silly question.'
> There were plenty of quandong ripe, but he wouldn't tell me.
> 'Look, Mr English,' I said.
> 'Yeah, what's the matter?'
> 'You see that pine tree loaded with that blossom?'
> 'Yeah. I see the pine dust.'
> 'That means quandongs ripe when that dust fall.'
> 'Come on, where's your missis? Take us out and show us.'
> Out come Mrs English, laughing, and we three went down to the pine trees. I chucked a stick, and oh, great clouds of pine dust fell.
> 'You see,' I told him. 'That mean a lot of quandong ripe out in the paddock.'

'All right,' he said. 'This afternoon I'll take you and your mate (that was Mrs English) out to get quandong.'
And when we went out, the tree was bending down, loaded with ripe fruit. Beautiful!

Emily was married at a far later age than Aborigines living the traditional life. Although an aunty 'gave her away in marriage' when she was a baby, according to the correct kinship rules, her parents refused to honour the contract when she reached the age of puberty. She said that her parents refused to give her away at thirteen 'to be knocked about'.

She was married in 1904, in a Christian ceremony. A Brother Casby conducted the ceremony in the drawing room of Milroy Station. Her husband, also a Muruwari from the Culgoa, worked on the station, although he had apparently spent many earlier years working in Bourke. Emily described him as 'a dark fellow like me'. She was very proud of her legal marriage. Years later, for some reason, she was checking the records at Brewarrina. She told the official the exact details of when she was married, where, by whom, etc. She delighted to tell this story.

'It's not registered here,' he said.
'Yes, it is. A minister, Brother Casby, married me.'
'E looked again and found it!
'Ever been to school?' he asked.
'No.'
'By gee! You've got a bloody good headpiece on you.'

The last comment was accompanied by self-appreciating chuckles. This incident is one of the many references there are to Emily's phenomenal memory, accurate to the smallest detail.

Married life was spent with both husband and wife working on stations — Milroy, Hillview, Tallangoona, Weilmoringle, Warrawina, and others. Emily's job was general housework: doing out rooms, cleaning windows and door knobs, washing, ironing, scrubbing, helping in the kitchen or waiting on tables. It was a sore point that, in the early days, there was no mop. 'Me old fella', as she called her husband, was employed on general outside work at the station. Sometimes Emily and her husband went on holidays, using a horse and buggy. They appear to have wandered over a wide area of southern Queensland and north-western New South Wales, picking up odd jobs here and there. They obtained money by rabbiting (a penny a scalp in those days), scouring fleeces, fencing — anything, it would seem, other than jobs offered in towns. It appeared to be a full and happy life, which ended when her husband died at Brewarrina, probably in 1940.

Emily commented on the number of women who, like her, were childless. She thought the matter odd. She had but one pregnancy, but the child died at birth. The memory was as vivid as a present happening.

I only had one by the first. Died a few minutes after it was born. I was silly, delirious, you know. Didn't know me mother that day. It

was June, very cold with mizzling rain. Mumma made a little fire and put me on. Made me right. But the woman looking after me, poor thing — she didn't know any better — she bathed me, dried me, put the thing on. I went out to it! Then Mumma came back.
'What's the matter?' she asked.
'I dunno. Something's wrong with me poor mate.'
And Mumma made that thing — *gawa* we call it. Rolled the dirt away, made a little hollow, put the fire in it, warmed the ground up, raked the ashes away, and laid me there. I was as good as gold next morning. Old people know what to do better than a doctor, you know.

The 1919 influenza epidemic struck the Muruwari camps along the Culgoa with devastating force. Twelve died at Weilmoringle and twelve to fourteen at Dennawan. Emily's account was corroborated by Robin Campbell and others. Death came with terrifying speed after the first symptoms appeared. Emily's endearing and tender-hearted sympathy was never more in evidence than at this time of disaster. Without thought for herself she used to go into the humpies where the sick lay to try to help them. No doctor visited them, nor was any Aboriginal hospitalised. The hospitals were far too full of sick Europeans.

Might be a little 'umpy there, and I'd go in to see if I could do anything. 'Don't go in there,' the whites told me. 'You can't help 'em. You'll get sick yourself. Keep out of there.'

She realised that they were speaking the truth and desisted, but was amazed that she did not contract the disease. 'Tough as iron' was her verdict on herself.

Vividly she recounted a conversation with one of the men in her camp who had become ill over night.

He was on 'is way to the shearer's hut to get some breakfast.
'You got it?' I asked 'im.
'By jove, missus, I feel sick!'
Went up and got tucker. Come back.
'E said, 'Can I have a bit of breakfast here, missus?'
I said, 'Yeah. You sit down. There's a billy of tea over there.'
'E 'ad a feed. Last feed 'e 'ad! 'E 'ad everythin' on 'is plate — cooked beautiful too. But 'e could 'ardly eat it.
'I'll leave this 'ere and give it to the others after,' he said.
I never seen 'im anymore. Next day 'e was dead. He got real yella in his mouth and eyes. Went away and flattened his-self. Never got up, poor fella.

Despite the lapse of years, Emily's voice still betrayed some of the shock of those terrible days. She told of three people at Weilmoringle who wandered off in delirium to thick lignum scrub, where they died. Another horrifying memory was of bodies being carried past the camp on the way to a rapid burial. A foot was sometimes seen hanging out from the cover of the blanket. Such experiences must have been devastating for those who believed strongly in the desire of the spirits of the dead to take their loved ones with them. The situation was made even worse by the fact that the living no longer had freedom to move camp after a death, as they did in former days. There was nowhere to move to: the only recourse was to put the whole camp through the smoke of burning leaves and trust that the spirits of the dead would then leave the living in peace.

Long association with station owners weakened Emily's beliefs to some degree, but she was unshaken deep down concerning most of them. Though she spoke little of her belief in spirits, she admitted to possessing some psychic powers. One morning we were talking about dreams. Unexpectedly her voice suddenly became solemn and, striking an emphatic note, she told me about how she knew if a sick person was going to die.

> You know, I'm telling the truth. Anyone who is real sick over there, they come and tell me. I think, *Hoooooooooo*. [Here she exhaled a long breath.] No, nothing will happen. Then she said softly, 'I can tell.'

I asked how she could tell.

> My stomach. I learnt it from my mother. You know, when I think like that, when I draw me wind like that, it gotta come out of me — from inside — if that person not gonna die. That *nanbadhara* — that noise — it comes up itself. I can't help it. When poor Mrs Darcy got sick, I'm thinking, thinking, all the time. Never come up that breath, that *paaaaaaaaaa*. [Here she released her breath.] I knew she was going to die.

As mentioned earlier, it was a very long time before Emily would admit that she knew any Aboriginal legends. 'Silly' was the term she accorded all stories. She listened, apparently sceptical, to the legends I told her. But, if I deviated from the version she knew, I was quickly corrected. I first tried to get her to tell me the story of Giyan the Moon that Jimmie Barker had recorded for Janet Mathews. She scoffed at the story and derided me for wishing her to tell it, but finally with great reluctance she told me parts. Some days later she broke into the conversation with the following comment, leaving me in no doubt about her real opinion.

> When you said 'stories' I thought about that moon. You know that moon? He got drownded right down in the bottom of the 'ole there. He got into the mud from the bank about as far away as your car. You can see that big 'ole where he was supposed to come out. It's there today, on the Culgoa, down from Weilmoringle. It will never go out of it.

On another occasion she commented, 'He wasn't the moon — he was a man blackfella.'

She remembered and told me, first in English, then more sketchily in Muruwari, a number of legends. An unexpected piece of information was gleaned from her one day after I had told her the story Radcliffe-Brown had obtained about Kiwi's seduction of the two wives of his father's brother, Bindjalanj. Then she broke in with a detail that Radcliffe-Brown's informant had not volunteered:

> He was a dirty brute, that Kiwi. I heard them talk about that. He had two dicks. When he used to do it to the one, he did it to the other. Straight out. Put one in there. Put another one in the other woman. Work 'is way in. Wasn't satisfied with one woman. Wanted the two straight out! He was going in for the good thing then, the dirty sod.

Then followed gales of hooting laughter, which reflected her love of the ludicrous. In Emily's version of the legend, Kiwi was the father of the two women. He composed a song about the incident, four lines of which Emily sang for me.

Another area of Aboriginal belief that Emily retained implicitly was in native medicine. She told of many incidents where native medicines had cured a wide range of diseases. She spoke of a wild onion cure for ringworm, of a solution of boiled saltbush leaves whose drawing properties cured a woman of breast abscesses, and of the numerous skin diseases (boils, measles, chickenpox) that were cured with the application of boiled or burnt emu-bush leaves (*Eremophila* sp.). She told how she herself was at death's door with the measles (which she called 'Barcoo rot'), caught on a visit to Bourke when she was twelve or thirteen years old. She travelled in a wagonette from Bourke to Milroy and then walked the seven miles to Mundiwa where her parents were. Her father burnt some emu-bush leaves, mixed them to a paste with water, and got her mother to paint the solution liberally all over her body. Her delirium, high fever and spots vanished overnight with this treatment.

Memories included some vignettes of social history, such as the use of Kanaka labour on the stations.

> I've seen some Kanakas, fetched up from down below [presumably Sydney], who used to wait on the tables. One man, Philip, oh, he was a big man. Another man, Dave, he's the one who cut his throat — there. [She pointed on her own throat to the exact spot.] But they saved him. He couldn't get a woman, you know. He went *wamba* [mad].

Her most vivid memories, however, were of happenings within her own culture. She described how the women used to get dressed up in their little trunks (special garments worn on these occasions) and hold a corroboree all night long. She recalled how some sang with clear voices, especially Jack Broome.

> My, he was good; he had a great lung. I've heard them sing all night till nearly sunrise. Corroboree *all* night. No spell! Kids and all, till morning. And one man's the singer. He used to sing for the mob. And they with their boomerangs rattling — *didadit, didadit, didadit*

— keeping time when they shake their legs corroboreeing. Bushes round their legs, round their arms. I've seen the gins too — young girls with their trunks on. I was in on that! Some of them looked good too. But some had bloomers on. They didn't know the difference! [She giggled at this.] I used to laugh at some of the girls. They knock off at sunrise, have a wash, have breakfast, put on their clothes. Walk about all day and then corroboree in the night with another lot wanting to see their corroboree. Oh, it was really good.

Emily's second marriage probably took place about 1942. It may best be described in the ensuing dialogue. I had asked her about her second husband and where he died.

He died here at Goodooga, poor old fellow. He was an old man. Ninety-three years of age. White man, 'e was. I've got the marriage lines there to prove it. [Here she pointed to a case under her bed.] Frederick John Hoilable [spelt 'Horneville' on the document when it was produced].

I asked where she had met him.

'At Brewarrina.'
  'Where did he come from?'
  'Victoria . . . Oh, a beautiful coffin 'e had.'
  'Did you know any of his family?'
  'No. Good man 'e was. Good for me. I wouldn't live with a bad man. No fear!'

Frederick Horneville was a drover. Emily accompanied him on his jobs but always remained 'at home' or 'in the camp'. When he became too old to work they made a permanent home under two peppertrees at the farthest end of the Goodooga Aboriginal Reserve. There, Emily continued to live after his death, till a number of unfortunate incidents, precipitated by helplessness and advancing years, drove her to seek the security of closer neighbours. She had a number of falls, which ultimately caused her to become bedridden. Once, her dress became entangled in a nail on the door of her house while she was carrying wood, and she fell heavily. Another time, while carrying two buckets of water, she fell over a log hidden by the long grass. These falls so impaired her mobility that she was forced to walk with sticks.

While in this crippled condition, and well into her eighties, she was assaulted and injured one night by a drunken youth, and spent some weeks in hospital. After this incident her neighbours took steps to protect her and the tiny house she was to occupy for almost the remainder of her days was built for her close to Ruby Hooper's house. Ruby's husband, Alec, built it out of materials that were paid for by Emily. Ruby offered to look after 'Aunty Emily', although there was no actual blood relationship. Ruby had no children at the time and, following Aboriginal custom, offered her services to this old member of their community.

Emily Margaret Horneville 119

Emily with Ruby Hooper and Ruby's daughter Yvonne. Ruby looked after Emily on the reserve. Later, when she was allotted a government house in Goodooga, she took Emily to live with her. Emily remained in Ruby's house until shortly before her death.

The house was big enough to contain a narrow bed, a home-made table and a few wooden boxes. The windows were barred so that no one could gain access, and during winter they were shuttered with a movable sheet of tin. The door boasted a padlock and Ruby locked the old lady in every night about sundown. A piece of tin sloped from the roof to the ground in front of the door to give protection from the elements.

For a time, Emily moved about as formerly, but another fall caused her hip to break. She described how it happened. Some 'dirty mongrels' came in and helped themselves to her water supply, spilling some on the ground of her house. When she entered, her stick skidded on the water. 'I had the river on my stick' was the colourful way she described it. Although she spent some time in hospital with the injury, the bone did not mend, so for the last ten or more years of her life she was bedridden.

In latter years she seldom left her home; but in it she lived a remarkably full life. In some respects she reigned like a queen, either dispensing largesse to the children who visited her or yelling at them to go away. She unerringly gathered all the gossip of the camp as she accurately interpreted every sound and movement. She questioned everyone who came by about the actions and plans of everyone she knew. However, particularly as she became more deaf and cantankerous she was left alone for long periods of the day. Despite this, she was very much at home in the environment she knew and loved so well. Through the doorway she could see the two peppertrees of her old camp, about a kilometre away. She could also watch the sky, and her long distance eyesight remained amazingly keen. It was possible for her to discern the tiniest clouds far off on the horizon, and she interpreted their significance daily: 'No, no rain in these clouds'; or 'It'll be raining by morning'. An iron fencing post had been driven into the ground beside her sloping iron shelter so that when the shadow of the two synchronised she knew it was about midday. She would watch that shadow move and comment, 'It's nearly twelve o'clock, isn't it? Look at the shadow.' Thus she kept a check on the time.

As we worked and talked together she frequently spoke of the vast and fascinating natural world that had been her domain for so long. It intrigued me how vividly she could bring that world to life as we sat in her little house, so alienated from it in fact, but not in reality. Emily never lost her sense of wonder at the marvels of nature. This keen appreciation of all living things was manifested by the detailed descriptions of the ways of ants, birds and animals, and by her oft-reiterated comment of how clever or beautiful natural things were. Of native bees she said:

> They are clever little fellows to make honey in any sort of tree with a hollow in it. In winter time bees don't work. That little place where they go in is all wax. They shut it up and eat some of that honey in the winter. Then, when the summer comes, they open that up and work again to fill their little combs up. Clever little fellows, aren't they?

She made a similar remark about how the goannas know when to come out of hibernation and how to gradually restore their strength after the long fast. She spoke of the skin of bilbies [small marsupial, kind of bandicoot]: 'They're a pretty blue colour. Just lovely!' How I wished we were both mobile so that together we could explore this natural treasure-house!

Emily's zest for life was further revealed in her love of certain foods. She passed comments such as 'Oh, for a good feed of emu. I haven't tasted emu meat for a long time'; or 'That *dhalimuganj*, that manna — little round things tasting of bread and honey. We'd pick them off the coolibah leaves and stick them together in a ball and eat them. Real good!'; and 'Yams! By gee, they were lovely one time. We used to cook them any road — in the ashes, boil 'em or in the round hole' [fire-pit].

She did not suffer fools gladly and was not afraid to acquaint them with the fact. 'I don't spare them. I tell them!' was ever her policy. Among other things she roundly condemned drunkenness, loose behaviour, government hand-outs of 'too much money', cadging children, dishonesty and meanness. One day she was particularly critical of the way white children catch frogs for fishing bait.

> White children lie on their stomachs to catch 'em. But they're stupid, white children! Stillborn! They will sit in the mud and when you tell them to get out of it they say, 'Good, good.' Dirty little brutes!

One of the most caustic comments she made to me concerned a linguistic point that to her was obvious, but not so to me. She remarked with supreme scorn at my bumbling, 'You'll never make a scholar, mate!' There was no mistaking her wrath when she was angry, nor her sympathy when she was moved. Her camaraderie with me she expressed by calling me 'mate', although sometimes it was 'ole darlin'.

Emily's accurate and long-reaching memory focused on many things. She demonstrated it most by her knowledge of physical features. One day she named all the rivers in correct sequence, commencing with the most easterly one and recounting them until she reached the Murray. On another occasion she named in Muruwari all the waterholes on the Culgoa, methodically placing them in sequence from the one furthest upstream to the last downstream.

At the climax of a recollection, Emily's voice would peak to a certain note, which would be retained over the next several syllables, each one being elongated as if to stretch the pleasure of her memories. Then her voice would return to its normal pitch and, in a rush of words, the telling would be concluded. For example, when recounting how, as a child, she used to eat *dhalimuganj*, she said, 'I used to g-o r-o-u-n-d t-h-e t-r-e-e-s, e-a-t t-h-e-m; [then quickly] suck-on-the-leaves, you-know. Like bread and honey — real good!'

This highly entertaining trait manifested itself when recounting an amusing story. Then fun-loving laughter would bubble forth, saving many a linguistic session from drudgery.

Just a few months before she died, Emily moved into a new house in town (one of six built by the government) that had been awarded to Ruby. There, she had a room to herself in a house that contained all modern conveniences. But she seemed to be *in* the household rather than *of* it. The kitchen and lounge room were filled with card players each afternoon, but few came to see her. She missed the familiar sights and sounds of the reserve. That tiny home on the river bank where she was still within reach of the bush and camp life was where she belonged. She had become a displaced person. When I visited her a few weeks after she had moved in, I discerned a certain wistfulness and disorientation. It was not many weeks before her mind became confused and her physical frailty increased. After several weeks in the Goodooga Hospital, she died on 22 February 1979 at the probable age of ninety-eight years.

It is indeed fortunate that she escaped the 'civilising' influences that wrecked the indigenous lifestyle of so many Aborigines and so frequently sowed the seeds of schizophrenia in the dispossessed. Almost to the end of her life Emily retained a rare independence of spirit and wholeness of personality which denoted a fully integrated individual. That she remained so comparatively unscarred may be attributed to an inflexibility of spirit that refused to submit to alien forces. In addition, she was fortunate that circumstances had allowed her sufficient freedom to escape much of what was unacceptable. She was lucky to have been fully grown up by 1912. Had she still been a child she would almost certainly have been compelled, as many were at that time, to leave the comparative freedom of station life for the miseries of a reserve or mission. When asked if she had ever lived on a mission, she replied emphatically, 'No! No! No mission for me! We didn't believe in the mission. Only go visiting sometimes.'

Thus, from a childhood mostly at Milroy and other places on the Culgoa, to adult life spent wandering far and wide throughout Muruwari territory and beyond, Emily knew a freedom of movement and spirit denied to most Aboriginal people of her day.

It grieves me that Emily's greatness was not appreciated. By European standards she would not be listed with the eminent in *Who's Who*. She served on no committees, was not a member of any prestigious group. She received no award for meritorious service. If Emily's intelligence and force of character had been fully recognised, she would have been amongst the leaders. As it was, she lived her life largely unnoticed and unsung. But if the ability to live a full life in the face of tremendous social upheaval and to retain an inner integrity of mind and spirit are marks of greatness, then Emily Margaret Horneville attained it.

Additional reading

Mathews, J. (1977). *The two worlds of Jimmie Barker: The life of an Australian Aboriginal, 1900-1972.* Australian Institute of Aboriginal Studies, Canberra

Radcliffe-Brown, A. (1923). Notes on the social organisation of Australian tribes: Part II. *Journal of the Anthropological Institute of Great Britain and Ireland*

9

Inyalangka

Helen Payne

'Langkie, Langkie!' The shriek of delight resounded across the camp, cutting into the still crispness of the desert's early morning. The call came from Lois, a plump exuberant eight-year-old who was bounding, arms outstretched, towards a group of elderly women seated on the bare, red earth beside the old hospital building at Ernabella. Seated in the group was sixty-year-old Inyalangka, affectionately called Langkie. She was the object of Lois's excitement. As she talked to the women around her, she rhythmically struck the ground with a short, curved stick held in her right hand. As Lois's shriek of delight broke the concentration of the group, Inyalangka raised her eyes and peered through the thick haze created by the fire that smouldered in front of her.

Her face broke into a smile as she saw her grandchildren approaching, followed by their mother. The older children were all running now, with Lois taking the lead. Imuna, their mother, quietly followed, carrying her youngest child, a chubby six-month-old baby.

After the initial bubbling excitement of the new arrivals' welcome had died down a little, Inyalangka, now nursing her youngest granddaughter, cast her eyes beyond the immediate group to the graded road that lay behind them and the grey Toyota truck that had brought the new arrivals to Ernabella. Already it was half hidden by the group of men who had gathered around it to talk with Donald Fraser, Lois's father, still seated in the driver's cabin.

Donald, son of George Fraser, was Inyalangka's eldest child. He had recently left Ernabella to take up residence at Kenmore Park, a cattle station now under the managment of Pukatja Community, an incorporated group within the Ernabella settlement. At the meeting held to select a manager for this property, Donald had been elected to the position. Accordingly he had left his home in Ernabella to live in the old station homestead located on the property. Inyalangka had openly expressed her sadness at losing her son and his family from Ernabella; none the less she was pleased that he had been chosen for the position, for, as she said, Kenmore Park is *Donaldgu ngura* (Donald's home country). Now that she no longer saw Donald and his family every day (as she had when they lived in Ernabella), she had become accustomed to returning with them to Kenmore Park to spend a day or two there and see her only grandchildren.

Often she went on these holidays alone, because her husband Tommy (or Minyungu), an elderly, very knowledgeable Pitjantjatjara man, preferred to remain at Ernabella. Like Inyalangka, Tommy was born in traditional Pitjantjatjara country located to the west of Amata. He rarely chose to accompany Inyalangka on her visits to Kenmore Park, yet he was always on the sharp lookout for an opportunity to return to his own country. Inyalangka usually accompanied her husband on these trips and would later tell me how happy they were to be in the bush, away from the worries and strains created by 'settled life'.

Like Tommy's country, Inyalangka's also lies to the west of Amata, her birthplace being very close to the intersection now created by the junction of the Western Australian, Northern Territory and South Australian borders. It was in this area that her older brother Dickie, and younger sister Anmanari were born.

Today only Dickie lives in this area; Inyalangka and Anmanari are both living in Ernabella. This is the home also of their younger sister Muwitja, who was born one year after Anmanari, shortly after the family's arrival in Ernabella.

Inyalangka first came to know Ernabella as a young woman. At that time Ernabella was a mission station, founded and supported by the Presbyterian Church. The mission offered many forms of employment in exchange for food, clothing and other European goods. The missionaries ran a large sheep-holding and Inyalangka, Tommy and most of her kin were at one time or another all employed as shepherds. This work gave them the opportunity of visiting particular places of totemic importance to them and maintaining a lifestyle similar to that of their forebears. Inyalangka, in telling me of her shepherding days, recounted how she and Tommy were often able to leave their flock briefly. Using donkeys and camels as pack animals (now left to run wild in the area), they would visit a nearby site of totemic importance where food and water were plentiful, and there enjoy a few days' holiday. Sometimes they would travel to visit one or other of her sisters, who, with their families, worked at shepherding flocks. Often, they brought back Anmanari's children with them. Always, on such occasions, Anmanari would have worked hard to prepare enough damper and secure sufficient food for her children to take with them on their holiday, so that they did not prove a burden to Inyalangka and Tommy.

It was in this country that Inyalangka gave birth to, and reared, her own children. The eldest, Donald Fraser, was born east of Ernabella near a bore now known as Donald's Well. The brush shelter (*wiltja*) in which he was born can still be seen and is easily viewed from a nearby vehicle track. Inyalangka's other children are Tommy's sons, Kulyuru and Litja, now men in their twenties. Both live at Ernabella, Kulyuru and his wife occupying the galvanised iron shed next to that of Tommy and Inyalangka.

Both sons are employed in full-time trade work in Ernabella and, in accordance with the traditions of kinship obligation, whereby every member of the society must help or assist those standing in particular kin relationships to him or her, they assist Inyalangka and Tommy in securing their daily needs.

Inyalangka must now rely on others to obtain her supply of firewood. She has required more wood than usual since serious tuberculosis attacks a few years ago, for her resultant coughing spasms are worsened by cold. Nowadays Ernabella residents must go quite some distance by truck to collect suitable firewood. However, not all family groups at Ernabella own vehicles, although they may have the use of one for community work.

Thus, on my most recent visit to Ernabella, because I had a truck and was regarded as a member of Inyalangka's family, I and my family became responsible for collecting Inyalangka's daily supply of firewood. Inyalangka, for her part, assumed the major responsibility as my teacher and supervisor, for my learning of women's *inma* (ceremonies).

I first met Inyalangka in 1976 when I made a short visit to Ernabella to see a woman whom I had first met in Adelaide and had come to know quite well. My return to Ernabella in 1978, this time accompanied by my husband and our two-year-old son, provided the opportunity of renewing my friendship with those whom I had met on my previous visit, as well as of undertaking, as a trained ethnomusicologist, a study of women's *inma*.

On this 1978 visit, as I stepped out of the truck, I heard women start to sing their traditional *inma*. Turning, I saw a large group of women seated on the lawn in front of the old hospital building singing. As I moved closer to the group, my eyes focused on the familiar warm smile of Inyalangka, welcoming me. I was not then aware that I would work very closely with Inyalangka and her family on this visit and that I and my family would be included in her family. I learnt of this latter decision one day whilst talking with Harry Purampi (the husband of Inyalangka's sister, Muwitja), and another important Ernabella man. They classified me as Inyalangka's 'sister' and my husband as Harry's 'brother'.

Shortly after my arrival, Inyalangka suggested a very perceptive program for my tuition in women's *inma*. When I agreed with it, she became my vigilant supervisor, making sure that the program was adhered to and that it received the necessary support from the rest of the community.

Weather permitting, the program involved almost daily *inma* performances. Often Inyalangka would coax some of the younger women, not so expert or interested in this aspect of their heritage, to come out and participate. Once, I heard her reprimand one young working mother, ordering her to leave her housework: it would wait for her, but *inma* would not! The woman duly came out to learn the dances in which Inyalangka sought to instruct us on that day. As Inyalangka well recognised, it was vitally necessary for the younger women to learn their *inma* if the *inma* were to continue in the area; but she was dismayed by other women's lack of interest. Indeed, on the eve of my departure she sadly remarked that now there would be only a handful of women who would come regularly to *inma*, because she would not be able to offer them a means of transport and would thus fail in her efforts to recruit participants. It was indeed significant that Inyalangka would have preferred the payment the women received from me for their *inma* to have gone towards the repair of their currently unuseable, tyreless '*inma* truck'. Although out-voted by the other women, who desired the money for daily personal needs, Inyalangka's suggestion publicly affirmed her own commitment to women's *inma*.

Indeed, Inyalangka's zest for *inma* showed itself not only in the encouragement she gave the other women, but also in the enthusiastic and quietly authoritative manner in which she led the performers at the appointed performance ground. Her instruction never diminished the element of enjoyment that was so much a part of every performance. So important was Inyalangka's presence that, when she was absent from the community for a few days, performances became either conspicuous by their near absence, or, if held, by the number of sections omitted. This highlighted Inyalangka's ritual status, for, according to tradition, certain verses cannot be performed without a person who stands in authority for the *inma* and has deep knowledge of it being present.

My elder sister, whose story I share with you in this contribution, died on the eve of the completion of this publication. In deference to the feelings of her relatives, the editors generously agreed to delete her photograph. We include instead, one of her younger sister—Anmanari—who also is mentioned in the text.

As this story still contains the *name* of the deceased, readers are advised not to display or read the story aloud in the presence of the bereaved kinsfolk.

Inyalangka's enthusiasm and agility in commanding and participating in performances sometimes caused what was intended to be a small-scale day performance to be continued well into the evening. Sometimes Inyalangka herself would still be dancing, painted and stripped to the waist in the customary manner, well into the night, apparentlly oblivious of the increasing chill of the air and the inevitable coughing spasms that would follow. Eventually she would be persuaded by me or another of her sisters to halt the proceedings on account of her health. However, she would only do so after having successfully arranged with the other performers to continue the performance the following day.

Usually *inma* would finish at dusk, and then I would take Inyalangka (and any other woman who wished to come with me) out from the settlement to collect the night's supply of firewood. On the journey, Inyalangka, and either Anmanari or Yuminia, a woman in her thirties, who was one of my constant companions and an excellent dancer, would sit with me in the driver's cabin. We used this time together to discuss the day's happenings, or to plan ahead for the next few days. Sometimes we sang again some of the *inma* we had performed that day, and Inyalangka carefully corrected my numerous mistakes. After we had filled the truck to capacity with wood (Anmanari and I collecting for Inyalangka, but every other person for themselves), if it were not yet dark, Inyalangka, Anmanari and Yuminia would spend some time showing me the plants in the vicinity and would name them in Pitjantjatjara and explain their traditional uses.

There was a carefree enjoyment about these times we spent together away from the settlement collecting plant foods and wood. They contrasted strongly with the dedicated seriousness of our journeys for *inma* instruction. One series of journeys, made for the purpose of teaching me the location and significance of the series of sites associated with a particular *inma,* stands out in my memory as epitomising the kind of working relationship that existed between myself, Inyalangka and her kin, particularly her sister Anmanari. The task involved travelling from site to site, retracing the steps of the dreamtime ancestors responsible for the *inma*. At each location, Inyalangka and Anmanari would take turns to explain the story concerning the ancestors' stay there and would outline the significance of the site.

As this particular *inma* path comprised many sites, the task was an exhausting one. It tried the dedication and tenacity of us all. When we finally returned to Ernabella late that night, after having worked since just after dawn, we had on board not only some rabbits that had been caught by Anmanari's daughter and shared amongst the group in the traditional fashion, but also some very quiet, sleeping women — a most unusual occurrence, as these women seldom slept in a mobile vehicle.

Just before my departure, Inyalangka, Anmanari, Yuminia and I enjoyed a final afternoon's hunting for *tjala* (honey ants). Our earlier rare attempts to secure this delicacy had failed, but this time, because the promised 'big rains' had come, I was able to leave the settlement with a small jar of this very sweet and highly prized food. On our way to where Inyalangka guessed that we might find the honey ants, she gave me, my husband and my child our Pitjantjatjara names. The names she chose were those of her kinsfolk: my husband was given the name Minyungu, her husband's name; my son was named Kayipipi, the name of her youngest sister's child; and I was given the name Yuminia.

On the day of our departure, most of my time was spent by the Ernabella radio telephone awaiting calls concerning our arrangements. I noticed Yuminia watching me, repeatedly beckoning me over to her. Finally, the calls completed, I was able to pay heed to her signals. Following her, I came upon Inyalangka and Anmanari, who led me to the spot where they had managed to keep my husband and son occupied. Inyalangka then took command and sat us in a row before her. My kinswomen then stood in a row facing us. In turn each came forward and made a speech to us, assessing the value of our stay with them. At the conclusion of their speeches, each gave us a parting gift, by which they said, we would remember them when we were far away.

As Inyalangka spoke, I saw before me an older sister, greying, knowledgeable, and generous in her sharing of experience and loyal support. I saw, too, an authority on *inma,* whose knowledge commanded respect from other women and who consciously used her ritual status, and the moral authority it implied, to foster a concern for women's traditional knowledge amongst the members of the generation that would follow hers. I saw one who had considered me worthy to learn, and to share, a heritage not my own — one who had accepted the challenge and responsibility of designing and supervising a program of tuition for me. She had patiently guided and encouraged me in this program as she would have done for one whose birth decreed a right to it. I was not born a Pitjantjatjara woman; but Inyalangka had taught me to appreciate what it means to be one.

The opening words of her speech to me that day were 'Yuminia, you came here knowing only a little; now you leave very knowledgeable, *nyuntu nyinti pulka'*. Those last words truly applied to the woman who spoke them to me: Inyalangka, *nyuntu nyinti pulka!*

Additional reading

Hilliard, W.M. (1968). *The people in between: The Pitjantjatjara people of Ernabella* Hodder and Stoughton, London

10

My Sister Who Mothered Me

Janice Reid

While I was living at Yirrkala in Arnhem Land the idea of writing about Aboriginal women never really occurred to me. As a fledgling medical anthropologist out to get my full complement of professional feathers I focused my attention on people's ways of coping with illness and death and their use of such resources as 'bush' medicines, the traditional healer, the health centre and the hospital. I was the fortunate student of people who diligently taught me Aboriginal concepts of the causes of illness and talked with me about their understanding of everyday illnesses and their management. But one person was more than a teacher: her name was Nangaypa, and she was my 'sister' and my friend.

Nangaypa rarely sat with me, as others did, to give formal instruction about her culture. By letting me share her daily life and family concerns she 'grew me up'. Despite the formidable barriers posed by my being a *Balanda* (European), she tried valiantly to mould me into a superficially passable community member — an honorary Yolngu. When I was asked to contribute to a book of biographies of Aboriginal women, I thought at once of Nangaypa. I fossicked through my field notes for biographical details about her birthplace, childhood, marriage and adult life, her family, jobs and responsibilities. I arranged the information chronologically and tried to mould my notes into a life history. However the portrait of Nangaypa I managed to cull from her occasional reminiscences was lifeless, nothing like the vivid, intimate and affectionate image of my adoptive sister which is lodged somewhere between my thoughts and feelings. My private portrait of Nangaypa, resulting from impressions gained during my field visits and her holidays with me in Sydney between 1974 and 1981, could not be captured in a conventional biographical narrative. I realised that, to describe Nangaypa, I would have to write about how I came to know her. This means revealing more of myself than is customary in anthropological accounts; it means describing some of those field experiences, painful and happy, which shaped and fostered our friendship. The Nangaypa I know is the person who mothered, taught, frustrated, delighted, comforted and puzzled me. It is this woman who is described here.

Yirrkala, founded as a Methodist mission station in 1935, is now a community of approximately 1100 Aborigines and 100 Europeans. The clans living there are part of the society W. Lloyd Warner called the 'Murngin'. In 1974 I arrived at Yirrkala equipped with the conventional anthropological paraphernalia: a typewriter, notebooks, camera, modest tropical clothes, camping gear, gifts and a research plan. My only previous field experience consisted of a three-month study of the social and economic aspects of wild pig hunting in a remote part of Hawaii. With considerable naivety I assumed that a research strategy formulated at Stanford University would easily be translated into action in Arnhem Land. This assumption was quickly dispelled.

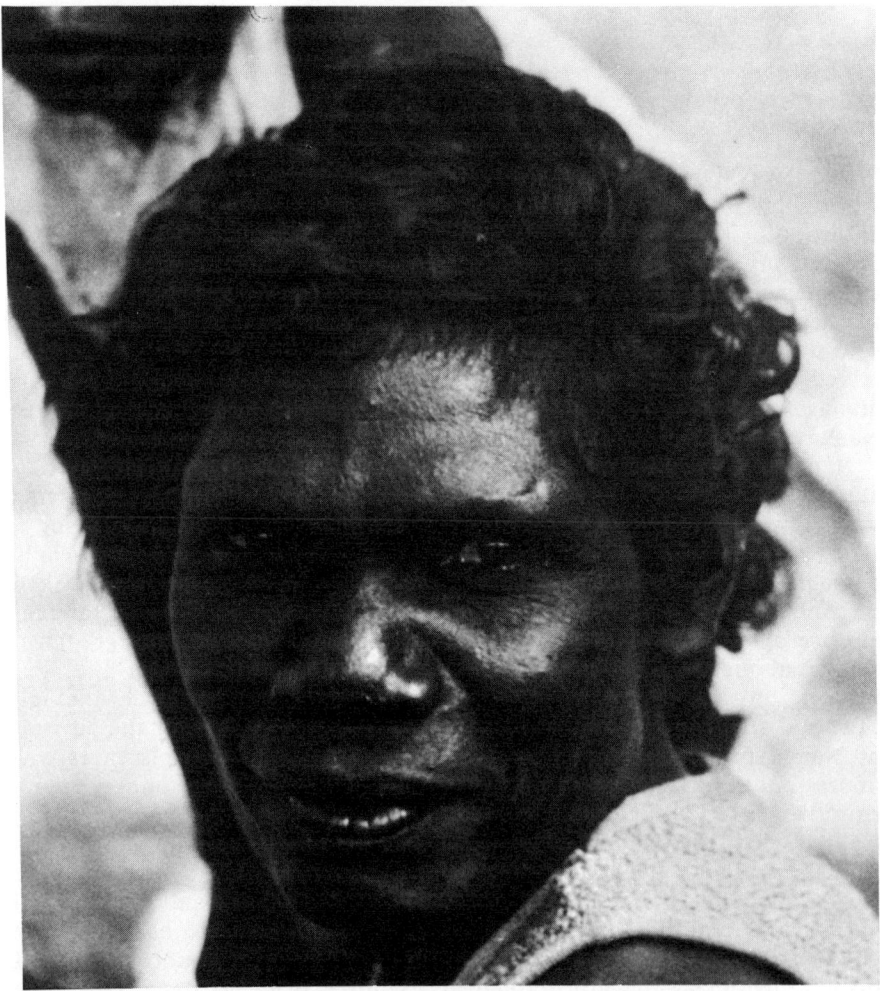

Nangaypa at Birany'buy in September 1975

My first priority was to find an 'informant' — preferably a woman — who would introduce me into the community, answer all my questions, interpret when necessary and be my friend. My training had given me clear ideas about the kind of person I would choose. She would be about my age and a person of standing, and would necessarily speak English because of my faltering knowledge of Yolngu languages. I would select her after I had surveyed the situation fully and assessed the suitability of various women.

Within a week a woman of about forty whom I had never seen before informed me, through an interpreter, that she would work with me. She did not want to work at the school anymore because they did not pay her enough. I was told that I would be her sister and that my name would be Djinyupa. My subsection, like hers, would be Bulanydjan, my moiety Yirritja, and I would be a member of the Gumatj clan, a prominent land-owning group of the area. Nangaypa's father became my father; her mother my mother. (Nangaypa's parents died in 1979 and since the names of the dead may not be spoken or written for several years after their deaths they are not referred to by name here.)

My relatives were innumerable. I was told not to talk to my many actual and classificatory brothers in a familiar way, and to avoid any contact at all (except through an intermediary) with my numerous sons-in-law. I was then instructed by a senior man of my mother's clan that I was to be a 'good girl'. This meant that I was to justify the community council's trust in allotting me an abandoned and overgrown house in the Aboriginal 'camp' by behaving impeccably. There was to be 'no trouble' in the house, 'no alcohol' and 'no one living in the house besides you and your [female] assistants'.

Very soon it was made clear to me that the social, economic, political and religious affairs of the community were carried out in the context of multiple clan and kin relationships and that I was expected to know who my hundred or so closest relatives were, what obligations and expectations were attached to each relationship and which kinship terms I should use when addressing them. The process of education that was intended to make me an adequate Yolngu was not only directed towards me. Children and infants were constantly told, particularly when they looked at me in fright and cried inconsolably until I turned away, that I was their *ngandi* (mother) or *yapa* (sister) or whatever our relationship happened to be.

Despite these initial (and customary) efforts to incorporate me into the kinship network, I did not know Nangaypa and she did not know me: our relationship was strained. When I visited her house I would be greeted by a flurry of nervous activity as dogs were dispersed, sheets spread on the sand near the house, cups and plates washed and children washed or dressed. Any sights or behaviours which Nangaypa thought I might find offensive she quickly suppressed. I was embarrassed. I tried protest and studious indifference but was unable to persuade her not to treat me as just another European stranger.

Before we could start our first joint research project, recording the genealogy of the Gumatj clan, Nangaypa's brother was taken ill and died in Nhulunbuy Hospital, 20 km away from Yirrkala. At the time of his death at least 100 relatives were camping in patches of bush outside the hospital so that they could be near him. His family was distraught with grief and, as is frequently the case when deaths occur in this society, they suspected sorcery. His loss was the more tragic because he was a middle-aged man and the father of a young family.

I did not know what to do. I wanted to go to the hospital and convey my condolences and sorrow to Nangaypa and her family but did not know whether I would be intruding on their grief. I went into town, having decided to sit on the periphery of the gathering, but when Nangaypa saw me coming she beckoned me to sit on the rug with her. A group of men sitting nearby were singing the sacred songs of the dead man's clan to the accompaniment of didgeridoo and clapsticks. Women and girls were dancing the stylised ceremonial dances which mime the themes of the song. Intermittently several older women wailed loudly in unison to the music, their wailing punctuated occasionally by sobs. One threw herself repeatedly to the ground to express and assuage her grief. As is customary for bereaved women, Nangaypa had been hitting her head with sharp objects, and patches of her hair were matted with blood from the cuts on her scalp. I sat quietly but awkwardly, not knowing whether I should stay or leave. Finally Nangaypa asked me anxiously if I wanted to start work on the genealogy. I was stunned. 'No,' I replied, 'not while you are upset and busy.' Milminyina, her adolescent daughter, who is a most capable interpreter and had been facilitating many of our conversations, rounded on her with an impatient 'I told you so'. I gathered that Nangaypa had been worrying for some time about my tolerance for interruptions to my work schedule.

As time passed and I showed, however clumsily, that I wanted to be treated as a member of Nangaypa's community and family, the quality of our relationship changed. When we were more familiar and more relaxed I began to learn something of her story.

Nangaypa was born in about 1934 at Yuḏuyuḏu on the western side of Melville Bay. Few people in her family had then ever met a European, for the only European resident on the eastern coast of Arnhem Land was the explorer and trader Fred Gray, who was harvesting trepang in the area. In 1933 neighbouring Yolngu at Caledon Bay had killed several of the crew of a Japanese pearling lugger. In Darwin and southern Australia outraged officials and citizens called for a punitive expedition; instead, the Reverend Wilbur Chaseling established a mission station at Yirrkala in 1935. Nangaypa's father was already a prominent man; later he was to become head of the Gumatj clan and a major figure in the land-rights struggle of the Yirrkala people and in their negotiations with the bauxite mining company Nabalco Pty Ltd in the late 1960s. Nangaypa's mother was the first of his thirteen wives. When I first met her she was an old, respected and important member of the Rirratjingu clan, the last surviving child of the man, Marika, whose name is now used as a surname by its members. A grandson described her as the 'head of the Rirratjingu for the maḏayin (sacred knowledge and objects) and the Law'.

Nangaypa could remember her mother teaching her to make her own small digging stick when she was a little girl, so that she could dig yams with the older women. She had her own dilly bag, woven by her mother from bark string, which she carried on foraging expeditions with the women. From her mother she learned the names, seasonal variations, mode of collecting, and attributes of the abundant plants, small animals and seafoods which it was a woman's responsibility to gather. The skills learned as a small child flowered into exceptional skills in adulthood; by the time I met Nangaypa she had a fine reputation as a vigorous and productive food gatherer.

Nangaypa went to school for a short time at Yirrkala, in a school hut then constructed of bush timber and coconut palm leaves. She recalled, 'There was no paper, only little blackboards and chalk for each of us.' But her energies were mainly focused on learning about the environment and its resources, and in acquiring the religious knowledge which, as an adult Yolngu, she would be expected to possess.

While still young, Nangaypa was betrothed by her parents to a man of the Galpu clan who lived in a neighbouring community. However, it was a Djambarrpuyngu man then living at Yirrkala who gave help and economic support to Nangaypa's parents, bringing them portions of any game or fish that he caught, as is expected of a prospective son-in-law. And so, when Nangaypa reached puberty, she began to spend time with this man, collecting food and becoming accustomed to his company. He was then working with the missionaries, and had helped to build the first store hut and cultivate the gardens. Within a few years Nangaypa became his wife.

Nangaypa's first son died in infancy. Her second son was born in 1958 and her daughter in 1960. During the 1960s her husband took a second wife. After he died the younger wife remarried and went to live at a neighbouring settlement, leaving her son at Yirrkala, to be cared for by Nangaypa as her own. Although pressed to remarry by the husband of several of her sisters, Nangaypa has insisted upon remaining a widow and independent householder. She said that she did not want any more children, particularly children who would belong to a clan different from that of her deceased husband. When her husband died he had been leader of the Dhudi Djambarrpuyngu clan at Yirrkala. Her son and daughter, when older, would inherit joint responsibility for the land, lore and sacred objects belonging to that clan.

As the resident population increased in the early years of the mission, game and other native foods within walking distance of Yirrkala decreased. Entry into the cash economy became inevitable, particularly as it was mission policy to encourage wage labour rather than distributing rations of food. From the 1950s onwards, as well as caring for her household, Nangaypa worked for European mission staff to earn the money she needed to purchase staples such as flour, sugar, tea, tobacco and material for clothes. She helped weed and cultivate the mission gardens, cleaned, ironed, washed and cooked in the houses of staff members, and taught younger women the domestic skills required in European households. For three years she took everyday charge of a European child. She also gained experience as a laundress, both at the central laundry in Yirrkala and at the mining town of Nhulunbuy, sorted and packed fish at the seafood processing and freezing plant near Nhulunbuy, and taught 'Yolngu culture' at Yirrkala primary school. In 1974 she began paid work with me.

These activities were never central to Nangaypa's life nor, I suspect, essential to her self-image. As her mother's daughter, as her husband's wife, and as one of the elder daughters of the head of the Gumatj clan, Nangaypa is an influential woman whose secular and ritual responsibilities are considerable. I first noticed this at the elaborate circumcision ceremony for her young step-son. Both in her own right and because her husband was dead Nangaypa took a major organisational and ritual role. She was also the central figure in the establishment of an outstation or homeland centre on Djambarrpuyngu and Rirratjingu land at Dambaliya, an island 15 km off the coast. A leader of the Rirratjingu clan told me in 1975 that he had designated Nangaypa 'boss' of the outstation: 'Nangaypa is a very important woman and boss of Dambaliya until her son and daughter grow up and take over and the old people step back.'

This outstation near the beach at Ruwakpuy on the south coast of Dambaliya was established in 1974 when many groups were leaving Yirrkala to move back to their clan estates. By 1975 twelve such communities had been established. A government grant allocated to the small group of people who had rights by birth or marriage to live at Dambaliya enabled Nangaypa to purchase a 3.5 m aluminium dinghy, an outboard motor, some tarpaulins for shelter and a two-way radio. The boat ferried people, dogs, food, small plants and trees for a new fruit and vegetable garden to the island. The outstation was intermittently occupied during the 1970s. Its members went to Yirrkala to work, attend ceremonies, or to receive medical attention when ill. In 1980 Nangaypa began to make arrangements to build the first timber and corrugated iron house and store at a new site, Gatilinya, also on the south coast of the island.

Dambaliya is not a new home. As a child, and later as a married woman, Nangaypa used to sail there with her family in dug-out canoes to collect seagull and turtle eggs, oysters, clams, mud crabs, yams, fruit and berries, fish, turtles, corms of the spike rush and other foods. During one of my visits, Nangaypa and others reminisced about earlier years. She recalled the time during World War II when a plane had crashed nearby. Her kinsmen rescued the injured American pilot, taking him by canoe to Yirrkala for care and eventual evacuation.

Dambaliya is no longer the isolated place of Nangaypa's youth. In 1976 it served briefly (with the owning clans' permission) as a detention centre for wayward Aboriginal boys from as far away as Central Australia. The island is sometimes visited by residents of Nhulunbuy who come by boat to fish, picnic and camp. Their presence makes Nangaypa anxious and angry. She successfully vetoed a request that a portion of the island be set aside as a target practice area for the Army. Unfortunately she can do little about the occasional outbreaks of acute food poisoning suffered by people eating fish caught near Dambaliya. Nangaypa and others are adamant in their opinion that this scourge was unknown before the opening in the early 1970s of the bauxite processing plant 15 km to the west. They believe, despite the company's denials, that the illness results from pollution of the waters by the plant's effluent.

Outstations were usually closed to European visitors, but as I was Nangaypa's sister, the Yirrkala community council gave me standing permission to accompany her to Dambaliya at any time. On my first visit in early 1975 the most senior Djambarrpuyngu man present sang sacred songs to inform the local ancestral spirits that I was coming and that I was an acceptable visitor. Nangaypa's mother later reported that the mythical serpent that inhabits the sacred waterhole on the island had raised itself from the water and peered at me while I was standing nearby. Nangaypa, I was told by Milminyina, then took a small spear, passed it under her armpits in the traditional way and threw it into the pool. The serpent, recognising this ritual gesture by a person who had a right to be on the land, disappeared.

As we sat on the beach at Ruwakpuy after our first day of food gathering and watched a large pink moon rise over a crystalline sea and the lights come on at Yirrkala and Nhulunbuy, Nangaypa talked of the island's history and recounted its creation myths. Looking back, I recognise that these occasions were a means of socialising me into the life of the Yolngu. Nangaypa was 'growing me up' by teaching me the values and obligations I must observe. Although our conversations were hindered by my poor Gumatj, our growing store of shared experiences — times spent laughing and working together, misunderstandings and annoyances, excitement and joy — was beginning to forge a bond of deep affection between us. This change in our relationship unexpectedly heralded a change in productivity for me. My first realisation of the effect it would have on my work came during my fourth month of fieldwork.

I was finding it particularly difficult to observe or elicit information within the 'camp', so had begun a survey of the attitudes of women to childbearing and family planning. I hoped that this undertaking might be more productive and straightforward. However, I was hampered by a dearth of respondents. I quickly became familiar with the highly effective strategy of passive avoidance employed by all those who did not want to be interviewed and yet did not want to refuse me directly. (I was to use this strategy to good effect myself on later occasions.) One day I unhappily told Nangaypa about my research problems. She listened thoughtfully but said little. The next day when I set out reluctantly in pursuit of respondents, I found resistance had all but vanished. For several weeks I was caught up in the euphoria of productivity. Although nothing was said it was obvious that the women who agreed to be interviewed were my sister's relatives; it was only when I had interviewed ninety women (and probably exhausted her circle of influence) that I ended the project.

After a time I discovered to my pleasure that the most active *marrnggitj* (healer) at Yirrkala was a close relative of Nangaypa's late husband. As she vouched for me and my work, he granted me several interviews, during which he described his life, his initiation and his work in rich detail. I was also able to talk at length with my close relatives about the causes of illness and to obtain numerous firsthand accounts of illnesses believed to have been caused by sorcerers. Nangaypa and I went on expeditions into the bush to look for and collect plants traditionally used as medicines. She and others described their preparation and uses. When a person was ill I was included as a family member in caring for the patient. In this way I was able to observe the management of a range of illnesses and to talk with relatives about their course. During funeral ceremonies I was expected to help with preparations and to take part, usually as a dancer with the women.

Nangaypa Dhamarrandji with her grand-daughter Djinyupa (the author's namesake) and a freshly caught goanna

Although I continued to pay Nangaypa and others a wage for the assistance they gave me, our relationship had begun to change from a contractual to a personal one. This change brought with it strains for us both. Although I can only speculate on her perceptions and feelings, it seems to me that I must have remained an intruder in her life and daily activities. For example, we had different agenda. I needed to complete certain tasks: to write up and file my notes, interview, observe and record. She, I imagine, wanted to minimise the amount of time she spent on my repetitive and tedious work and to maximise that she devoted to agreeable pursuits. More than once I declined invitations to go hunting, shopping or visiting because of some task I had not finished.

In addition, Nangaypa had the taxing task of teaching me certain basic skills. As a Yolngu I simply did not excel. My fires went out. I never caught a mud crab. My major success was learning how to open and gut rock oysters quickly. Though I was no more productive as a hunter or gatherer than a five-year-old, I was invariably given the choice items found on women's foraging expeditions. I could find only half as much firewood as adult women and had the greatest difficulty carrying a small load on my head without losing half of it. I forgot who my distant brothers and sons-in-law were and thus embarrassed myself, them and Nangaypa by speaking to them directly. Such *faux pas* always elicited a howl of recrimination from everyone present. I suspect that I was seen by my Yolngu kin as shy, unpredictable, well-meaning and likeable, but basically incompetent.

Eventually I became more sensitive to the unspoken demands of different situations, remembered what to call my many relatives, could manage to communicate in simple Gumatj, learned to dance at ceremonies, and to tell one tree from another. I still experience a stab of retrospective mortification when I recall my social mistakes. One day I left the main group hunting mud crabs and, with a sister, Maypilama, and her children, clambered through a broad and muddy expanse of mangroves to a beach where we could harvest rock oysters. After a few hours I announced my intention to return to the other women. Maypilama looked alarmed and said that I would get lost. Insisting I would not, I set off, tracing our footprints through the disorienting maze of mangroves. Flushed with pride I emerged only 100 metres from the main camp. When the women saw me they looked agitated, asking, 'Where's Maypilama?' I indicated the beach. They asked incredulously if I had come back alone. I responded, proudly, that I had. As if by silent signal, several women began to wail. Between refrains they explained that travelling alone I was liable to attack by a sorcerer who had reputedly been seen in this part of the country. After all, I was supposed to know about the dangers of sorcery as I questioned people about it all the time and I had been told many times that sorcerers attacked people out walking alone. I was gratified by their concern for me. It was not until much later, reflecting upon the incident, that I suddenly realised that it was not for me they were crying, but for Maypilama and her children, whom I had left to return alone.

I found that the demands of my work often conflicted with obligations to my kin. Because I could see that Nangaypa was using up considerable social capital by asking relatives to assist me, I felt obliged to conform, to be a good family member and to give material help when asked. Once it became clear to me where my obligations lay and whom, therefore, I could politely refuse (using the technique of passive avoidance), I found that few unreasonable requests were made of me. I gave time, money, food and possessions, knowing that they were scant repayment for the enormous debt I owed Nangaypa and her family. I knew that equivalent gifts and services would be forthcoming from my relatives if I asked. Even when I did not ask they showed their concern for me. Once, after I left Yirrkala, I happened to mention in a letter that my grant had ended and I had not yet found another job. Immediately a bank cheque for $60 arrived from one of my Yirrkala daughters — 'just to keep you going'.

My ready access to a small number of friendly Europeans at Yirrkala was quickly perceived by my family as a resource. They expected me to be able to facilitate an occasional ride to town or the use of a sewing machine or oven. I found it difficult to explain that these friendships were delicate, and that there was some antipathy among mission staff to anthropologists. I myself found relationships with Europeans at Yirrkala difficult to sustain, though I did appreciate the familiar companionship they offered. My desire for such social contacts sometimes conflicted with my personal and work priorities. When I had to make a choice between attention to European acquaintances and Aboriginal family I invariably chose the latter. Consequently I lost several European friends, who were (justifiably in terms of their expectations) hurt and angered by my confusing behaviour.

I also found it difficult to deal with the strains created by incompatibilities between my family role and the aims of my fieldwork. My family naturally expected that I would work predominantly with the clans to which I was most closely related, and that I would be reserved and careful in my relationships with other groups. However, the canons of fieldwork teach that too close an association with one set of families can limit opportunities to work with others and so bias one's findings. Moreover, if I acted solely as a Yolngu woman would act, my access to information from the men of the community would be restricted. I had heard of 'culture shock': now I experienced its meaning. The strain of trying to anticipate the behaviour expected of me and explain my deviations began to take a toll of my composure. I was torn between the desire to gain Yolngu acceptance and the desire to be myself. I felt that the boundaries of my identity were becoming blurred. I wanted to be both close and distant, both with my kin and yet alone, both sister and anthropologist.

For much of my time at Yirrkala I did as expected and confined my enquiries to people of the clans with which I was affiliated. But as the months passed, and because I was allotted a house in a different residential section of Yirrkala distant from that in which Nangaypa lived, I became acquainted with the people who lived in other camps. Their willingness to work with me encouraged me to cross social boundaries. Yet I felt that my association with distant classificatory kin sat uneasily with Nangaypa and wondered if she felt I was being disloyal and possibly placing myself at risk. The fact that my research needs extended beyond my family role was something I found difficult to explain. To declare that the opinions and experiences of one group in the community were inadequate for a scientific study would have given offence. When I was juggling visits to my own family and other people I was constantly seeking excuses for my aberrant behaviour, always worried that I would hurt people who cared for me. Milminyina told me that on the night of a death in my area of Yirrkala, Nangaypa and another sister had cried for me, fearing for my safety in a distant and troubled camp. Yet Nangaypa, ever gracious, suggested I participate in the subsequent funeral although she would not attend.

Not all the members of my immediate kin group, though, were as supportive as Nangaypa. Throughout 1974 and 1975 one of my relatives, a young leader, avoided or ignored me and opposed my various requests to visit his outstation, to interview his wife, and to live closer to Nangaypa and her family. He was not alone in his lack of sympathy. Several young and influential leaders were openly hostile to researchers working in their community. Their attitudes can be appreciated when viewed in context.

Yirrkala is a politically sophisticated community. It had experienced the trauma of losing an unprecedented land-rights case in the Supreme Court of Darwin three years before I arrived. It was the focus of parliamentary inquiries in 1963 and 1974 (and in 1978) and received frequent visits by dignitaries and many government officials. The community was also troubled by a rapid staff turnover, the establishment of a large bauxite mine and processing plant on Yolngu land, the associated growth of the European town of Nhulunbuy nearby, and the growing problem of alcohol. Those young men who had received secondary schooling and other training outside Yirrkala were among the most consistently proud and outspoken of the Yolngu resisting European encroachment on their lives and lands. I found their antipathy towards Europeans understandable and felt both ambivalent about my role in the community and acutely conscious of my responsibilities to family and community.

I left Yirrkala in August 1975, planning to return for several months in November. Just before I was to leave Sydney to go back I received a letter from the Council stating that 'permission has not been issued to you for your visit this time'. I was stunned and upset but wrote to say I accepted the decision. I guessed that my return had been challenged by the leader who had shown opposition to my work. In late 1977 I was elated when he unexpectedly invited me to attend a meeting he was to address in Canberra. When I saw him again his greeting could not have been warmer. He addressed me as his sister and our previous differences were not mentioned. I suspect that some familial pressure had been brought to bear, particularly by Nangaypa, but she never alluded to this crisis in the years that followed.

Between 1975 and 1978 Nangaypa and her daughter or sister's daughters visited me twice in Sydney. I kept in touch with my family by letter and telephone and was told of events in the community by visitors from Yirrkala. In April of 1976 I received a telephone call from Nangaypa to tell me that her daughter's husband-to-be, who had been seriously ill for over a year, was close to death. She asked me to 'come home' to see him before he died and to attend his funeral. But I had not then recovered sufficiently from the rejection of my request to return the year before nor from the stresses of fieldwork. After several days of deliberation I decided not to go and sent a telegram and letter trying to explain why. In April 1978, when Nangaypa's mother was ill and her family feared she was near death, I did go to Yirrkala to see her. During this trip I also presented copies of my thesis and published articles to the council and community. I returned again in June as an adviser to the House of Representatives Standing Committee on Aboriginal Affairs, then carrying out an inquiry into Aboriginal health.

Early in 1979 three elderly women died within weeks of each other. All three were wives of Nangaypa's father; one was her own mother. Nangaypa's uncle rang to ask me to return for the funeral. Before I had made a decision, news came that Nangaypa's father had also died. I caught a plane two days later and stayed for a month, until the ceremonies had been completed and both parents had been buried. During these emotional and demanding weeks I saw more clearly an aspect of my sister that I had only glimpsed before — her untiring commitment to her social and ritual responsibilities.

The ceremonies for her mother were held at Nangaypa's house. A large shelter of bush timber and stringy bark had been built to house the coffin. Nangaypa's father's funeral was underway two houses away, where his body, lying in a coffin, had been placed in an equally large paperbark shelter. In association with these funerals the Yirrkala community also held a Djungguwan and a Ngärra ceremony. Both are sacred and secret ceremonies which are held infrequently and through which men must pass to gain access to the most significant religious knowledge of their clans.

During this time Nangaypa was an assertive and determined organiser and an enthusiastic participant. She divided her time between the two funerals, for she had responsibilities at each. She painstakingly participated in painting clan designs with ochre on the young men — a very unusual and probably new role for a woman. When the women assembled to wail at the final viewing of her mother's body, Nangaypa, though deeply affected by grief, stationed girls behind several women to disarm them if they hit their heads with knives or stones. When the ceremonies lagged, or too few people danced, she stood and loudly berated the assembled gathering for their neglect of their duties. When some of the young men failed to appear during the burial, Nangaypa herself danced the sacred goanna at the edge of her mother's grave — a dance usually performed only by men. When they still had not arrived a while later she angrily gathered her belongings and walked away, beckoning me to follow. She refused to return until a car was sent to collect her and she had been assured that the young men would come and participate.

On the last night of my stay the ritual washing and purification of participants was held. The clan leaders insisted I join the women. We sat in the ceremonial sand sculpture at sunset and were doused with buckets of water while the men sang the clan songs over us, their clapsticks ringing the beat. Then the men were washed and the women danced. I was pushed to the front and motioned to lead. For once my hands, feet and body felt the music and I knew I had it right. The onlookers laughed with delight and shouted praises. But I knew their commendations were as much for Nangaypa as for me — tributes to the perseverance, patience and skill which mark her life and which, after five years, had transformed an intractable European into a momentarily passable Yolngu.

Additional reading

Reid, J.C. (1983). *Sorcerers and healing spirits.* Australian National University Press, Canberra

Reid, J.C. and Mununggurr, D. (1977). We are losing our brothers: sorcery and alcohol in an Aboriginal community. *Medical Journal of Australia* Spec. Suppl. 2, 1-5

Reid, J.C. and Yunupingu, L. and D. (1978). Caring for the aged and dying in an Australian Aboriginal community. *Australasian Nurses Journal* 7 (12), 22-6

Warner, W.L. (1958). *A black civilization.* Harper and Bros., New York (First Edition, 1937)

11

Running Free: Three Kugu-Nganychara Women

Diane Smith

> . . . men with men, women with women. Just us three women in camp again — no man.
>
> . . . I'm running free now, working for myself . . . I please myself. No one boss me.
>
> Mayimuntha Holroyd

Minhathana and her two adult daughters, Yippanah and Mayimuntha live on an Aboriginal outstation south of Aurukun, northern Queensland. I arrived at Aurukun in May 1978 to carry out anthropological research, and after three weeks I travelled to the outstation. Yippanah was the first person to greet me and subsequently we became 'mates — just like really sisters'. This account focuses on Yippanah, her older sister, Mayimuntha, and on their mother, Minhathana. It is a compromise between what these women decided to tell me and what I wanted to know. All of us were concerned to maintain our personal integrity and to exert some control over what we were divulging. The events in which these women participated are commonplace in Aurukun society and the roles played by them as mothers, daughters and sisters, as widows and mourners, and as 'women alone — no man' are part of the essence of Aboriginal sociality.

Aurukun was established in 1904 as a Presbyterian Mission and continued as a church mission, more recently under the Uniting Church of Australia, until 1978. Located amidst vast bauxite deposits, Aurukun became the centre of a series of protracted conflicts concerning mining and Aboriginal self-management. Aurukun is no longer a reserve area, but was made a Queensland Government shire in order to effectively open the way for mining.

During a boat trip to the Kendall and Thuugu Rivers in 1953, the missionary the Reverend W. F. McKenzie recorded Yippanah's name and that of her family among a list of people still living in the bush. In 1978, Yippanah spoke about meeting McKenzie:

He came to Holroyd [River] and told my mother he wanted George and Artarmon [Yippanah's two younger brothers] for the mission. He wanted to try and give her axe and some food for them [raucous laughter from the women following this statement]. She too cranky. That old lady got really cranky at him and just tell him 'no' and he went away. Later on we all go to the mission for a while, everyone walk to Aurukun. He wanted to round those people up just like cattle and drive them into the mission.

Yippanah's family, like many others living between the Kendall River and Christmas Creek, were reluctant to settle permanently at Aurukun and were some of the last to do so, preferring to walk occasionally to the mission or to Edward River (a government settlement formed in 1930) for tobacco, flour, tea and sugar. Her family did not move into Aurukun permanently until the late 1950s. Even then they returned to their 'country', which lay between the Thuugu and Holroyd Rivers, for 'bush holidays'. Consequently, many people such as Yippanah and her brothers and sisters were 'born in the bush' and can remember having their 'small time' living with their parents on their own land. Furthermore, a number of old people, such as Yippanah's mother, Minhathana, have spent most of their life in the bush — not on the mission.

In mid-1975, Yippanah lived with her second husband, Sam Kahathuugu, their two children, Andrea and 'young Headley', and her mother in a bush camp 80 km south of Aurukun. From approximately 700 in the early 1970s the population of Aurukun by 1978 had dropped to 400, a direct result of people moving to the outstations.

The outstation where Yippanah and her family now live was established in 1976 by her husband's brother's son at a major wet-season camp on the banks of the Kendall River about 3 km from the coast. This site is located on one of a series of low sand ridges which run inland parallel to the coast. A swamp, now dry, forms the western boundary of the site, where wells have been dug. It is a domesticated landscape, the direct result of deliberate burning by Aborigines over time. The central campsite itself has been cleared, leaving only trees that provide shade, fruit, medicinal ingredients, or manufacturing material. The ubiquitous sand soon swallows up all rubbish and personal possessions that are left lying around.

When I arrived at the outstation at the beginning of June 1978, twenty-eight people (seventeen adults and eleven children) were living there permanently. Amongst these people five dialects were in active daily use: Wik-Mungkana, Wik-Iiyanh, Kugu-Mangka, Kugu-Uwanh, and Kugu-Mu'inh. Though these languages were not mutually intelligible to everyone, most people said that they could 'hear' or understand all the conversations carried on around the camp. People on the outstation today are invariably bilingual, often multilingual, as they were in the past. Most children and young adults do not speak their own language, but Wik-Mungkana, the community language taught at the Aurukun school. Adults at the outstation prefer to speak their own language and encourage their children to do so. They refer to Wik-Mungkana as 'that rubbish language'. A few elderly women speak no English at all, whereas some younger adults speak it with considerable fluency and flair. Yippanah and her sister instructed me in their own language, Kugu-Uwanh.

A number of families maintained autonomous camps in which they slept, cooked and ate. There was one single men's camp, five extended family camps and one nuclear family camp. These flexible camps changed composition frequently because of quarrels, desire for companionship, lack of food, or visitors arriving and leaving. Yippanah's camp was near to where her mother's brother and his family were living. These two households formed a closely knit and publicly recognised sub-unit within the outstation camp. They were planning to set up their own outstation, under the direction of Yippanah's uncle, about 20 km further south in their own country, north of the Holroyd River. Yippanah's husband regarded their present camp as being in his country, but her primary affiliation was with her father's country, to which they intended to move.

Yippanah's camp consisted of three lengths of corrugated iron used as wind breaks. These were secured lengthways along the ground by wooden stakes driven into the sand. Arranged this way the sheet iron could be shifted as the wind changed. Her possessions included blankets, mosquito

Empadtha outstation. Yippanah making a fishing net using string made from cabbage-palm leaf

nets, digging sticks, clothing, towels, cooking equipment, such as plastic dishes for making damper, billies for tea, a saucepan, sharp knife and some cutlery, an axe, machete and small earth oven. Private possessions usually included pipes and tobacco, string bags and bush string, bees wax, hair combs, a magazine and mirror. Clothes were stored in a pillowcase, which could also be used as a pillow.

I was incorporated into the camp of my son's namesake. I had to call him 'son-in-law' and maintain the semblance of an avoidance relationship with him. He argued that I was not 'really poison aunty' (a relationship which meant that we must avoid each other socially) and that we could talk with each other. He erected my tent for me with this comment: 'This just for work. You can't stop by yourself.' So it was decided that I should live with his family, and my interaction with other families at the outstation was through my position as a member of his family. Everyone regarded this as the proper arrangement.

Yippanah's camp was only a few metres from mine. During my first few days everyone was concerned about her husband's health. He became completely immobile, and Yippanah devoted her attention to him. She cooked special soft food for him to eat — yams, or custard and tinned fruit. She also used bush medicine, an infusion of leaves to bathe him. This, she explained, was to relieve his pain. At night she sang to make him sleep, and during the day, people from a nearby outstation visited the old man to sing for him.

Yippanah is about forty-six years old. Tall, with sharp, fine features, she is wiry and very healthy because of her life spent mostly in the bush. She believes that she carries her 'own law strong'. She is multilingual, speaking Kugu-Uwanh, her own language from her father, as well as Kugu-Mu'inh and her mother's language, Kugu-Mangka. Her English is good and she partly understands a number of other local languages.

Mayimuntha, Yippanah's older sister, who was then at Edward River, is the eldest of a family of six. She is about fifty-six and was also born in the bush. However, she has spent more time at European settlements and missions than her younger sister and attended the mission school at Aurukun. Mayimuntha, with a dry perceptive humour, has established a no-nonsense working relationship with Europeans. She has been a council woman at Edward River.

Minhathana, the mother of Yippanah and Mayimuntha, is proud of being a bush woman. Strong and capable despite her seventy-eight years, she is fastidious and intent on doing things the 'proper Aboriginal way'. She speaks only a few words of English and is one of the few remaining speakers of Kugu-Mangka. My conversations with her were invariably humorous events, with myself, Yippanah and Minhathana all talking at once, and Yippanah passing information from one side to the other. Minhathana and I rarely attempted to talk directly to each other: I was 'poison aunty' ('mother-in-law') to her, and she studiously upheld the avoidance behaviour associated with that relationship. I often listened as the 'old lady' talked to her daughter, who would then translate for me. She remembers the past when, as a young girl, she used to visit a small island off the mouth of the Holroyd River. According to Yippanah it was 'all the same beachside, good for hunting, yams; camping places too'. Minhathana and her children, camping near the Holroyd, survived the cyclone which completely obliterated this island in the 1940s. She is one of the most knowledgeable adults in the outstation camp. Others check facts about past events with her and she willingly recounts tales of days in the bush. According to the mission records Minhathana was married in 1920. It was her only marriage and she had no co-wives. Her husband died about 1968 at Aurukun, and I rarely heard Yippanah or her sister talk about him.

As young girls during the 1930s, Yippanah and Mayimuntha lived with their four brothers, parents and mother's mother on their father's 'country' at Thuugu River. Yippanah recalls that:

> We walk 'round one family. All different families all over for the dry; then we camp together one place for wet — Grannie, that old lady there [Minhathana], Mayimuntha, George and Artarmon together ourselves. The young boys no school then . . . that other sister bin die, well I take name from her. We stop by ourselves out bush, beachside Thuugu [River] for the wet. My father come back for the wet. He work sometimes on [cattle] station, run 'round 'nother place for dry, different place different people. My old lady look after me. My really grannie from my mother look after them children . . . OK in bush — we know that country; plenty food for everyone.

People are willing to talk about the 'old mission time' at Aurukun in the 1950s, which initially appears as a sort of golden era, though some stories are tempered by descriptions of harsh realities of mission life. Yippanah remembers her days at Aurukun mission with both humour and criticism. 'All the same pharaoh days eh?' is her comment when recounting how she had been chained at the ankles to a tree by the resident missionary because she had given him cheek. According to her she had refused to follow one of the mission laws, whereby wrongdoers were publicly punished by a member of their own family. In similar accounts given by other people this usually meant giving them a 'belting' with a rubber hose or strap. Yippanah was called upon to give such a belting to her younger brother for 'girlfriend trouble'. Displaying nervous embarrassment at the thought of doing such a thing, she explained, 'Well I can't give my own brother a hiding.' A similar response to the missionary's orders had caused her to be chained to the tree in front of the 'mission house' in full public view. Later still, when she was 'running free' after the death of her first husband, she once again incurred the wrath of the missionary, this time for her own 'sweetheart trouble' and she returned to the south. 'I stop bush now, I don't want to go back' is her conviction.

Yippanah was married twice. Both were what are now called 'bush marriages'. When young, she was promised by her family: 'My mother and brothers, my father, grannie [mother's mother] and grandfather [in this case her mother's father], they all talk for me.' She grew up knowing who her husband would be and went to live with him permanently when she was about seventeen. Her husband would then have been about forty. He already had one wife, a woman from a country on the upper Kendall

River. Yippanah called her co-wife 'older sister'. She remembers her first days as a new wife vividly:

> I was frightened . . . my first time with man — nothing man before. I just a young girl. Well he promised for me. OK with husband, but I want to stop with own mother, own camp. By 'n' by he get angry own husband, get cold. OK he come, I do cooking, get water. We sit together one fire, one blanket, we pull together for work.

She spent the early years of her marriage living in the bush with her husband and co-wife. Her first baby, a girl, died there. 'Really small time just new baby. No doctors then. We have bush nurse . . . Baby sick and die.' Her second baby, also a girl, was born in the bush and survived. The years spent with her husband, co-wife and first child are remembered as being 'good years'. She remembers occasional trips to Aurukun or Edward River to obtain tobacco and flour. Her husband travelled along the 'beach road' and sometimes Yippanah accompanied him, carrying her infant. She is proud of their independence and self-sufficiency. 'We carry own law strong. New generation nothing. Before own law strong.'

Her husband died about 1962 and Yippanah was left a 'new widow' with a nine-year-old daughter. She was now a 'single woman' and talks of this period as being able to 'run free', of being independent with no responsibilities and no one to 'boss' her. Soon her parents began 'pushing' her to marry a certain man who was also regarded as a 'promise'. Both families agreed to the union but it was not to Yippanah's liking. 'I not wanting to marry him. He too young; stop Aurukun all the time. I don't like his language, [so] I go to Edward River [settlement] and stop there with Mayimuntha. I give my brother to his sister instead.' Yippanah's brother did indeed marry the sister of her rejected suitor, and whilst there is a tradition of 'brother, sister marry brother, sister' to explain such marriages, it is clear from the way she talked that she feels she had a determining effect upon her brother's marriage and that it represented a substitute of sorts for allowing herself to escape an unwanted union.

When Yippanah remarried it was to a man of her own choosing. She admits, however, that her brothers, and mother and father 'all have to 'gree [agree] for that man — both families, both sides, 'gree.' She was about twenty-nine and her second husband, 'young Sam Kahathuugu', was then in his late forties. Today it is also spoken of as being a 'promise marriage', a 'straighthead marriage'. The latter term is commonly used by people to refer to those marriages which satisfy the major local Aboriginal requirements for obtaining a spouse; namely, one should not marry 'too far away' geographically and one should not marry 'too close' genealogically.

Yippanah is obviously proud that both have been proper marriages, 'real bush marriages'. 'I got no boyfriends, only my two husband both promise.' She continued to live in the bush with her second husband, and they eventually had a daughter and then a son (born at Aurukun). When these children grew to school age, Yippanah and her husband settled more permanently at Aurukun.

Mayimuntha married a man from 'Edward River side . . . really from Holroyd River country'. She now has a married son and daughter with children. Another son, in his early twenties, is as yet unmarried. Her husband died in 1967, but unlike her younger sister she has never remarried.

Yippanah had begun her first marriage as a second and therefore junior wife, but she stressed the power that she wielded over her husband because of her youthful attractiveness and because of her ability to bear children (unlike his first wife). According to Yippanah, when children come you are really married. She remembers her co-wife as a mate who helped teach her to be a 'new wife'. Whilst acknowledging some jealousy, her comments emphasised the importance of female support and companionship: co-wives could 'bail up' on their husband if he did not provide enough meat for them; they could refuse to cook or gather food for him; and they could remove themselves from his camp and set up another together. This supportiveness was firmly pointed out to me as a direct criticism of my own ethnocentric view about polygymy. After Yippanah, Mayimuntha and I had been sitting together for some time talking about married life and about the relationship between husband and co-wives, I said, 'Oh yes, that's when one husband got two wives.' I was firmly corrected by Mayimuntha, who replied, 'No, when two women got one husband.' Yippanah nodded in agreement.

Invariably, women are married at a young age to an older man and, as the number of widows at the outstation camp seems to indicate, they frequently outlive their husbands. After a suitable period of mourning, they are required to remarry. Yippanah says that there are proper procedures regarding marriage arrangements. 'Parents talk strong for a girl to marry husband from promise. Can't break law from father, big brother. They strong; by 'n by, girl they kill'm . . . Big fight from girl; spear arm, leg.' It is apparent, however, that as women grow older they have more say about their marital careers. They are able to choose their future spouse, to postpone their remarriage for a period of time (to 'run free'), or even to decide not to remarry at all.

Mayimuntha, a widow of long standing, says, 'I never marry again. I shame from my husband to marry 'nother man.' Women are sometimes said to feel 'shame' about remarriage because they worry for the well-being of their children. Mayimuntha also admits to less altruistic motives. 'I'm running free now, working for myself, for my mother and children. I please myself. No one boss me.'

Mothers are often said to hold on to their children: 'Well that mother always have to keep those children behind.' A similar attachment operates with grandchildren. Mayimuntha has a number of grandchildren, whom she loves and over whose welfare she keeps a close watch. 'Grannie always have to spoil their grandchildren. Those children always look to grannie to buy them things.' She also talks strongly about keeping her last unmarried son with her as long as possible. 'I hold him yet. All right, I let him marry good girl, not someone cheeky to me, someone who works hard for her husband.' Yippanah expresses similar feelings about her second teenage daughter. 'I can't let her go, she my last daughter.' It appears to be a reciprocal desire, for daughters frequently want to stay with their mothers. Yippanah pointed out a common conflict when she stated, 'Not growing up husband from small, growing up mother. Mother really boss. If woman don't like husband, don't follow — stay mother.' Thus, countering the necessity to marry and establish one's own family, is a contrary tie affirming attachment and loyalty to one's natal family.

It is about ten days after my arrival at the outstation and the day begins with familiar scenes. Yippanah and her mother rise about 5.30 am, usually before anyone else in the camp. She puts a billy on the fire, which has been burning all night, and talks quietly to her mother. They laugh and tease each other, call the children to wake up and get to work, get cross at the lack of response, then laugh again. Yippanah walks to her husband's well, about 100 m away on the edge of the dry swamp, to get water, taking along a flour tin with a wire handle. The well usually needs to be cleaned out in the morning to remove the small frogs, leaves, collapsed sand and sometimes a snake. She sits down at the edge of the well and uses the large bailer shell, which is always left there, to clean up the well and collect the water from it. It is the dry season, the water is only about 12 cm deep, but it takes only a few minutes to rise back to that level after the well has been emptied of rubbish. Yippanah arrives back in camp balancing the full tin on her head. She then makes a damper. It is cooked in the ashes of the fire and eaten with jam or syrup. More sugary, warm tea is consumed. Headley, her ten-year-old son, is running around teasing or playing with Yippanah's only dog, while her daughter Andrea, about fourteen, lies on her mother's blanket flipping well-worn playing cards expertly onto the sand.

Other people in the camp wake about 6.00 am when small trails of smoke rise over each sleeping area as tea and damper are made. As the sun rises over the wall of trees at the eastern boundary of the cleared ground it becomes increasingly hot in the unprotected sleeping areas. Yippanah and her mother begin shifting from their night camp to the family shade, a group of trees some metres away. Minhathana's 'brother' comes over to carry Yippanah's husband to the shade. He is too weak to walk now.

With her husband settled, Yippanah goes to the well again to wash clothes. It is a large load, so she fills a number of flour tins with water from the well. Yippanah is looking after me because I am, in her words, 'just a young girl', a comment indicating my obvious inexperience in bush living rather than my age. When I arrive with my load of dirty clothes, she quickly incorporates me into her system. I am immediately told that no soap or washing power is to be used near the wells, otherwise 'big rain come up and you might get sores all over'. I help her carry the tins of water from the well to the nearby shade area where the washing is carried out. It seems to be women's work.

Yippanah sets one of her cut-down flour tins on four upturned fruit tins and builds a fire underneath it. For the next hour and a half we are occupied with boiling water, hand-washing and rinsing clothes, which are then draped over the branches of a fallen tree to dry. My son joins children who are playing around the outstation tractor. When the washing is done we return to her shade. Minhathana is sitting on her blanket talking with two women who have arrived from a northern outstation. Yippanah lies down on the blanket and rests her head on her mother's lap. She listens as her mother and the two women reminisce about earlier days spent together at Thuugu River.

Towards midday Yippanah takes her cousin, my son and me for a walk into the surrounding scrub. She is looking for cabbage-leaf palm so that she can make some more bush string for a bag she started a few days ago. She also wants to show her cousin the best tree root to use for dyeing. Yippanah stays on the well-known paths, only veering off to go to specific trees, and then she uses her sharpened machete with great efficiency. The whole trip takes about one and a half hours, during which time she sets a relaxed but business-like pace. On the return walk she spends time pointing out various edible foods and medicine trees to me.

The sound of loud crying hastens our return to camp. Yippanah's husband has died. All the men and women have gathered around her shade. Her two children are standing silently to one side of their father's body, their heads bowed down. The women are wailing loudly and two of them are singing a Kendall River *wuungka*, a women's mourning song. At the same time they are dancing, thumping their feet flatly against the earth in a rigid, shuffling-cum-hopping motion. Arms are outstretched, with the palms of hands held upwards.

Yippanah throws herself down beside her husband's body, crying loudly. Her mother and her husband's daughter-in-law cover her with their arms and bodies. The daughter-in-law stands up and pulling a branch from a nearby tree, starts hitting the two silent children about the shoulders and head. Meanwhile, people from the neighbouring outstation camp have come across the river in response to the crying and a shotgun 'message'. As they arrive the wailing increases in intensity and some more older women join in the singing and dancing, which continues intermittently for the next three hours. I am taken downstream to the second outstation, which has a radio, and I try to raise one of the nearby settlements to inform relatives about the death and to notify the State Government authorities. An official acknowledgment and acceptance of the stated causes of death are required by the Coroner's Department at Thursday Island (some 300 km away) before any burial can proceed. People at the camp fear that the authorities will request the removal of the dead man to Aurukun for an autopsy, their main concern being that 'he got to be buried own country'. We contact Edward River but have to wait till the following day for a reply from Thursday Island.

As I return a number of things are happening simultaneously. The 'dead body', as Yippanah's husband is now called, is carried by the adult men to the main camping area away from the ridge line and then covered with a blanket. The remaining people in camp collect their blankets, swags and mosquito nets from sleeping areas and set up a tightly-packed new camp around the dead body, for which some sheets of corrugated iron and a blanket provide a screen. That night Yippanah and her mother sleep with two older women further away from the dead body but still within the confines of the group. Her children sleep away from her with another family.

Wood fires are started around the perimeter of the small camp and kerosene lamps are hung in the nearby trees. People are wary of strangers, and torches are flashed periodically into the surrounding scrub. The camp boss has his shotgun near at hand. People wake up often, and low moaning and singing continues far into the night. A number of men and older women stay awake. 'We had to stay up all night watching that dead body. If we don't, then he might get up and walk around.'

Early the following day people slowly shift away from the vigil camp to yet another centrally located area on the sand ridge. Yippanah is now referred to as the 'new widow', and she and her mother also re-establish themselves, this time about 9 m away from the rest of the group in a hastily prepared tiny iron shelter. Their own blankets are arranged so that she will be fully concealed. Yippanah has eaten nothing since our return to camp the previous day. She has spoken only to her mother in whispers. Her children continue to stay with Minhathana's son. I and my son have joined my 'son-in-law's' family, in a nearby daytime shade area. In fact, only a thin line of low trees separates his camp from the widow's, so that the two families still form a unit. The sleeping spot allocated to me by my 'son-in-law' is adjacent to the new widow's.

In spite of her supposedly restricted, invisible status, Yippanah is not excluded from the rest of the group. Towards mid-morning the women who had initially been crying with her, and with whom she and her mother had slept the previous night, come over to the widow's camp and talk to the 'old lady' Minhathana. Yippanah sits behind her mother and listens quietly. The women discuss with Minhathana the arrangements being made for the funeral, and the circumstances of the death are reviewed in detail: how the dead man looked, what he had been eating, how he had said he felt, and the continued help given to him by everyone in the camp. There had been no blood on the man at death, which meant that he had not been a victim of sorcery. No 'bad words' had been said to him by anyone at the camp, and no one had been 'cranky at him'. Whatever the cause of death, it is agreed that it must have come from 'outside', from 'strangers'.

No one else talks to Yippanah. Her young cousin explains to me, 'Only women go up to the new widow, or talk to her — no man can. When the funeral nearly finished then its OK. But she don't want to talk to anybody or see anybody. People talk gently to new widow.' During the days that follow, Yippanah's daughter Andrea comes to sit with her mother and grandmother for extended periods. Sometimes she sleeps there during the day but always leaves at dusk. Yippanah's son, Headley, walks past and whistles so that his mother will look at him, but he does not talk to or sit close to his mother. Yippanah's own mother remains with her day and night.

The day after the death Yippanah's uncle supplies the two women with some damper, tea and a small catfish. Days later Yippanah explains to me that as a widow she is not allowed to eat big fish or other big animals: 'no meat from wallabies, pig or killer [cattle], or big birds. Little fish, yams, European food OK'. It is now Minhathana who collects water for her daughter, but from another well, as the dead man's well is considered to be poison (*ngyanycha*) to everyone in camp, particularly to his family.

She also gathers the wood that they need for their night-time fires. Yippanah does not participate in the funeral arrangements, though she is kept informed of their progress by the two female visitors. When permission is finally received from the Coroner's Department it is decided to have the burial immediately. People are unwilling to have the dead body in camp for another night.

When the burial service is carried out late that afternoon Yippanah remains in camp with her mother. I walk with the remaining residents to the nearby burial area located on the same sand ridge but further inland from the river. All the men co-operate to dig a grave. The body, now carefully shrouded in cotton sheets by a woman from another outstation, is brought on the tractor and placed on the eastern side of the grave. The dead man's nephew reads a long passage from the Bible and then leads the singing of European hymns. Yippanah's uncle then takes over and he and the adult men sing a series of local songs. There is renewed crying when four young men lay the body in the grave, which is then filled with sand by the men. After a few minutes everyone returns to the main camp.

Four days later the new widow has still not moved from her camp. Her face and hair have been blackened with charcoal in order to prevent her husband's spirit, which is still wandering the camp, from recognising her. Five days after the death the outstation boss (the dead man's brother's son) initiates the 'warming up'. He does not participate in the ceremony, however, as he is said to feel sad. It is organised and carried out by

A traditional pur-ayanchi, used by Yippanah and her husband as their wet-season shelter

Yippanah's uncle. This particular ceremony signals the re-opening of the camp area for general use again and a resumption of everyday activities. It represents part of the final expulsion from the camp of the dead man's spirit. Gradually people become less nervous and resume their normal camp activities. During the days following, the 'outside' camping sites used by the dead man for hunting or fishing, for cutting spear handles or for dinner camps when travelling, are also 'warmed up'. People have not yet ventured away from the immediate confines of the central camp area. There has been no hunting or fishing; everyone has been dependent on whatever European food they already had. After the outside camps are 'warmed up', people will be free to resume their economic activities.

The 'warming up' begins with people collecting branches from a nearby tree and tea-tree bark. With this material a number of fires are built at the southern end of the camp area. Everyone except the young children participate. Yippanah, accompanied by her mother, emerges from her widow's camp for the first time. Together they sit down at one of the fires, crying loudly. A dozen adults advance on a *pur-ayanchi* (a low shelter built of cabbage-palm leaf) which was the dead man's wet-season camp. Yippanah and her mother walk over as well. They are still crying and now beating themselves on the head and shoulders with branches. A large fire is built near the *pur-ayanchi*, and people dismantle the cabbage-palm leaf and wooden supports, throwing them onto it. Yippanah and Minhathana crawl into the shelter and collect all the rubbish and possessions until the sand floor is thoroughly clean. Everything they find is put into a plastic bag by Yippanah's uncle. Later it will be burnt with the dead man's clothing and his spears. Now there is nothing left of the shelter; everything has been burnt.

Yippanah's uncle digs a hole about 75 cm deep in the sand. Into this he shovels the ashes of a nearby fire said to have been used by the dead man. The hole is then filled and new ashes, from one of the fires used to burn the *pur-ayanchi*, are scattered on top of it. Later, my son-in-law makes the comment, 'new ashes on old fire' and explains, 'Now people can use that fire again.' The area is free from *ngyanycha* restrictions and people will be able to camp there in the future without fear. People then move to Yippanah's daytime shade where her husband died. The site is cleared of all possessions and these are burnt. The cooking fire is buried and new ashes put on top of it. This time Yippanah and Minhathana and her two children, who have now joined her, are 'smoked' (to protect them from the dead man's spirit) by having smouldering tea-tree bark waved around their heads and bodies while men and women wail loudly. Two infants in the camp, my own son and my son-in-law's granddaughter, are also 'smoked', as children are said to be particularly susceptible. The proceedings end abruptly here and Yippanah quickly returns to her camp. Minhathana remains behind to view the final burning of possessions and the distribution of specific articles that are to be kept. She takes some cooking pots back with her to the widow's camp. Headley is given one of his father's spears; the rest are burnt. Yippanah calls out to her approaching mother, 'They close that door properly?' Her mother replies, '*Kana, kane ola*' (finished, finished for good).

The ideal ending to these events would have been the widow's ritual release by degrees, from physical and social seclusion and from food and language restrictions. But ten days later Yippanah's 'uncle' also died. He had been Minhathana's 'brother', my 'son-in-law', the 'boss' of our camp and one of the two men in the region possessing the highest ceremonial authority. The events begun by his death were momentous. I will relate them as they affected Yippanah and her family.

Now there was suddenly another 'new widow', and Yippanah was released from her more personal restrictions, specifically her physical seclusion. She was now called upon to assume responsibility for looking after her own mother, who was now a more central mourner than herself. She also had to look after the new widow, who had no close relations in the camp to care for her. This time it was Yippanah who went for water and collected wood, though she still avoided her husband's well, as well as the one belonging to her uncle. Both were *ngyanycha* to her. Only one well could be freely used by all residents. The new widow and her children were forbidden to eat meat and were unable to cook food for themselves or for others. Yippanah had been under a similar restriction, but was now compelled to cook for the new widow. Her own children returned to her and she cooked for them as well. My cooking equipment was confiscated because utensils from the camps in which the two deaths had occurred could not be used.

Yippanah was required to make a premature re-entry into daily life yet was still not a full participant. She did not talk directly to any man. All her communications were specific and directed at a limited number of women. During the day, she stayed in the vicinity of her own camp as much as possible. She participated in all subsequent mourning ritual and attended the funeral service held for her uncle, but sat to one side behind everyone else when she went to the burial area as her husband's grave was also there. Yippanah 'should not look on it', commented her young cousin.

During the week following the second death, the outstation population greatly increased as additional relatives arrived, including Mayimuntha. Yippanah was overjoyed and, on first meeting, the two sisters and their mother cried together for some time. Mayimuntha (whom I met for the first time) had brought much-needed food supplies and said that she intended staying with them until 'things settle down'. Yippanah's four brothers arrived by boat from Aurukun a few days later and stayed two weeks. When they left, Yippanah and her children, Mayimuntha and Minhathana formed a single camp. They were left alone — all widows with no men to 'run' their camp. 'I'm all by myself now,' Yippanah said to me as her brothers left. The women made no attempt to integrate with other families; they remained autonomous, and during the months that followed established a group that became a social focus for other women at the outstation.

About eight weeks later Yippanah, Minhathana and Mayimuntha, Yippanah's uncle's family, I and my son, and a number of related kin who had stayed at the outstation after the mourning ceremonies had ended (about forty people in all) began a 'company' move to set up a new outstation. The three women had been constantly 'pushing' for this and talking to people about the need to carry out the 'promise left behind from that old man' (Yippanah's uncle), that an outstation be established on their own country further south. It was an uncomfortable two-day journey on the back of two trailers drawn by tractors. Adults, children, dogs, building equipment and food supplies were all mixed up together. The country through which we travelled was dry and dusty. Minhathana and another old woman from the outstation gave directions about which 'road' to follow and where to camp overnight. Excitement grew as we travelled closer towards our goal. The smoke of fires burning on the horizon was interpreted by Yippanah as being the 'old man', her 'uncle', watching his relatives coming into his country. 'This is my really home from my father,' Yippanah called out to me as we reached a specific location. 'We going back right to the centre.' We arrived at our destination late in the afternoon of the second day. The site chosen for the camp was Pu'an, one of that country's two major wells, which are owned by a pair of ancestral brothers. Upon our arrival, people crowded together and cried loudly for their recently deceased relatives and for their country. Smaller groups walked around the area calling the names of ancestors and pointing out remembered camping spots. Our new camp was located near the well, only 200 m from the beach.

On this land my three friends were respectful in their behaviour and meticulous about the way in which they cleared the ground for sleeping. Mayimuntha commented, 'Well I can't break those trees, these young shoots. I just got to leave them, let them grow up; otherwise big rain come up.' It became apparent that the women regarded their presence as being vital to the well-being of the country itself. Human habitation was seen as a domesticating force. 'This place gone all scrubby 'cause no one living here' was Yippanah's opinion. When people looked at the overgrown camping sites and the tall grasses in the dry swamp they commented that the country needed to be burnt. During the weeks that followed, Yippanah, Mayimuntha and Minhathana and I travelled from the main camp following 'old roads' inland from the beach, seeking out familiar places remembered from 'bush days'. Under the guidance of Minhathana my two 'granddaughters' located the birthplaces of Yippanah and her elder brother. Trees growing at the sites were said by Yippanah to be the product of childbirth blood which had seeped into the soil. They were called *yuku nganka thanhthe* (tree/thing spirit/soul) and the health of the person born on the site was linked to the well-being and survival of the tree. 'We have to look after them [trees],' Yippanah commented to me as she cleared leaves from the base of the tree growing on her brother's birth site. 'That tree like remembrance for family, for grandchildren to remember that person.' Mayimuntha's response was similar: 'We look around and feel sad for our old people; no old people here, all gone. But those new ones coming up behind — well that's the next generation. All those ones across — when we go they'll be behind to look after this place.'

Life at the new outstation quickly settled into a familiar routine interrupted only by trips to Edward River for supplies. Shortly before the wet season started a large number of people left to buy final provisions and equipment from Edward River. Yippanah's children went on the tractor for a ride. The only people left in camp after the tractor had gone were Yippanah, Mayimuntha, Minhathana, my son and I, 'Just us four women in camp,' commented Yippanah. We were to be alone for two weeks because the tractor broke down. The women did not particularly like their situation: being alone in the bush they were vulnerable to the attack of 'strangers'.

During the two weeks, we occupied a number of daytime shades according to the focus of activities: we set up a shade inside the bush when digging for yams, or for protection when the 'old lady' became nervous of 'strangers'; we rested under their own family shade at the main camp when making fishing nets or cooking; we moved closer to the well when washing clothes.

It is early morning and we have shifted from our regular night-time sleeping camp to the coolness of the main shade. The tractor has been gone a week and Yippanah and her mother anxiously scan the horizon for any sign of its return. In the daily running of the camp it is Mayimuntha who makes the effective decisions. 'She biggest one; she decide,' says Yippanah. '*Ngaya ina ya'a* (I'm nothing).' When our breakfast of tea and damper is over, Mayimuntha directs Yippanah and me: 'You have to go fishing . . . well you two got to fish for old lady.' So Yippanah, Minhathana, myself and my son walk to the beach to catch the once daily incoming tide. Minhathana sets up her shade nearby. As usual, it is meticulously constructed. After clearing a circular area in the sand she lays down her blanket, cup and can of water. She builds a small fire using four or five twigs laid at angles to each other, with their points touching like the spokes of a wheel. In this way she keeps a small fire alight and conserves her wood. Minhathana is never without a fire, her Erinmore tobacco or the wooden pipe which she carved. She sits down, draws deeply on the pipe and looks across to the beach.

Yippanah digs up small crabs for us to use as bait, and we cast our lines. After each catfish is dragged onto the beach, the 'poisonous' spines are broken off. The fish are then buried in shallow holes dug in the sand to keep them fresh. In an hour we have caught ten large catfish. 'We stop now; *kana* (finish),' Yippanah calls out to me. 'By 'n by waste them then no fish tomorrow. We just fish for fun now.' We wash the fish in the sea; then Yippanah strings them, through gill and mouth, on her 'steel' (a one-metre piece of steel rod commonly used nowadays for digging yams). We join Minhathana and head back, in leaps and bounds, across the scorching sand to the main shade area.

Yippanah and I clean our fish. The fat stripped from the intestines is then put back into the fish, which are washed in a drum of water and thrown into the coals. The 'mother' catfish (which contain two large sacs of eggs) are favoured eating by the women. Yippanah, who carefully arranges the fish on the fire, together with a billy of water for tea, is a superb bush cook. Her mother eats only those fish cleaned by her daughter. I am 'mother-in-law' to her and cannot give her food.

Back at the main camp Mayimuntha has been working on our wet-season shelter. For three days, she, Yippanah and I have gone out early in the morning to cut lengths of straight wood. The post holes have been dug in the sand by Yippanah using her yam-digging skill to great effect. Mayimuntha joins us at the shade when we return, and we sit down to relax and eat. We discuss the prolonged absence of the tractor and by implication settlement life and the altercations and wooings of various married couples or 'sweethearts'. We joke about our solitary state: 'We must be all the same as that old man just living all alone in the bush — just the same. We all silly women, just us three women — just living all alone in the bush by himself.' 'Poor little boy [referring to my son], you lost in the bush; just the same we all silly women lost in the bush. All of those men gone away — men with men, women with women. Just us three women in camp again — no man.'

In the days that followed the comment 'no man in camp' became an indirect criticism of the way in which we had been abandoned by the other residents to keep the camp running ourselves. Our food was running low, we had no meat except for the fish we caught each day, and our staple diet consisted of damper, yams and tea. Hunger often induced tension. Lighthearted teasing became deliberate and provocative, especially when the absence of male support was raised. 'You got nothing son?' was a critical remark made by daughter to mother. 'They should be here helping us. They make me cranky.' Quarrels would sometimes arise over relative workloads or access to 'private' possessions or 'private' space:

> 'You get water for tea.'
> 'No. You not my boss.'
> 'Yes I am. I'm your mother. I'm your boss.'
> 'No. I got children myself now. I bin married. You not my boss now.'

After a too earnest quarrelling session our camp would divide into one or more independent camps. Usually, these were only a few metres apart, but they made their point. Such rows did not last long, and, normally, good humour was quickly restored. Mayimuntha, because of her status as 'boss' within the women's camp and her even temper, played the mediating role in these disagreements. She was expert at calling upon a sense of family responsibility and the supportive ties amongst the women. She also injected humour and entertainment into our lives.

Although Mayimuntha was considered to be boss, the relationship between the two sisters was a reciprocal affair. Yippanah was able to offer, and use, her knowledge of bush life to assert her own priorities when she wished. Mayimuntha would ask for Yippanah's help when looking for bush medicine or bark. She would also ask her sister to accompany her when she went out to look for yams, to use her eyes. Yippanah was adept at spotting the withering flowers of yam vines which Mayimuntha often missed. While the three women maintained a strong sense of 'private' space and possessions, and were able to order their own independent activities accordingly, their household camp was a co-operative one. Provocative statements like 'You got to give me that tobacco. You my sister — I can ask you anything' or 'You my daughter — you got to get fish for me' were positively responded to, not simply because of accepted obligations close kin have to each but also because of the mutual affection these women felt for each other.

On other occasions I had seen Mayimuntha intervene on Yippanah's behalf in fights with other adults, or chastise Yippanah's children if she thought they were being too cheeky. 'You got to do what your mother says. You be good to your mother. I'm your big mumma. She my own sister. Don't you boss your mother. You nothing. I'm the boss, so don't you think that you can be the boss for my sister.' Similarly, Yippanah would teach her own children the 'proper respect' for their grandmother Minhathana. 'That old lady my mother. I'm her daughter. She your grannie. You shouldn't go cranky on her, tease her ya'a. She my own mother.' While Yippanah's brothers spent most of their time working at the 'mission', she and her mother had stayed together out in the bush. It was Yippanah who continued to look after her ageing mother and who constantly assumed that responsibility.

An observation made by Yippanah was very revealing about the sisters' relationship. She and Mayimuntha were making 'bush' fishing-nets and engaging in some friendly competitiveness in the process. Yippanah remarked, 'You know, my sister and me, we just the same as those two brothers from old time that make those first nets. Two brothers then; two sisters now.' She was referring to two ancestral brothers who travelled through her country and who at a particular spot — now the story place for the fishing-nets — had stopped and made the nets for the first time. People say they know how to make the nets from those two brothers.

Yippanah (right) and her elder sister Mayimuntha with their finished fishing nets at the 'widows' camp'

Yippanah regarded her sister and herself as actively continuing that tradition; they were in Yippanah's words, 'carrying the law' for the nets.

Life on the outstation camp was not easy. Initially my energies seemed to be devoted entirely to coping with the rigours of daily living — sleeping on the ground, adjusting to the heat and mosquitoes, caring for my son, collecting water and wood, cooking and washing clothes — while learning a new language and an unfamiliar etiquette. The events following the two deaths left me exhausted. I was immediately involved in prolonged mourning ceremonies, funeral services, the singing of spirits back to their own countries, 'warming up' ceremonies and the relocation of camps. I also had to refrain from calling my own son's name. He had been named after my 'son-in-law' and following the latter's death that name could not be used. My son was called *thaapicha* ('namesake' of the deceased) and was seen to be closely linked with the dead man. (Yippanah now referred to my son as 'uncle' rather than 'small daddy', as she had previously.) He was seen as being particularly susceptible to his namesake's spirit. I was unable to use my tent following the death of my son-in-law because he had erected it. When his spirit was sung back to its country it was said to have come from the tent. For a number of weeks I was involved with the harassing assessment of the causes of the two deaths.

When I first arrived, my son-in-law had spoken to me with enthusiasm about his intention to move to his own country. He outlined his plans and asked my advice about certain things. After his death I felt unable to maintain my stance as the outside observer. When people decided to set up a new outstation, and asked me to accompany them, I was anxious to do so. From that time I lived with Yippanah and her family. They concentrated upon my education: I was regarded as being 'just a young girl' and in need of advice and protection. As a married woman with a child, I was also ready to begin learning other aspects of 'women's business'. That, by the end of six months, I was able to live each day with relative physical and social ease is a tribute to them rather than to my own skills.

The situation in which we women found ourselves, 'women with women — no man', was not thought to be unusual. The phrase 'women with women' was an assertion of companionship and supportiveness; it was not a negative reaction to men, nor the chattel throwing off her chains, but was an acknowledgment of a well-established female bond based on mutual needs, friendship, and the common biological experiences which are part of women's business. The fact that the phrase 'no man in camp' was often followed by another — 'no meat' — emphasised the women's recognition that the duties and responsibilities assumed by men could not be taken for granted. We were 'meat hungry' for some time because no male relatives were residing with us. The comment 'no man' also acknowledged that the three women were relatively independent — 'running free' — and that they preferred to be like that. The three widows remained sedentary, whereas the men travelled constantly. However, they maintained a lively interest in men and spoke enthusiastically about their specific relationships with them and about co-operative ventures. The women's camp was full of humour and wit. They were satisfied with their own performances: 'I'm working for myself; I please myself. No one boss for me. I do it my own good time.' It became apparent that co-operation, fulfilling kin-based responsibilities and having relationships with men did not entail any loss of individuality for these women and also that co-operation and competition were not necessarily incompatible social processes.

12

Two Women of Jigalong

Myrna Tonkinson

Maggie Milangga and Patricia Burungu are women of two generations who live in the Western Desert community of Jigalong, Western Australia. Their lives have much in common, but they have also experienced vastly contrasting events, mainly because of the difference in their ages. Maggie is in her late fifties; Patricia is in her early thirties. The similarities and differences in their experiences are typical of the continuity and change common to the lives of Jigalong people, and particularly the women, as they have moved from a nomadic desert existence to the sedentary conditions of a mission settlement over the last forty or so years.

Maggie belongs to Milangga section and Patricia to Burungu. They call each other *juwari* (sister-in-law). In the classificatory kinship system that operates at Jigalong, relative age does not affect the terms used between individuals. I call Maggie *yagurdi* (mother) and Patricia *ngunyari* (brother's daughter); there is nothing inconsistent about this. As 'sisters-in-law' Maggie and Patricia observe a friendly but restrained relationship. They play cards together and talk to each other, but they do not joke together. Patricia has an avoidance relationship with both of Maggie's sons and is therefore careful when visiting the older woman, who lives in one son's house, not to encounter these men. Despite this, the two women interact with each other regularly.

During the time I spent at Jigalong, ten months in 1974 and ten weeks in 1978-79, I came to know these women well. Both are brilliant raconteurs, and I have spent many pleasant hours listening to them talk about their experiences and express their views. Their styles are quite different, but each is skilled at developing the dramatic aspects of a story. They would speak a mixture of English and their own language as my comprehension of their languages is limited; but Patricia particularly shows a preference for using her language, Manjilyjarra, when she is telling a story or describing an event. She will often start off in English and gradually switch to Manjilyjarra as the account progresses. This is natural enough since, despite her excellent command of English, she can be much more eloquent and expressive in her own language. She has a dry and pungent wit and frequently uses clever aphorisms. Maggie speaks Gardudjarra, which is mutually intelligible with Manjilyjarra. Her stories

Maggie Milangga

reveal an eye for the comic aspects of situations and also a deep sentimental quality. Ideally the women's stories should be heard from their own mouths, but I shall attempt to describe the two women, quoting them as much as possible, and attempt to convey something of the texture

Patricia Burungu

of their lives, how they differ and how they are similar. (I render the mixed quotations here in English, remaining as faithful as possible to the style in which they were delivered.)

I first met Maggie and Patricia in 1974. My husband, Bob, had been well known to the community since 1963, so I was immediately put into the appropriate section to be a correct wife for him, and most people expected me to 'follow' Bob in deciding on my kinship relationships to them. Since Bob is Banaga I had to be Garimara. Bob calls Maggie 'aunty' rather than mother-in-law; I call her mother. Bob calls Patricia *ngunyari* (sister's or brother's daughter) and so do I.

Maggie was an old friend of Bob's; he had been friendly with her husband, one of the older men, whom he greatly admired and respected. Their sons Colin and Reggie are Bob's close friends and call him *wajirra*, which means a very close cross-cousin. I thought Maggie a striking figure with her very dark skin and almost white straight hair parted in the middle and falling almost to her shoulders. Few women at Jigalong wear their hair this long. She is slow and dignified in movement, usually having one arm behind her as she walks, a characteristic posture at Jigalong.

I developed a comfortable relationship with Maggie, visiting her home regularly, where she would talk to me about 'the old days' in the desert as well as about contemporary matters. Sometimes Bob and I would go with Maggie and her older son, his wife and children and another close woman friend to collect yams.

Although Maggie conversed with me freely and taught me many things, she made it clear in a subtle way that she would not discuss secret women's business with me in any detail or talk about contraceptive methods. I respected these wishes and never pressed her for information. When I returned to Jigalong in 1978 to spend the summer months (December and January), I asked if I could write about her life for this book and she consented.

Patricia was not at Jigalong when I first arrived there in 1974. She was working on a station and then spent several weeks in hospital in Perth. She returned to Jigalong after I had been there about two months and immediately went to work as a teacher's aide in the kindergarten.

I had taught the kindergarten class at Jigalong for the first eight weeks of the school year, though unqualified and inexperienced. Another young woman, Helen, who was bilingual and experienced with children, worked with me, and together we were able to keep the children occupied and happy.

When Patricia arrived she joined Helen and the teacher. I maintained a close relationship with the kindergarten, making visits and taking the staff and children out occasionally for picnics. In this way I began to see much of Patricia. We went with other young women to nearby waterholes to swim, or Patricia was sometimes part of a group I would take out to gather yams and other 'bush tucker'. Women called on me frequently during the winter months to take them on yam-digging trips, for at that time only one Aboriginal woman at Jigalong had a driver's licence and use of a car. I found Patricia lively, witty and outspoken. Physically she stood out because she is taller (about 165 cm) than most women at

Jigalong. During my second stay at Jigalong, I continued to see a lot of Patricia and asked her to tell me her life story also.

The older woman, Maggie, was born in the desert east of Jigalong, in her mother's country. She grew up there, although the family paid annual visits to the land belonging to her father.

> My mother, she was Gardudjarra, and my father he was from north of there, Warnman; from that country where they got aeroplane landing everyday now — Telfer [now a prosperous gold mine and a closed town]. Yes, that country belong to my daddy. He belong there and his mother again, my *nyami* [grandmother], she belong that way again. My father went from there and got my mother. He went south and married her, and he stop there in my mother's country . . . We used to go to mother's country. Yoh, we used to go on foot. Mummy and Daddy, they carried my little brother, Pincher. We bin naked fella that time — no clothes. We never know [clothing].

Maggie recalls her childhood with pleasure and nostalgia. Like most older people at Jigalong she speaks of the desert as a bounteous land, although she also tells of the hardships experienced there. In the winter they lived near her mother's parents. Her mother had a younger brother and two younger sisters, who also lived in the same place. During the summer, her family left the grandparental hearth and camped at waterholes with a larger group of people. After rain they broke up into smaller units.

> In the hot time we stop one place — big water place. We used to get *girdigirdi* [hill kangaroo] in the evening: they come for a drink and *mardu* [Aboriginal person] there wait'n for them. While they drinking, *mardu* spear them — finish! Now they cook that meat at night so it wouldn't spoil and next day we get a good feed . . . Oh, there was plenty lizards there too. You could go there now, Rudall [River] way, and see. Too much — you can't eat 'em. Fat! Big one! Oh, don't say! And we had bush tucker, like wild carrot, and *minyara* ['wild onion']. That one come up after rain finish and it get hot again . . . Sometimes we were hungry, no meat, no vegetables, but we had water. My mother used to carry it in a dish. We would sit down in the shade and drink water. Then evening time and early morning we would walk to 'nother water place. We had no sugar bag, no honey, that side, so we learn 'em from Moolyella people. But we had *wama*, sweet stuff from flowers and from leaves, like sugar. You only got to make a bed underneath that tree and shake the bush and you got 'im, sugar *properly*! Couldn't boil nothing that time — no billy can, no tea. Only water we used to drink.

Maggie has a wealth of stories and anecdotes about her desert experience. Some of them are poignant and others humorous; many (of both types) concern early encounters with white people. One such story (translated by Robert Tonkinson) goes like this:

> We were way out to the east along the stock-route and we were travelling — might be going south. There was this white man who was travelling alone with camels; he was following the stock-route. As soon as he saw one or two Aborigines, he would lift his hat and take out his teeth. He had loose [false] teeth you know. He would take out his teeth like this and make as though he would bite us with them. We were frightened and we ran away. He would go on and do the same thing again to another lot. He scared us by showing us his teeth.

The younger woman, Patricia, was also born in 'the bush'. Her parents had by that time established a base at Jigalong but had not yet settled there permanently: they travelled between her father's country and Jigalong. Her father had six wives, of whom her mother was one of the youngest. He was much older than her mother and died while Patricia was still a small child. Patricia had an unusual childhood. The second of her mother's six children (three from her father and the other three from her mother's second husband), she was brought to Jigalong by her parents when she was still a baby. Because her mother was ill and had to go away to hospital, Patricia was left in the care of the first missionaries at Jigalong.

> My other mother [Sister T] looked after me when I was little because my mother was very sick. The mission was just starting. After that my mother came back from hospital and went away with my father. I still lived with the missionaries; I never went back to the camp. Sister T left, and I lived with the Stevens family. They had some bigger kids . . . Then they left and I lived with the school teachers. I lived in their homes until they built the dormitories. Then I lived in the dormitories with the other girls.

Despite having spent her early childhood living with European missionaries, Patricia maintains that she did not feel different from the other children and that they treated her like everyone else. However, it is with a certain wistfulness that she describes another unusual aspect of her childhood. The school children who lived in the dormitories were allowed to visit their families after school each afternoon, and they lived with their families during the school holidays.

> After my father died and my mother went away, I had no family to visit in the camp, so I started visiting Djabudi's family and Nyangabidi's family. They grew me up really these two. I was close to them, but they are not really my brothers . . . they are from a different country — not *walja* [close kin] — but they always looked after me.

Patricia stayed at school longer than most children at Jigalong did then, or do now. She completed the six primary grades offered but did not go away to high school. Comparing her school experience with that of present-day children, she says:

> In some ways it was better then; some ways it was worse. The teachers were more rough: they used to cane us. The *mardu* [Aborigines] used

to get wild about that. Some of the teachers were cheeky. Some bad ones came one after another. The school is better now. In my time, we only went up to grades 4 or 5. I and a few others went to 6, but after that there was nothing.

Patricia did well in school; she is literate in English and speaks it fluently. Reminiscing about her childhood, Patricia recounts:

We had a lot of fun, but the school was very strict. The missionaries used to lock us in the dormitories at night and let us out in the morning. In the days, boys and girls could play together, but after supper we were locked up separately. Sometimes we would climb out the windows though . . . The parents were not allowed to come up and visit the dormitories, but we could go and see them after school. If they tried to take their children away to camp, the missionaries would threaten to get the police . . . Oh, we didn't mind staying in the dormitories. We didn't know any better — we were proper stupid. Holiday time they would let us go and camp out. I used to stop with Nyangabidi and Nayidji and Dada [his two wives]. We used to walk everywhere from Jigalong to Noreena Downs, right up to Marble Bar. After I finished school I worked as a housegirl for the missionaries. I used to get two pounds a month. And I didn't spend it: I always saved it until the travelling shop came around. Once a year they came and sold clothes and jewellery and all that.

Both Patricia and Maggie were betrothed to young men when they were children. In this respect they are like most females in their community, and indeed in the Western Desert culture of which Jigalong is a part. (Nowadays, however, very few women actually marry their 'promised men'.) A girl's parents promise her to a man directly or through his parents. Over the years the man makes gifts to the girl's parents, and when the girl reaches a marriageable age (when she is thirteen or a little older), she goes to the man as his wife. This is the ideal bestowal, although actual bestowals vary considerably. Accordingly, then, both women were given to their promised husbands. Maggie recalls some of the details of her marriage thus:

My mummy and daddy took me to Moolyella [near Marble Bar] trying to put me with *bilyur* [promised spouse] . . . I was a big girl then, but no *bibi* [breasts] yet . . . That's the first time I saw horses. I never know. Old people there in Marble Bar showed me. I was afraid them horses would bite, but they told me it was all right. Then I saw camels and I was frightened. Real long fella, that one. Bush camels — nobody was riding them. Well, mother and father took me there; they show me horses and the tin mine. My *bilyur* was there. I stop with him there a long time — never see mummy and daddy. We never went back to the desert; we stop in this country. Early days we *had* to stop with old man — not like now. He was a rough one — cheeky. Used to give me lots of hidings . . . He didn't have any other wife. I stop there with him until he died. I was worrying for mummy and daddy, so later I came this way and stop with them . . . No, I had no children from that old bloke.

Although fascinated with some aspects of town life, such as cars, new foods, houses, Maggie missed the desert and her family. She also recalls that town life was unhealthy for many Aborigines.

I never saw people with colds and sick eyes until I went to Moolyella. Sometimes *everybody* would be sick — eyes shut tight, can't open 'em self, got to use fingers to open 'em. That was bad time . . . One time whole mob was sick. They had like cold, but different one — different. They just dropped dead for no reason, poor fellas. *Mabarn* [Aboriginal doctors] couldn't help them. We couldn't cry for them, couldn't bury them — nothing. We were sick ourselves; we might have finished [died] too. So white fellas picked them up and take them away, buried them. And gave us rations — sugar, flour, onions.

Widowed while still in her teens, Maggie was later bestowed on another man by her parents. As is customary, about five years elapsed between the death of her first husband and her marriage to the second. She stayed in Moolyella for two or three years after her first husband died, and then walked to Jigalong with a group of other people. While she was there with her parents they arranged her second marriage, which she describes as peaceful and happy.

Good fella, that one. No fight, nothing. My mother and father give me to him. I stayed with him *long* time, till he died. Got two boys with that man. He was a good man, poor fella.

Maggie speaks with nostalgia about her dead husband and is adamant that she will not remarry. 'I don't want no more man — too much trouble. I just stop here in my son's place.'

Patricia, too, found her first husband cruel, and she did not remain with him.

I worked as a housegirl for a while and then I got tired of it here. A lot of people were packing up and shifting. So I walked to Ethel Creek with my aunty. She was going to visit her daughter. I stayed there and worked for a while, but I didn't like it: the white fella [manager] was rough. He used to hit some of the men, and if you weren't very careful he would sack you. So I went to Roy Hill. My mother wasn't there then; she moved earlier to Nullagine. We stopped at Roy Hill, and Gatagulungu [Patricia's classificatory mother] tried to marry me off to this man. I didn't like him — well not exactly. He was all right. I went with him okay; and the first night I went to camp with him we slept separately. Next morning he got up and gave me a hiding for nothing. Well, the mail truck was coming through and I jumped on it and came straight back to Jigalong. That man married my sister later. He didn't try to get me back and no one tried to force me to go back to him . . . Too many, too many, they promised me to, really. The

> first one didn't really want me because he had a girlfriend. She was a bit older than me and they used me as an excuse to get together. He used to pretend he was getting together with me but he would camp with her. We were all friends. They ran away together after. Anyway, I ran away from that [second] man and went to work at Walgun [a station neighbouring on Jigalong]. One weekend I came to Jigalong and stayed with his mother and her old husband. I really liked them although I didn't want their son. Well, [her second husband] arrived back from the station where he was working, and one day he started giving a row to them two old people saying that they should give me to him. My father-in-law said 'no', but the old lady said, 'You go and camp with him for one night and then come back to us.' But after I stayed one night he wouldn't let me go back. He used to watch me ... I was his first wife; we are age-mates. He was a *marlulu* [initiate/novice] when I was a *durndurn* [adolescent girl]. The first two [promised men] were lot older than me.

Patricia describes her current marriage as a fluctuating experience and expresses some uncertainty about its future. She recalls that the relationship with her husband was good until about five years ago when he went away to Strelley and brought back a young women as his second wife. This surprised Patricia as her husband had not informed her of his intentions.

> I wasn't angry because he was getting another wife, but I was upset because he never told me what was happening ... He really changed after that. I left him for a while, but I went back. But it was no good. That girl used to ignore me all day and only come back before he got home from work. I said to her, 'Why don't you talk to me? We two *Burungu* [i.e. belong to the same section, co-wives]. You just acting like he is your father and you only waiting for him to come home every day!' She wouldn't cook or anything. When I complained to him, he just took her side. I tried to get along but I got fed up with it. So one time when we all went to Strelley — they were in one vehicle and I was in another — I said to him he would have to choose one of us. So he left her behind when we came back to Jigalong.*

She also recalls a period several years ago, when her husband was jealous and violent. She refused to tolerate his behaviour and asked her brothers to caution him. 'My brothers told him to stop hitting me. They said, "You have sisters too." ' The violence ceased and their relationship has since been amicable. She contrasts this with her experience with her first husband. 'I didn't know how to talk then; I was stupid then. I was a *durndurn* [adolescent girl], and I didn't talk up for myself.'

The plight of another young woman who had been beaten by her husband several times was commented upon by Patricia.

> She's got brothers. If they man enough they can tell him [the husband] not to hit her ... Some of these men get funny when they get a young

---

*At the time of publication this marriage had ended.

wife; they get very jealous and they start to beat up their older wife, or sometimes they beat their young wife.

However, she is not opposed to polygyny. She has stated on several occasions that in some households with two or three co-wives they work well together and are friendly and helpful towards each other. She notes too, however, that there is sometimes conflict over children.
On the matter of polygyny Maggie also speaks favourably.

No, I don't mind two wives. My husband only had me; but look at some of them others. They got two or three, and they help one another and no fights most of the time.

Maggie has two sons, who were born while she and her husband worked at Talawana Station.

They been born bush, my kids. White-fella took me to Balfour Downs [a neighbouring station]. Kimi [Maggie's sister-in-law] and Bunda [Maggie's classificatory daughter-in-law] were there. I sat *waiting* — waiting for two days before he was born. That was the first one. It was all right. Kimi and Bunda helped me . . . That's like a bushyman, you know? No doctor. We took that little fella back to Talawana . . . Second baby born Talawana. Them same two [women] helped me again. We were all working at Talawana that time. Good place Talawana. The first one was big then, walking around [three or four years old]. He didn't like little brother — he was jealous . . . I still worked on the station, but I stopped riding horses when I had little one . . . Yoh, I had only two boys. I never lose any . . . when we been desert, bushyman, people never had a big mob of kids — not like this lot now [she whispers with some distaste]. They used to have two or three. My mother had three, and Nyangabidi mother had three, like that. Not like some of them now got eight, nine . . . Two was enough for me.

Her sons are grown up and married now. Her older son has three children, the younger one has two. Maggie adores her grandchildren and reared her oldest granddaughter at Jigalong for about two years, so that the child could attend school. She returned at weekends and holidays to her parents, who were working on a neighbouring cattle station. They now live at Jigalong, but this granddaughter maintains a close relationship with her grandmother.
Patricia has a son aged sixteen and a fourteen-year-old daughter. She also assists with the rearing of two younger boys and a girl, relatives of hers, whose mothers are dead. She says she would like very much to have more of her own, but unfortunately this has not been possible. She never mentions a younger son and daughter who died accidentally about six years ago. Her grief was acute and continues. As is customary among many Aborigines she avoids any reference to them even now.
The birth of Patricia's first child was difficult. She spent several weeks in Port Hedland awaiting the delivery, and when her son Gregory was born, both were ill.

> He had to go away to hospital in Perth. I came back to Jigalong and went back to work in the hospital. When he came back my milk had dried up so I had to feed him with a bottle . . . [My husband] used to look after him at night, used to feed him. I had him all day . . . When Peggy was born I had no trouble. She was born here at Jigalong. Not long after that we all went to live in Meekatharra. [My husband] left us there, and he went with six other men to work on a station . . . I was all right, had lot of family there. I lived with Aunty Carrie. Then my baby got sick and they put her in the hospital, and I just looked after the older one. We used to get rations from the Welfare — no money, those days.

Patricia's children still attend school. Gregory is in the post-primary class at Jigalong; Peggy attends high school in Denmark (in the south-west of Western Australia) where she lives with a European family. Their mother would like both of them to receive as much education as possible, even if it means that they will have to live away from Jigalong. This is an unusual attitude. Most parents at Jigalong do not have higher educational goals for their children. Most are reluctant to send their children away from home to be educated or for any other reason.

Maggie and Patricia have had some similar work experiences. Both have been employed on cattle stations, where they worked as cooks and houseworkers. They have accompanied men out on mustering trips, on which they have cooked and done odd jobs in the mustering camps. These experiences they also share with many Aboriginal women all over the pastoral areas of North Australia, where Aboriginal women have made a major contribution as workers in the industry. Patricia and Maggie also had jobs in the mining industry, another activity in which Aboriginal women have participated. Although twenty years separate their experience, both worked in the tin mining industry in the Pilbara.

There have also been differences in the work experiences of Patricia and Maggie. In part, these are indicative of the changes in the community and the lives of individuals resulting from contact with Europeans and years of living in a mission settlement.

About her station experience, Maggie speaks with nostalgia and animation, though she feels that now she has done enough and is enjoying her retirement.

> I used to cook, used to ride horses too — out on the muster. Night-time we used to take turns watching cattle: man and woman took turns. Talk about tired, don't say! I used to get so sleepy. When I had my babies I used to leave 'em in the camp and go and cook [at the homesteads]. I made bread and damper with the flour. Yeast bread [but] not that dry form. That only come in lately. We had the wet yeast — hops. You mix up the flour, water, sugar, hops — mix 'em up and leave 'em all night. Next morning you make bread. Good one. Cook 'em in a camp oven. *Good* bread all right. And we had meat — bullock meat. No sheep, no goat — only bullock. I used to make roast or stew or curry. Sometimes we had salt meat or dried meat. No tin food; not much vegetable. Oh, sometimes we had onions and potatoes

— nothing more. No fruit. Not much bush tucker — *minyarra* ['wild onion'] sometimes; and watermelon, big rain time. Sometime when no bullock then we had treacle, or we might get kangaroo, emu, *marundu* [lizard] . . . No weekend off — I worked every day. Sometimes the men would go out hunting on weekend, but we didn't go — all the women would stop at home . . . Pinkeye [summer] time we come to Jigalong, see all our family (my husband and me had a little sulky) and camp there little while; then go back to Talawana.

For the past five years Patricia has been employed as a kindergarten teacher's aide, following a short training period in Port Hedland. A number of fully qualified teachers have commented on her ability and the consensus is that she could become a fully qualified kindergarten teacher. She has seriously considered going to Perth to do a three-year kindergarten-teacher training course. She said of her work in the school:

Oh yes, I like it. I like working with the children . . . Helen [another teacher's aide] and I work together well and the new teacher is very nice. She's doing a good job. . . . but I would like to go back and get more training to be a kindergarten teacher. That would be another three years . . . I wouldn't mind going to Perth, only thing is I would like to see Greg in school first. I filled out the forms all right [for him to go to trade school in Geraldton] but no word yet. Peggy's okay in school at Denmark . . . No, I won't be homesick. No worries; and my family, they won't worry.

To my suggestion that she might not want to go back to Jigalong after three years in Perth, she replied: 'No, I belong to Jigalong; this is my home properly. I'll come back. I've been to plenty places before, but I always come back to Jigalong.'

However, it is now unlikely that Patricia will pursue a teaching career. She resigned from the kindergarten at the end of 1979 to work in the hospital. She said she wanted a change, despite her success in the school, and is now happily carrying out her job as health worker.

Maggie, like almost all women her age, is deeply involved in the ritual life of the community. She attends women's rituals and is a 'boss' for some. She also holds the status of a cook in one of the important ceremonies involving senior men and women. Maggie says she enjoys going to the bush for women's ritual. 'I go all the time all right; but I am old fella . . .'

She does not understand why so many of the young women at Jigalong do not go to the bush and participate in women's business: '. . . they are terrible. I don't know why they don't go . . . maybe they shame.'

She implies that the younger women are so influenced by European ideas and values that they are rejecting their traditions, particularly in the areas of ritual (and the observance of marriage rules), and that they are embarrassed by these traditions. Maggie notes, however, that Patricia is one of the few young women who do participate.

Patricia is active in both public ceremonial life and women's secret ritual. She regularly accompanies older women to the women's ritual area to be instructed in 'women's business'. In addition, Patricia is one of the young women who consistently get up and dance during those public rituals in which the entire community can participate. Not long ago, with assistance from her husband and others, she drove her own car from Jigalong to Balgo (about 1600 km) for ceremonies. Many of the Jigalong travellers were reunited with relatives whom they had not seen for a generation. Some they had never met. Patricia spoke with pride and with animation of her experience on this trip, which included learning a new ritual from the Balgo women. When they returned to Jigalong, Patricia and a few other women, along with some Balgo visitors, taught the new songs and dances to other Jigalong women.

Patricia and Maggie are both keen card players and they usually play for money, although neither is a chronic gambler. Both of them accept the prevailing view that it is antisocial to get large winnings and withdraw from the game. Maggie says she does not want to win a lot of money at cards because 'somebody might do something to me; they might get jealous. No good that one'.

Both women enjoy going out in the bush to gather wild foods. Maggie is very skilled at finding and digging up wild yams. In the winter months she often goes out to collect yams, usually in the company of her son and daughter-in-law and sisters. On many occasions I have taken Maggie and other women on yam-gathering trips. The winter days are gloriously clear and warm. The bright blue skies make a brilliant background for the green mulgas on which the yam vines usually climb. Winter is also the time for collecting the bunches of yellow flowers which cover the desert oaks [banksias]. These flowers are sought for their nectar; they are either sucked on the spot or taken home to be immersed in water to make a sweet drink. The search for yams involves looking for cracks in the ground, pounding the earth with metal crowbars and listening for the particular sound that indicates their presence. When the proper spot is located Maggie and her companions dig skilfully and usually succeed in removing the yams without damaging them. They then roast them for immediate consumption or take them home to share. Sometimes Maggie accompanies relatives on hunting trips or to visit neighbouring stations. Most of the time, however, she leads a quiet, sedentary existence, staying close to her own house. Patricia is much more mobile, and shows a greater interest in the world outside the settlement. She has a car and a driver's licence and she travels two or three times a month to Newman, the nearest town, about 150 km away. She is often accompanied by her husband, male and female age-mates and sometimes her children. Patricia also makes trips into the bush, to picnic or to camp. Visits to distant Aboriginal settlements such as Strelley and La Grange are also undertaken willingly by Patricia, either in her own car or in the community's bus or truck. Maggie, on the other hand, chooses not to make such journeys. In 1978 Patricia and another young woman from Jigalong came to stay with me in Canberra and also to visit Sydney. They enjoyed a number of new experiences and were especially fascinated by Sydney, which they found both exciting and awesome. After about two weeks, however, they were terribly homesick and were anxious to return to Jigalong.

Maggie and Patricia are both respected in their community. Each in her own way is a source of leadership and strength. The former is respected because of her age, ritual seniority and the fact that she is a dignified and strong woman who has never caused trouble. Her white hair and calm confident air attract the attention of outsiders who meet her. The latter, though much younger, has distinguished herself by mastering many European skills while retaining full membership of her own culture. Patricia recently served for a year as the chairman of the Jigalong Community Council. Though several women have served on the Council, she was the first woman chairman and one of the few women to have held such an office in any Aboriginal community. She was elected with the support of several senior men and women, including one of her two 'brothers', who might himself have stood for the position. Her supporters came from both of the major groups at Jigalong. Patricia is extremely articulate and even-tempered, and these qualities serve her well during community meetings and disputes, as well as in the Council, of which she is still a member though no longer chairman. Her participation (and that of any woman) on the Council is constrained by the necessity to observe avoidance rules: even as chairman the onus was on her as a woman to avoid her 'sons-in-law'.

Both women are positive about their community and optimistic about its future, though concerned about its problems. They worry most about interpersonal conflicts and about the difficulty of controlling the violence which erupts when people become inebriated. Maggie is concerned about the rebelliousness and non-conformity of some of the younger people, such as the girls who refuse to marry the men to whom they are promised, or those who elope with their lovers. She would like to see more young people involved in the ceremonial life of the women. Although nostalgic for the desert, she considers Jigalong her permanent home. It is 'good country', and she expects her children and grandchildren to remain there leading a happy life. Patricia is also committed to remaining at Jigalong. Over the years many of her relatives have moved to Strelley (one of her brothers is a leader there), and she too has spent time there, but Jigalong is home for her and her children. She is impatient with the slow pace of housing development, and she would like to see better educational opportunities for children. She also expresses irritation at the reluctance of many of the older male council members to assert their leadership role when there is uncontrolled drinking and fighting. 'Some of them just run away and camp somewhere else. They don't do nothing.'

Patricia and Maggie are fine models for the next generation of women of Jigalong.

Additional reading

Tonkinson, R. (1974). *The Jigalong Mob: Aboriginal victors of the desert crusade*. Cummings, Menlo Park, Calif.
────── (1978). *The Mardudjara Aborigines: Living the dream in Australia's desert*. Holt, Rinehart and Winston, New York

13

Aunty Ellen: The Pastor's Wife

Diane Barwick

Ellen Campbell Atkinson, widow of a clergyman and caretaker of the church which was his memorial, was one of the most respected elderly ladies of Mooroopna, in northern Victoria, when I met her at the end of 1960. I saw her almost daily for four months; then only on rare visits before her death in 1965.

I did not know her well. How could a twenty-two-year-old stranger from Canada really share the concerns and appreciate the memories of an Australian Aboriginal pensioner? She was a widowed grandmother coping with illness, poverty and isolation in a small town where the prejudices of teachers, employers, landlords and officials still shaped the fortunes of her family and friends. I was a graduate student beginning an anthropological study of the Victorian Aboriginal community, introduced to her by a nephew who had taken me into his home with generous kindness.

I did not plan, all those years ago, to write her life story. I do so now as a tribute to a woman who deeply influenced my life. What she taught me about the responsibilities of daughters, wives and mothers reinforced — and made me appreciate — the example and loving instruction given by the women of my own family. What she told me of the past has shaped my work for over twenty years. All that I have written has something of Aunty Ellen in it. But she died before I found the old documents and photographs which confirmed the accuracy of her reminiscences, before I could show her my written accounts of the history I first learned from her.

Aunty Ellen had to tell me of the past to make me understand the present. Her way of explaining her life and that of her community was to talk of the relatives who had been important to her, and of her beloved husband, Edwin Atkinson, 'the first Aboriginal ordained as a pastor'.

To tell her story I must write about Ellen and Eddy, weaving together the memories she recounted and the fragmentary records of their lives preserved in government files, church magazines and newspapers. Her biography must be a family history, because family ties were the framework for her perception of the past and the essential source of her identity.

Aunty Ellen's domestic routine, her restricted outings, her roles as possessive mother and fond grandmother were superficially like those of

Ellen Campbell Atkinson and Edwin Atkinson. Wedding — Echuca, 3 May 1911 (Photograph courtesy of Alick Jackomos)

other elderly women in the town. But her Aboriginal identity set her apart: her life chances had been determined by government policy decisions made before she was born. Her opportunities, like those of her ancestors and descendants, were limited by other Australians' intolerance of cultural difference, by their poor opinion of Aboriginal capacities. Yet Aunty Ellen's influence on the world beyond her household was greater than that of the other old women of Mooroopna just because she belonged to an Aboriginal community. She and Eddy had four children, fifteen uncles and aunts, twenty-five brothers and sisters, seventy-three nieces and nephews and innumerable cousins. As she said, 'Everyone calls me aunty, related or not; even some white men.' She was pleased that some outsiders felt close enough to her community to adopt this term of respect. She was delighted when I dared to use it.

I cannot now reproduce the rich detail of Aunty Ellen's reminiscences and instruction from my scribbled notes. The tape recorders then available were bulky and unreliable. Anyhow their use was inappropriate to the kind of participation I sought in the life of her community. I learned others' opinions of her, then and later. I saw her among friends and relatives at church and community gatherings and at home with family and visitors. We talked alone as I helped her clean the church or while we rested in her house, surrounded by mementoes of her husband's career. During that long-ago summer, she told me something of her life and worries, and a good deal of the history of her people. Much of what she told me I did not fully understand. I was then too ignorant of the past to encourage her reminiscences and seek her opinion on events which the documents compiled by officialdom cannot explain. I did realise, hearing about her forebears at Coranderrk Aboriginal Station in Victoria and her own life at Cumeroogunga Aboriginal Station in New South Wales, that it was impossible to write about modern life without examining the history of administration in these States.

At first our conversations were limited to the topics appropriate between strangers. I was shy and afraid of being impertinent; she was kind yet implacable in her skilful management of interviews. She had played an important role in interpreting *koories'* (Aborigines') needs to *gubba* (European) sympathisers during forty years of church work. Initially she saw me as yet another inquiring *gubba* to be instructed and gently manipulated as a potential resource for her community. But our relationship changed, just because I was a young girl without relatives and needed help. Her people have, I think, a special kindness for waifs and strays bereft of family, perhaps because their own identity is based upon kinship ties. Several men of the district told me that as lonely youngsters during the depression years they had been sheltered by Aboriginal families, just as I was befriended and protected. When I turned to Aunty Ellen for advice and emotional support, she showed me the fondness of a grandmother, calling me 'my girl' and expressing anxious concern about my finances, my diet and the suitability of my fiancé. My own mother could not have bettered Aunty Ellen's inquisition about his habits. My marriage won wry appreciation from her kin, whose sole criticisms of Aunty Ellen suggested she was a mite possessive in rejecting her daughters' suitors.

She had been most happily married: 'Everyone loved my husband, both dark and white. He was good and gentle. Our life together was always happiness'. But she had good reason for her warnings. Between 1939 and 1959 a whole generation of her community had grown up in shanties on the riverbank at Mooroopna, despised by most townsfolk and ignored by officials. Some had found recreation and solace in Eddy's church; many had turned instead to alcohol.

> My married life was really happy, but I always tell girls to think well. The nicest girls get terrible husbands . . . Go slow, you are married all your life . . . You can't change a drinking man. They'll promise you a nice home and comfort and everything. Sometimes you get it and sometimes you don't . . . Be sure — better single than a drinking man!

In 1958 ten riverbank families had been re-housed in the isolated Rumbalara settlement belatedly built by the Victorian authorities. Others were scattered in standard housing in Mooroopna, Shepparton and more distant towns. This experiment in assimilation had its costs. Many had found their standard of living was worsened by high rentals; some regretted their isolation among 'white' neighbours; most resented the humiliating supervision of their domestic lives by government officials.

In 1960 Aunty Ellen lived in a weatherboard Housing Commission cottage with her elder daughter Muriel, a spinster, and a crippled teenage grandson whose mother had died at his birth. Her eldest child, Geoff, and his family were permanently employed on a nearby farm, where they made packing boxes for tomatoes and fruit, the main crops of the district. Her youngest child, Lawrie, a seasonal worker, was then visiting Leeton, where the younger daughter, Daisy, lived with her small children. Aunty Ellen welcomed my visits because she was lonely. She could not get about easily and most of her relatives and friends were tied to distant homes caring for children or working long hours in orchards and canneries.

The isolation troubled her: 'We used to live among our people; now we never see them any more. If only we had a car we could get over to see my sisters — they are widows and lonely — and we could go to Rumbalara. I often think I'd like to visit some of the old ones down there'. But her fortnightly pension of £10 (plus her daughter's earnings as cannery hand, fruit picker and hospital cleaner) barely covered rent, food, clothing and medical expenses. She could not afford taxicab fares, the only means of reaching her dispersed community.

In fact she had more contacts than others because her house adjoined the Aboriginal church built by voluntary labour with donations from the Churches of Christ. The opening in 1957 had been attended by three hundred guests, she told me. She had wept when they handed her the keys: 'It was the church they promised Eddy'. But he was dead and only his nephew, Pastor Doug Nicholls, stood beside her. On the riverbank their church had been a bough shelter: 'Then, when we moved down here, we used to rent a hall, a little supper-room, in Mooroopna for the services. We saved and saved from the church collections and finally we bought this block of land for the church. Now we're trying to pay off the church'. There had been no resident pastor since Eddy's death.

Services were conducted by ministers from Melbourne and Shepparton, assisted by her son Geoff. In 1961 she was afraid 'the white Shepparton

Official opening of the Church of Christ at Mooroopna, 1957. Ellen Atkinson with Eddy's nephew, Pastor Doug Nicholls
(Photograph courtesy of Alick Jackomos)

people may take it over'. Maintaining an independent church was important to her. It was not just Eddy's memorial but a symbol of the achievements of the Cumeroogunga people. They had survived the greed and unthinking benevolence of other Australians and remained a proudly distinct community.

Aunty Ellen's reminiscences rarely revealed any bitterness towards individuals: she had 'many white friends' and genuinely pitied 'ignorant people' who openly displayed prejudice. But she and others spoke with anguish of the loss of land once reserved for Aborigines, and were dismayed by continuing government efforts to 'break up' Aboriginal communities. I had assumed that Aboriginal land and group identity were protected under treaty agreements. I learned how the absence of land rights and compensation had affected her life and the lives of her ancestors.

We were talking of recent policy decisions and their consequences, and the closing of her childhood home, Cumeroogunga, when she explained that her family had been forced to leave 'an older mission, Coranderrk, near Healesville'. They had crossed into New South Wales to settle at 'Maloga Mission that was before Cumeroogunga'. The Coranderrk folk had 'battled for years' to keep their land. She recalled that 'John Green, who was manager, he helped the people'. I was more interested in the protests that had occurred in her lifetime, yet because I had heard only criticism of the many nameless officials who had ruled the lives of Aboriginal communities, I asked why this manager was remembered kindly. She explained that 'John Green was a good man, the old ones said, a father and a brother to his people at Coranderrk. They were loyal to him when there was trouble with the Board, back in my father's time'.

Her words prompted me to investigate the history of Coranderrk, formed in 1863 by survivors of the clans composing the Woiworung, Bunurong, Taungurong and Jajowrong 'tribes' of central Victoria. Green won their loyalty by encouraging them to 'manage themselves' but the Board for the Protection of the Aborigines took control of this successful farming settlement and dismissed him. From 1874 to 1884 the Coranderrk residents fought the Board's plans to remove them and sell the land. Coranderrk became a 'permanent' reserve but the Board simultaneously adopted an 'absorption policy' which required all young 'half castes' (the official term for Aborigines who had some European ancestry) to leave the reserves they had struggled to develop.

Aunty Ellen's parents were among the exiles. She had fond memories of her father Alick Campbell, a famous shearer, horseman and storyteller. 'He used to gather all the children round him, telling the old yarns. He was a great joker, too.' From the records, I learned that Alick (1851/53-1922) was a Baraparapa 'half caste' born near Kerang on the lower Murray River. The orphaned lad worked for fifteen years at Ganawarra Station, where, in 1872, he earned £1 a week plus rations. When the Aboriginal women and children of this region were persuaded to join Coranderrk, Alick sold his horses and followed Emma Jackson Patterson. They married in 1873. On 26 February 1887 Alick, now a widower, married Elizabeth Briggs Charles (1857/58-1936), who like him had seven children. Alick and Lizzie then had four daughters: Jemima (who died in infancy), Maggie, Louisa and, after their exile from Coranderrk, Ellen. The fifteen surviving children were 'all one family', Aunty Ellen recalled, but the three youngest were particularly close to their half-sister Alice: 'There were four of us Campbell girls'.

Aunty Ellen described her mother, matriarch of one of the largest families at Cumeroogunga, as a 'strong Christian' who had 'helped her people'. The records showed she was a daughter of the 'half-Tasmanian' John Briggs (son of More-te-woe-te-yenner of Cape Portland and George Briggs, a free seaman of Bedfordshire) and his 'quarter caste Aboriginal' wife, Louisa. Aunty Ellen had vivid memories of her grandmother, Louisa Briggs, who died at Cumeroogunga in 1925 just before her ninetieth birthday. This 'good Christian woman who went on working for the people to the end of her days' had delighted her grandchildren with tales about shepherding and the Victorian gold rush. Aunty Ellen could still 'remember her telling about meeting one of the old gangs — not the Kelly Gang, another — who asked to spend the night in her hut'. Like her surviving sisters Aunty Ellen was tiny and had exceptionally curly hair. She explained that the Briggs family were of Tasmanian descent 'like Truganini, whose skeleton is in the museum', but said that Louisa was a tall woman with 'straight' hair. 'My mother's mother came from a coast family. They lived on the coast south of Melbourne.'

Years later I found a document recording a 1924 interview with Louisa and her daughter, Lizzie Campbell. Louisa, who had pale blue eyes and 'almost straight' hair, explained that her father was 'John Strugnell, a white man', and her mother Mary was the 'half caste' daughter of Marjorie, 'a fullblood of Melbourne'. Louisa was reared in the Bass Strait Islands like her half-Tasmanian husband, John Briggs. Other documents named the sealers who had kidnapped Louisa's mother and grandmother from Point Nepean, south of Melbourne, about August 1833 and identified John Strugnell as a London chimney sweep aged seventeen when transported in 1818. John and Louisa had their first child on the goldfields of Western Victoria in 1854. After working as shepherds they were admitted to Coranderrk in 1871. John, an experienced ploughman, was 'worth' 10 shillings a week in 1872; Louisa, an expert midwife and practical nurse, earned that wage as matron of the orphans' dormitory in 1876. The Briggs family was indeed prominent in the long campaign to prevent the sale of Coranderrk but, like other 'half castes', were exiled from 1884. Few of the skilled Coranderrk workers could find secure jobs and homes. Most soon joined the impoverished Maloga Mission across the Murray. Without implements, livestock and more land this private mission station could never be self-supporting. In 1888 New South Wales officials forcibly removed most residents to the nearby Cumeroogunga reserve.

Meanwhile Alick Campbell had returned to Ganawarra. His earnings as stockman at Coranderrk had supported his family in comfort but now he found the employer's ration scarcely fed two. Even with the elder children 'working for themselves' he was 'barely making a living'. The Board ignored his pleas to return 'to give the children schooling', but finally the Campbells were re-admitted to Coranderrk because Alick's first wife was dying. The Briggs family were forbidden to rejoin Lizzie

(Aunty Ellen's mother), who remained here after her first husband, John Charles, was accidentally killed in 1884. It was not until September 1892 that Alick and Lizzie Campbell and their infant daughters were exiled as 'under-age half castes', although their elder children had been sent out to domestic service from the age of fourteen.

It was impossible to find work during the 1890s depression but Victorian and New South Wales officials co-operated to ensure that no more 'half castes' joined Cumeroogunga. When the Campbells pleaded to return to Coranderrk they were advised to give up their family to the Department for Neglected Children. Instead they took refuge at Maloga, which was forced to close in 1894. The Victorian Board sent six blankets in response to their May letter requesting aid as Alick was too sick to work and they were 'in want of warm beds'. In August Ellen was born at Madowla Park, the Victorian pastoral station where Alick earned 10s a week as stockrider. In 1895 her parents pleaded for rations and clothing for their fifteen young children. The Board secretary refused, cautioning Alick that he had 'heard you spent several pounds in drink not long ago'. In 1896 a Melbourne court committed three of Alick's children to the Maloga missionary's new refuge in Victoria (already seen as a threat to the Board's 'assimilation' policy). All pleas to reunite the family at Coranderrk were rejected. Finally the children were restored on condition the Campbells made 'a solemn declaration' to settle at Cumeroogunga and never seek Board aid or return to Victoria. Their final entitlement, eight blankets worth £7 3s 5d, was sent to Echuca in 1897. When the Coranderrk community again petitioned the Board to let the family come home, an MLA offered his support. He was told that Alick and Lizzie constantly wrote to Members of Parliament but their return to an Aboriginal reserve was 'against the law'.

This law was amended in 1910, but officials continued to interpret very narrowly their power to assist needy 'half castes'. Meanwhile a similar dispersal policy had begun to affect Aunty Ellen's happy childhood at Cumeroogunga. The ambitious farmers from Maloga and Coranderrk had invested their earnings from seasonal work in the development of some twenty farm blocks on the arable portion of this 2965 acre (1198 ha) reserve. This acreage would have supported only five European families, yet by 1908 a township of 46 cottages with its own shop, school, church and farm buildings housed 394 Aborigines. Rations were given only to destitute children and old people. This district produced little but sheep and wheat, and there was no work in the immediate vicinity for five months of the year. From the 1880s until the great Riverina pastoral stations were subdivided in the 1920s Cumeroogunga men dispersed each year to earn standard wages as drovers, fencers, shearers and harvesters. At home, rabbiting, fishing and timber-cutting were the main sources of supplementary income. The 'half castes' forced off Cumeroogunga by policy changes — and those who crossed the Murray to prevent the New South Wales Board from apprenticing their children as servants in distant localities — generally sheltered in a makeshift camp at the Barmah punt on the Victorian shore, where New South Wales officials could not intervene.

Sometimes they did enlist co-operation from the Victorian Board to uphold their powers of guardianship over minors. In February 1911 the Victorian Board agreed to obtain a police report on the welfare of 'the half caste girl Ellen Campbell', then working with her family at Strathmerton pastoral station. The local constable was asked to keep her 'under surveillance as required'. But with her father's written consent, Ellen, a 'domestic' aged sixteen, was married at Christ Church, Echuca, on 3 May 1911. She and Edwin Atkinson were then residents of Cumeroogunga.

Eddy Atkinson, who was born at Cumeroogunga on 8 August 1888, was eighth of the nine children of Aaron Atkinson and his wife, Louisa Frost of Mathoura. Aunty Ellen remembered her father-in-law as a skilled shearer, clever carpenter and 'a leader of his people' until his death in 1913. Aaron was one of eight 'half caste' sons and daughters of Kitty of the Wollithiga clan (part of the Pangerang tribe), and from her and her mother Old Maria, who lived until 1879, he had learned a good deal of the language called Joti-jota. Maloga, a selection cut from the Upper Moira run, was part of Wollithiga territory. Kitty's family were among the first to join Maloga, despite bitter opposition from local employers who had long relied on Aborigines' willingness to work for a pittance so they could remain in their homeland.

The Maloga pioneers and the exiles from Coranderrk were the respected elders of Aunty Ellen's childhood. Their hunger for land and independence shaped her life. Her distrust of officialdom had seemed reasonable in 1960 from what I knew of recent insensitivity. Later, reading the old letters which revealed how arbitrary policy decisions had shaped the fortunes of her community, I began to understand her insistence that ties to family and familiar territory were the only lasting source of security. The benevolent schemes of remote officials had always ignored the loyalties of Aborigines and the prejudices of other Australians. To Aunty Ellen the consequences were clear: 'Everywhere our people are living on the rubbish tips, and there's never been anything given to them to pay for the land'.

The loss of Cumeroogunga particularly grieved her. In 1960 I heard the few remaining residents tell members of the Victorian Aborigines' Advancement League how they had petitioned for years to farm what remained of the reserve, then leased 'up to our doorsteps'. Their pictures of the vanished township and Aunty Ellen's stories of the prosperous wheat-farming community of her youth made me explore official records to discover why this model farm had disappeared. Documents confirmed their oral history: Cumeroogunga families had indeed farmed their land successfully — until policy required the 'half castes' to disperse, and their land was used by Europeans.

The New South Wales Board had resumed the farm blocks in 1908, alleging that they were mismanaged. The Cumeroogunga men who had cleared and fenced at their own expense over twelve years, believing they had secure title, were told they had only a permissive occupancy. They protested. Board reports said discipline was maintained by 'the removal of certain undesirable residents'. They had equalled or bettered county averages for grain production, yet were dispossessed because distant officials needed to expand station income to subsidise welfare work elsewhere. The new policy of exiling young 'half castes' halved the population between 1908 and 1921. Wheat-growing ended in 1918, and from 1921 the Board leased most of the reserve to a European neighbour.

Aunty Ellen's youth had been financially comfortable and full of gaiety. Like others of her generation she felt nostalgia for 'the sports and singing they used to have at Cummera':

> Good times we had there! The good old days on the mission were best. I often think we should never have left: no rent to pay there! But there was no work for us . . . I used to like dancing; we danced a lot before I was married. We stopped then, when we went into the church. There's no harm in clean dancing! It was the waltz then. My mother was very strict — we girls always had to have a guardian to bring us home from the dances.

The Cumeroogunga folk had lived much like their working-class neighbours until the 1920s, when lasting drought and changes in the regional economy limited seasonal work. They bought food, clothing and household necessities at the Cumeroogunga shop, at Echuca, or from the 'Afghan' hawkers who travelled the region. Until the pumped water supply failed in the 1920s they had abundant milk and vegetables and charming flower gardens. This small reserve was never adequately stocked, but Aunty Ellen recalled how fish and game procured at the Moira lakes made up for the lack of meat:

> We used to cook turtle, fish, swan or ducks on ashes. We used swan and emu eggs (they're rich!) for cakes, birthday cakes. We used to have wonderful meals. You try it: you scrape the coals away, lay gum tips on the ashes, put the fish on — split, skin side down — or turtle upside down on saplings. You can tell when the turtle's cooked — there's a narrow split where the opening is in the shell for the legs. Always remove the four 'stones' under the arms without breaking them. They're like gall. Our old people used to say it was something to do with lightning.

Cumeroogunga folk earned respect as workers, and acceptance in the sporting competitions, church activities and musical entertainments of the district. Australian Rules football was 'a way of life'. Their team won the premiership of the Moira League several times before World War I and during the 1920s. Aunty Ellen's father-in-law, husband and sons had been star players, and she had a connoisseur's appreciation of the game:

> The Cummera All-Blacks were a great team. They played together and they played scientific. Each man supported the others. They won the premiership time and again. Becky Murray still has the big cup. The players gave it to their teacher, her father, Thomas James. My Eddy was rover for the Cummera team; her husband, Bob Murray, was rover for the Barmah team. They played opposite in many matches. Old Mr Riordan of the shoe store here was a rover for the Picola

team. He and Eddy often joked together about how they used to play. He tackled Eddy in the store one day; he sidestepped and Mr Riordan fell. He laughed and said, 'You're still one of the best, Eddy.' The dark players mix up on the local teams now; they don't have their own team. They don't do as well now.

Ellen praised the influence of Thomas Shadrach James, who was teacher, preacher and doctor to three generations. He was an Indian from Mauritius who married Eddy's aunt soon after he came to Maloga in 1881. He was the salaried teacher at Cumeroogunga until 1922 and remained a leader of his adopted community until he died in the 1940s. The school, choir and church he founded shaped the lives of Eddy and Ellen.

Although popularly called 'missions', all New South Wales Aboriginal reserves were managed by public servants. Organisers of the non-sectarian Aborigines Inland Mission began visiting Cumeroogunga in 1906, and in 1913 sent one of their first 'native evangelists' from Karuah to live with James and assist him in a 'Christian revival' campaign. Eddy, Ellen and many of their closest relatives were 'converted' at these meetings. They became deacons and organists of the independent church which bolstered morale while the Board dismantled the model farm at Cumeroogunga and tried to disperse the families who had developed it. Monthly magazines issued by the Aborigines Inland Mission provide precise dates for many events remembered by Aunty Ellen. Eddy was first mentioned in July 1921, when he and James preached at the 'Barham Native Convention' on the lower Murray, attended by congregations from Cumeroogunga and the Moonah Cullah Reserve near Deniliquin. Church work increasingly absorbed Eddy's time after his uncle retired in 1922: 'Eddy was his nephew and took over his preaching. Doug Nicholls was Eddy's nephew and it passed on to him'.

Ellen's four children were born between 1919 and 1927. As wheat-growing had ended and the reserve was leased, 'Eddy used to do a lot of carpentering and fishing. We used to camp and fish along the Murray and sell the fish in towns'. Ellen worked beside her husband at harvesting tasks. In season they would 'go up for the good pea and bean picking in New South Wales', then move to the Victorian fruit-growing towns, camping for a few weeks wherever work offered but always going 'home to Cummera', where they could subsist on savings. Eddy's ministry was unpaid but 'we'd go hungry rather than beg', and anyhow they could be certain that relatives would help.

When I lived with Aunty Ellen's community, people still felt bound to care for needy relatives. In teaching me about the obligations of kinship she frequently explained how community loyalties had survived decades of hardship:

We've had nothing this week — and we've had nothing before. But we've never begged; we've battled along. Our families always help each other. At Cummera, when Eddy first began to preach, we got no pay. Sometimes we had nothing to eat. Our sisters — his and mine — used to help us; they shared their meals. Once we had no dinner but we couldn't tell a lie when Eddy's sister came for the singsong and asked how had we finished so soon. We had to say we'd had no dinner. Eddy's sister was upset: 'Oh, Eddy, why didn't you come over? What sort of sisters would we be if we didn't share with you?' She brought dinner to us.

The elder children of Edwin and Ellen Atkinson. Muriel, born 1923; Geoffrey, born 1919 (Photograph courtesy of Alick Jackomos)

In 1961 many remembered Eddy's inspirational preaching and assured me he was 'better than Billy Graham on the radio'. In 1924 Eddy and his well-dressed congregation had impressed two visiting researchers, who reported that the services resembled those of 'any ordinary country village of Nonconformist type, where the preacher is earnest and the singing hearty'. The 'black crêpe de Chine dress, black silk stockings and patent high-heeled shoes' of the organist indicated that Cumeroogunga folk could still afford good clothing. But in 1924 only 147 people occupied the remaining houses. Another 118 exiles were camped in bag huts across the Murray at Barmah.

In 1924 church members built a hut in the Barmah camp for an Australian Inland Mission (AIM) 'missionary' (who remained for a year), and the hawker Mehra Navi Bux, husband of Ellen's half-sister Alice, provided an organ and the use of his shop premises for church services conducted by Eddy. In May 1925 Eddy was appointed an AIM 'Native Helper'. His and Ellen's brothers and sisters, prominent members of the Cumeroogunga–Barmah church, were delegates to the AIM Auxiliary meeting in Melbourne in September. Afterwards the AIM founder visited. Her report praised Eddy's services in the old Cumeroogunga church and his Sunday meetings at Barmah, Ellen's management of the Sunday School, and the fervour of their children, Geoffrey and 'Muriel, not yet two, who sang a Sunday School hymn'. They had just purchased a harmonium, still in use at the Mooroopna church in 1961 when Ellen told me about it:

> Eddy was in the church for 40 years, and that little organ is about 35 years old. I couldn't play when we bought it, but the music came to me — a gift from the Lord. I played for all the services and the Sunday School too. Eddy's two sisters learned to play; they were always trying to get at the organ.

Ellen remembered with pride how Eddy's converts had offered themselves as AIM 'missionaries to other Aborigines':

> My husband Eddy converted a lot from drink to be Christians. One of them was a crippled fellow at Cummera, Robert Peters. Eddy saved him, and later he went up preaching at Darlington Point, and worked there preaching for years. We've got a book on him.

In 1928 AIM magazines printed Eddy's letter describing this conversion, noted Eddy's subsequent promotion to 'Native Missionary', and published his address to a Melbourne meeting in which he explained how he had supported his family while serving as evangelist for 15 years: 'I labour with my hands like the Apostle Paul and receive no salary from any Church or Society'.

For New South Wales Aborigines the great depression lasted from 1928, when the Board's report noted that the new Workers Compensation Act and the obligation to pay award wages had caused many to be 'thrown out of employment', until 1939, when the Board complained that a State policy of 'granting preference to white workers' still prevented many from obtaining unemployment relief work. By 1928 Eddy spent much of his time travelling between seasonal workers' camps on the Murray to conduct communion services. By 1930 his health was so poor that Echuca church workers came to help with services. In 1931 the railwayman W.B. Payne was named an AIM Associate Worker at Cumeroogunga and took charge while Eddy was in hospital. Eddy had been the main speaker at the 1931 Wakool Convention and both he and Ellen went to the Moonah Cullah Convention in 1932. The AIM founder, again a guest in their home afterwards, reported that unemployment had increased the Cumeroogunga population to 220 and Eddy's church, 'enlarged twelve feet', was 'packed to the utmost capacity'. Although too ill to go as planned to 'a new mission field', Eddy was able to relieve the AIM workers at Moonah Cullah in December 1932. In early 1933 he and Ellen attended the Barham Convention, visited Robert Peters at Darlington Point, then travelled 330 miles in their buggy (with all four children) to the Goolagong Convention. Later they went to Moonah Cullah to help raise funds for a 'Native Helpers Training College'. Six of the seventeen Native Workers in New South Wales were Eddy's Cumeroogunga converts and AIM activities now linked all reserve communities between Cowra and Brewarrina. These networks, supplementing and even transcending kinship bonds, became important as the tribulations of the 1930s prompted Aborigines to organise protests drawing public attention to their plight.

At the first Cumeroogunga Convention in January 1934 a new independent church was host to visitors from Darlington Point and Moonah Cullah. The Atkinsons then went as missionaries to Brungle

Church of Christ Sunday School, Cumeroogunga c. 1938. The photograph shows W. B. Payne (standing at left) and Mrs Payne (standing at right), Eddy (standing, third from left), Ellen (centre row, third from left) and their daughter Daisy, born 1925 (front row, third from right) (Photograph courtesy of Alick Jackomos)

reserve but illness brought them home in June. By December a second church was flourishing at the Barmah camp. Little Muriel was now able to play the organ for Sunday School hymns.

But in 1935 AIM magazines reported problems. Payne, funded by the Victorian Churches of Christ from June 1933, ceased to be an Associate Worker in March. After June the Atkinsons were not listed either. After a visit by AIM officials two European missionaries were transferred to Barmah. The former representative Payne was accused of 'dividing the Native Church and taking with him a portion of it'. The AIM continued work at Barmah until 1950 but Eddy and Ellen were no longer involved. The AIM blamed sectarian sentiment — but this interpretation ignores Aboriginal opinions about independence, paternalism and the merits of rival patrons.

Aunty Ellen spoke warmly of her 'great friends' the Paynes, who shared the same August birthdays as she and Eddy and 'always celebrated together'. She entrusted her daughter Daisy to them from about 1935 'so she could get a better education living at their home in Echuca'. Her sacrifice was necessary: in Victoria Aborigines had always had a standard education, both on and off the reserves, but separate schooling and an inferior curriculum had been condoned in New South Wales since the 1890s. Cumeroogunga always had qualified teachers, but Thomas James's successors did not bother to enrich the restricted Aboriginal syllabus. As Aunty Ellen said, 'Education at the mission was only about fourth grade — but still we got more than our children.'

Cumeroogunga workers paid taxes on their earnings in Victoria as well as New South Wales, but both States refused them sustenance and unemployment relief work, and both Boards denied that able-bodied 'half castes' were entitled to aid. When J.G. Danvers became manager of Cumeroogunga in January 1934 whole families were subsisting on the new child endowment benefit. As there was no work in the three months between shearing and fruit-picking, he ignored Board policy and gave rations to all willing to renovate the station. But tools and stock had been removed, agriculture was impossible since the water supply had failed, and two-thirds of the land was leased. Conditions worsened from late 1936, under Danvers' unsympathetic successor.

In Aunty Ellen's opinion the 'great leader' of those days was Eddy's uncle, William Cooper, who had left Cumeroogunga a few years earlier in order to claim the age pension. This he spent on his campaign to petition the King for land rights, voting rights and Aboriginal representation in the Federal Parliament. The ideas came from his reading about North American Indians and Maoris. He had collected 1814 signatures from all over Australia by 1937, but because of official opposition the petition never left Canberra. The Aboriginal league he had formed in Melbourne and another formed in Sydney by William Ferguson (father-in-law to one of Ellen's nieces) did provoke an inquiry into New South Wales reserves by a Select Committee in November 1937. The testimony of Danvers and another ex-manager confirmed what Aunty Ellen later told me about Board policy: half of the Cumeroogunga cottages had been burnt or pulled down to discourage the return of families absent for seasonal work. Now 172 people were crowded into 24 cottages and 113 more occupied huts of scrap iron and wheat bags. Another 50 'expellees' camped across the Murray.

These officials said discontent was justified. The Board's inspector visited for a few hours a year and referred all complaints back to the manager, so residents openly 'said "What is the use of reporting the matter to the Board? . . . no-one takes the word of an Aboriginal" '. One of the few local sympathisers was the lay preacher Payne, who visited weekly. Danvers praised the sophistication and ambition of the Cumeroogunga folk, attributing this to their superior education under Thomas James. The Select Committee was told that many had furnished their homes comfortably, wholly by their own earnings. In fifty households there were 12 radios worth up to '29 guineas'. Eight families had old cars or trucks, and some others had horses and buggies or gigs. But without wage employment they went hungry.

The inquiry lapsed and this evidence was not made public until 1940. Cooper and Ferguson tried other tactics, even a vain deputation to the Prime Minister, J.A. Lyons. When Jack Patten became president of the Sydney association he tried to visit many reserves. When he read extracts from the 1937 inquiry evidence to some 300 residents of Cumeroogunga (many of them relatives) they believed his warning that the Board planned to create a 'closed compound', take control of their earnings, and remove their children to institutions. On 3 February 1939 police seized Patten on a charge of 'inciting Aborigines to leave their reserve'. About 170 people then crossed the Murray to camp at Barmah, some of them on the Bux family's land.

The New South Wales Board, unable to admit that their policy had caused this flight into Victoria, used ridicule and false propaganda to break the 'strike', which provoked unprecedented press attention and questions in three parliaments. The strike was not irrational. Since 1936 legislation had empowered the Board to remove Aborigines to reserves, and the quarantine imposed by police during an outbreak of polio in January 1938 had proved that people could be forcibly confined at Cumeroogunga. The community was already angry about the new manager's use of police to expel 'unauthorised' residents. Cumeroogunga folk had long resented Board control of benefit payments and wages earned by minors; the recent compulsory deduction of half the 5s endowment for the scanty ration given to needy children had caused real hardship in many households. Moreover, the new manager had warned many parents he would enforce the Board's long-standing policy of removing children for a brief institutional training before apprenticing them to years of domestic service. Parents had been unable to intervene or even locate children taken earlier, who had endured miserable conditions with distant employers. Older people remembered several 'raids' when police assisted Board officers to remove children forcibly. Everyone knew which girls had escaped in 1919 by swimming the Murray.

The strikers wanted a public investigation of serious grievances: the leasing of their land and destruction of their homes; the inferior education and lack of job training at Cumeroogunga; and the inadequacy of Board rations, worth much less than unemployment relief. They told Victorian newspapers 'we might as well be hungry here as over there'. Doug

Nicholls, then a famed Melbourne football player, said his relatives were better off in Victoria, where they could qualify for the dole after three months' residence.

Meanwhile they had only fish, rabbits, and a little food and money collected by Cooper's league in Melbourne. Ellen vividly described their hunger, anxiety and discomfort in the nearly flooded camps after 'Eddy moved over to be with the people. He was their preacher and he said he ought to be with them, to preach when they needed him'. At a public meeting on 26 February 1939 Eddy told the press how the new manager had antagonised residents. The *Shepparton News* gave details:

> Pastor E. Atkinson of the Church of Christ said that as a religious and spiritual adviser of his people for 28 years he had been forced to leave the station, as the manager told him to remain neutral and not to help the people who had left. He had then crossed the river, 14 days after the others, as he had been entrusted with money for his people's food, and he considered the manager unfair. The people had suffered much from persecution by the manager since last October, when a petition for the removal of Mr McQuiggan had been sent to the Board. They objected strongly to brutal remarks and insults addressed to them.

The Board refused to consider any inquiry until the strikers came home. After six weeks Cooper and other elders persuaded many to return to test the Board's good faith. On 22 April the press reported that twenty-two familes had again returned to Barmah because of the manager's intimidation. Because they 'belonged' across the Murray all were still denied the dole, but on 26 July the Victorian Minister for Sustenance approved relief for five families, pending an inquiry, 'since Aborigines should have the same sustenance rights as white men'. The Victorian Board publicly protested that this would encourage more Aborigines to immigrate, and that Aborigines would desert the Lake Tyers station to obtain the dole.

On 11 October a second Aboriginal deputation urged Victorian Ministers to grant sustenance for all and provide a school for the twenty-eight children being taught by Eddy's niece, Hillus Briggs, because the Barmah school was overcrowded. They claimed entitlement because Cumeroogunga workers had long paid Victorian taxes on their earnings for four months each year. The Ministers refused, announcing that the New South Wales Board had assured them that conditions at Cumeroogunga were very comfortable. On 1 November this Board announced that no inquiry was needed.

In fact the New South Wales Public Service Board had conducted a confidential investigation of Board administration in 1938. The report, released in 1940, strongly criticised the leasing of Cumeroogunga and recommended major reforms. The manager was removed and the Board itself was reconstituted as an Aborigines Welfare Board. But wartime restrictions prevented renovation of reserves and delayed plans for vocational training, a major focus of the supposedly new policy of 'assimilation'.

Wartime manpower needs, and the bitter anger of many strikers determined never to return, encouraged migration to the developing towns of Mooroopna and Shepparton. But in these and other fruit-growing centres permanent jobs and standard housing were always scarce. In May 1941 Melbourne newspapers criticised the riverbank camps, where up to 300 Aborigines lived in the picking season. Ellen's sister, Mrs Shadrach James, one of the few able to rent standard housing in Mooroopna, wrote a spirited reply: it was ridiculous to expect pickers to 'build elaborate homes during their few weeks stay'. She reminded the public of the Aboriginal war effort: this community had given many fighting men and had freely offered their services to raise funds for the Red Cross and the local hospital.

Two-thirds of the Cumeroogunga community were now in Victoria and as always the Atkinsons went where Eddy saw the greatest need:

> When we left Cummera to get work we were all at Barmah. Then we came out here to Mooroopna to work in the orchards at the fruit drying. We were all out there. We used to have the old organ there and have services out in the orchard. Lovely, it was. Sixty or so would come. Then my husband held Sunday School under a big plum tree. They all used to come. My husband used to preach. He had a licence to marry people of our colour.

In 1940 many Aborigines found well-paid factory work in Melbourne. The Atkinsons soon followed. Eddy had spent a fortnight at Coranderrk in 1910 and Ellen had visited there as a small child (she remembered 'the raspberries there and the lovely jam the old women made'), but aside from the recent Cumeroogunga migrants they had few acquaintances in the Victorian Aboriginal community. It did not matter. Their church work was welcomed by people who treated them as kin:

> When Muriel was about 17 she went to work in Melbourne. Eddy, the boys and I went down to Gippsland, near Lake Tyers, for three months, with the organ. We took singing and church to those people. They'd never had it before. They were kind to us down there. They called us brother and sister, aunty and uncle. They knew of my family. I'd never been there before; it was lovely, near Lakes Entrance. We'd never seen the sea. The boys took a collection and paid Muriel's fare there on the bus.

For a while they lived in Melbourne, where their son Lawrie became a noted footballer. Eddy's church services, held in various homes, deeply influenced his nephew, Doug Nicholls.

During the war years Cumeroogunga had only 150 residents, mostly invalids and elderly folk. Eddy and Ellen had returned there by November 1941, when *Pix* magazine published a brief biography of Edwin Atkinson, described as an ordained minister of the Church of Christ 'licensed to marry Aboriginal people of that district'. He was an expert mechanic and builder who earned his own living as a bush worker and seasonal factory hand. Their comfortable home contained a radio and they now had an old car.

The car enabled Eddy to visit the thriving Aboriginal church in Melbourne. The Churches of Christ paid Doug Nicholls an honorarium when he became its pastor in 1944, but Eddy still received no pay. He and Ellen were now grandparents. The last of their older relatives — the pioneers of Cumeroogunga — was dead by 1947. Ironically, Eddy and a nephew were able to farm a portion of the reserve once again, as tenants of the lease-holder:

> Les Briggs and Eddy used to have shares growing tomatoes at Cummera. They shared in the profits. A drunk from Balranald wrecked the garden once. Eddy went to him (he was always gentle) and talked. Eddy gave him a Bible, and he carried it always. He couldn't read, but had people read it to him. When men asked him to the pub he'd hold up the Bible and tell them 'No, I'm a Christian'. That was another soul Eddy saved. Eddy never turned a drunk away, always asked them home with him and looked after them. He converted a lot. I always speak to drunks on the street when they come up calling me aunty. I don't like people who won't speak. It's wrong to be ashamed of your own people.

Their last years at Cumeroogunga were rewarding. In 1943 the division between AIM and Church of Christ adherents was healed when Eddy and Ellen, the station teachers and the Barmah missionary conducted united services at both churches to pray for the men away at war. Over at Mooroopna, AIM representatives led services at the home of old Thomas James, and later at the home of his son, Shadrach, husband of Ellen's sister, Maggie.

The riverbank camps between Mooroopna and Shepparton became permanent as postwar housing shortages drove many Aborigines out of Melbourne. They were exploited as a convenient pool of seasonal labour, but employers and local councils refused to provide facilities for them. Workers would not and could not retreat to Cumeroogunga when not wanted, as they had done for half a century. From 1939 to 1959 they reared their families in bag huts in an area flooded two or three times a year. Those who built more substantial homes risked all they owned, as they had no secure tenure and could be evicted at any time. For twenty years the Rodney Shire Council complained that these camps threatened the health of local citizens, but it refused to provide sanitary carts or remove garbage. Campers had to supply these services and carry all their water from the river.

In June 1946 Shadrach James, as secretary of the Aboriginal Progressive Association of Victoria, led a campaign to persuade the Victorian Government to erect a church and community centre and provide housing at reasonable rentals. On 8 November the press reported that Pastor Eddy Atkinson and his wife had come from Cumeroogunga as 'missionaries' to the Mooroopna community. He was described as a keen self-taught student of theology who had served as lay preacher for twenty-five years. The public was reminded that he had led Aboriginal football teams to premiership. His wife was 'an organist of ability' who had trained and led Aboriginal choirs. They were appointed by the Aborigines Mission

Committee of the Churches of Christ, which planned to build Eddy a church to his own specifications. Eddy hoped to form a council of Aborigines to manage the church, then 'we will endeavour to bring them together to conduct their own affairs'.

The Minister who headed the Victorian Board had visited three months earlier. He now announced plans to buy Daish's Paddock, the only area on two miles of riverbank which was never submerged. This 150 acre (60 ha) site would provide campers with homes, gardens and pasture for cows. In December 1947 these plans were abandoned. A Board report had declared that 'the majority were legally white people . . . and consequently the Board has no jurisdiction over them nor responsibility for them'. Ironically, Shadrach James had just been appointed as the first Aboriginal member, but as the Board met only once a year he had little influence. Policy was controlled by the Minister, his Under-Secretary and a clerk. Daish's Paddock became the shire rubbish tip. The Aboriginal 'humpies' remained. Only the widowed sisters Ellen and Maggie eventually saw the completion of the church and government-built homes their husbands had worked for.

Local resentment of the immigrants increased as the camps grew. In March 1947 the press quoted Doug Nicholls' reports of victimisation by police and increasing discrimination in cafés and recreational facilities. Local councillors retorted that the formerly 'benevolent police policy' now had to be 'modified'. The council could not control Aboriginal campers (estimated at 'six hundred' in picking season) as they were on government land outside the municipal boundary. Local citizens wanted this area for a park. The press also interviewed Eddy Atkinson, who upheld his nephew's charges of growing prejudice. Aborigines could not 'mix socially' with town dwellers. Their football team, which had won last year's premiership, was now barred from local competition. He had 117 children in his Sunday School. The Aborigines' only social centre was his church, described by the reporter as 'three walls and a roof made of hessian, and a few forms'.

Yet when Aunty Ellen reminisced in 1961, as we sweltered in the house which consumed her income, she recalled her years on the riverbank as a time of financial and emotional security, something she had not known since her youth on Cumeroogunga:

> Eddy preached all for nothing over there. When we came over here the church paid him £3 a week. It wasn't much, as we had our family to care for. Our people used to live down on the riverbank here. They had nice little houses — huts really — that they built themselves. It was lovely and cool there, and we didn't have to worry for the rent. Our people were all together, helping each other. We had a place Eddy built — nice it was, too. Lino and furniture and everything . . . But when the floods came we often had to carry our belongings and move, and then go back and rebuild the huts and put more earth on the floor and the lino down again. Our people are all good swimmers: we were all taught to be able to swim across the Murray! The little children used to swim in the floods. They never got drowned . . . We built a big bough shelter for the church — as big as this lounge room. We

swept it out every day. It was so cool, we used to put tables in and have our meals there sometimes . . . We had socials and singing. Eddy used to have a half-ton truck, to get round to the people. He used to be asked to preach at different churches, and we had a family choir. We were asked to sing at all the different churches: Geoff and his father were tenors, Lawrie a bass, Muriel a soprano, and Daisy and me altos . . . We used to have a concert party that travelled by bus around the towns. The men all played guitars, Muriel on the piano, Geoff always played the gum leaves — people liked that. We all sang.

The next generation of Cumeroogunga folk continued William Cooper's political activism through the organisations he and William Ferguson had founded. In 1943 Eddy had contested the election (won by Ferguson) for a seat on the New South Wales Board. But the two Aboriginal members had as little influence on policy as Shadrach James on the Victorian Board.

The extension of the Federal franchise to some Aborigines — those entitled to vote in the States — gave some hope of political change in 1949. In May, Eddy and Ellen were among the twenty who interviewed the Minister for the Interior in Canberra. Their deputation, led by Ferguson and Shadrach James, sought voting rights for all Aborigines and an Aboriginal member of Parliament. They urged the Commonwealth to take control of Aboriginal affairs in all States, replace police protectors with Aboriginal welfare officers and administrators, and undertake development schemes modelled on postwar reconstruction programs. The Minister said Federal control had been rejected by a recent Premiers' Conference and an earlier referendum. He was sufficiently impressed to recall four women delegates to discuss the role Aboriginal women might take in administration of the Northern Territory, the only area where the Commonwealth had jurisdiction.

In August 1949 Eddy and Ellen were among the delegates from all over Victoria who met at Shepparton to interview the Federal member, John McEwen, who was deputy leader of the Country Party. He offered to introduce a private Bill for the referendum needed to establish an Aboriginal electorate. But the Commonwealth rejected all appeals for direct Aboriginal representation in parliament because of 'constitutional difficulties'.

Eddy and Ellen could vote in Commonwealth elections from 1949. But they did not live to see the adoption of some of their ideas by a Commonwealth Government department in the 1970s. In their last years they were busy with local problems. Aboriginal campers were still denied aid in Victoria, and police were increasingly used to control them. Victoria was not represented at the 1951 Commonwealth conference which adopted a national policy of assimilation. The government declared there was 'no native problem in Victoria'. When Aboriginal organisations protested, the minister retorted that the Board was only responsible for nine 'fullblood Aborigines'. Conditions in New South Wales were little better. There were no improvements at Cumeroogunga. The new Board's assimilation policy aimed at dispersing such 'segregated' communities. Cumeroogunga was to be closed in 1950 but the shire council publicly opposed resettlement of the eighty residents at Mathoura. Only three families (including Ellen's sister Louisa) consented to be relocated in nearby towns. After the station was closed in 1953 the population of the unsupervised reserve increased. But the land was not theirs to use.

The Mooroopna community lost homes and belongings in the disastrous floods of March 1950 and the State Relief Committee provided tents. The press reported that the 'grateful Aborigines' declared they had 'never been better housed'. Eight months later Eddy and Shadrach assisted Housing Commission officials to prepare a report on their needs. Eddy explained the history of Cumeroogunga. There they once had homes and work but 'when employment ceased they could not live'. Shadrach, who had led a vain deputation to ask the Victorian Premier for housing, argued that the government had an obligation to assist Aborigines 'because of earlier dispossession'. Both pointed out that Aborigines were relatively well off at Mooroopna, where their labour was needed for eight months at the tobacco factory plus four months at the cannery. Officials were appalled by the huts and deplored the council's refusal to provide any facilities. They reported that the three camps were flooded at least twice a year. Occupants then had to 'move the makeshift shelters on to Daish's Paddock until the owner drives them out'.

A second official report described the Atkinsons' home in 'the best camp' in April 1951. Eddy, Ellen, Muriel, and two young orphaned grandsons occupied a neatly built three-roomed hut lined with plaster sheets. Linoleum covered the earth floor. Next door was the equally neat wooden home of their daughter Daisy, who had trained as a nurse. The report said Ellen was eager to move to a drier site because of her severe asthma, but Eddy insisted he must be housed near the people who needed him. The local Ministers' Fraternal supported his plea, saying Eddy was not merely spiritual leader but 'constantly at hand to aid in all domestic affairs'. Eddy had a church salary of £3 10s a week — but the Housing Commission rental was £3 10s a week. Officials admitted this was too high for Aboriginal camp-dwellers, who could pay no more than £1 5s. But the Board and the Housing Commission rejected all pleas for special housing for Aborigines. Because church supporters guaranteed the pastor's rental the Atkinsons were among the first offered standard housing. Eddy was then sixty-three.

Ellen lost her husband on 2 November 1952, 'just one year after we came to this house — after all his years of struggle. Eddy worked so hard for the people. The doctor told me his heart just gave out. So few of our people live to get the pension'. The townfolk were sympathetic: 'When my dear husband died the neighbours sent food. Everyone was good. I didn't have to cook for a week'. She told me Eddy was buried at Mooroopna: 'We couldn't take him home as he would have wanted'. I assumed that the expense was too great, but learned that this was not the real reason why Eddy was the first elder to be buried away from Cumeroogunga. In the 1960s the Victorian Aboriginal community always united to raise fund for funeral arrangements, and many were buried at the reserve cemeteries where their forebears lay. People still believed it was important for their dead to 'go home', 'lie in their own country', 'be buried where they were born'. I was later told that Ellen had been persuaded to let the church bury Eddy in town. A sympathetic clergyman recalled that a local church committee had been 'triumphant at breaking this burial tradition. They thought it superstition'.

At first Pastor Nicholls travelled to take services in his uncle's church. Ellen vainly urged officials to appoint her son Geoff as pastor. Instead ministers from Shepparton and Melbourne took control. The mission board's paternalism had long annoyed many Aborigines. In 1950 its secretary had publicly complained of their alleged drunkenness and immorality, asserting that they must be reformed and 'absorbed into ordinary society'. His *Argus* article had also ridiculed Shadrach James's insistence that special housing was necessary.

Meanwhile the AIM was recruiting youngsters from Cumeroogunga and Mooroopna for its missionary training college. An AIM official reported that seventy-five Aborgines attended the evening services conducted by Shadrach and Geoff at Mooroopna in June 1954. But in August the press reported that the Mooroopna church was divided. Shadrach's 'breakaway movement' had begun as an attempt to lead the whole community 'away from the Churches of Christ Mission Committee', but most church members had 'responded to the appeal of Pastor Doug Nicholls'. Followers of Shadrach's 'non-denominational church' met at his home. He attended the next AIM convention, but the movement collapsed on his death in 1956. Years later a Church of Christ official told me that he had blamed Shadrach's personal ambitions at the time, but afterwards understood that most members had wanted 'an independent church, their own to control. Yet we were too paternalistic to trust them to manage it'. This division of her family and community grieved Ellen. She was grateful for the genuine kindness of some clergymen and wanted Eddy's church to survive as his memorial. But she also resented the paternalism and regretted that Geoff was not helped to carry on his father's work.

In 1954 the press was still criticising official neglect of the Mooroopna camps, the largest 'Aboriginal settlement' in Victoria. The New Deal Committee organised by Geoff's friend and employer, Don Howe, and a few other citizens had helped eight families to rent Housing Commission homes. In 1952 the Commission and the Board had rejected the council's offer to sell Daish's Paddock for home sites: both refused to build 'a segregated settlement'. A 1955 council deputation was told the Board could not aid 'part-castes' and the Commission could not house anyone at less than standard rental charges.

In 1956 public concern forced the government to commission a State-wide inquiry. It was conducted by a retired Chief Stipendiary Magistrate, Charles McLean, assisted by the Board's clerk. He spent only a few hours on country visits and then talked mostly to officials. When Don Howe learned McLean was 'told nothing but the bad things' about the Mooroopna community, he took him to meet Geoff Atkinson, selected a year or so earlier to manage Howe's farm and box-making industry, which employed fourteen Aborigines. Geoff and his wife convinced McLean that the 59 adults and 107 children still camped on the riverbank and rubbish tip could be rehoused and employed as successfully as the 31 adults and 55 children already in town houses. McLean's 1957 report strongly criticised local attitudes to the hundreds of Aborigines whose seasonal work was 'of considerable importance to the district'. Most citizens' only concern was that they 'should be kept out of the town, in the interest of "tidiness", and that someone else should do something about them'. He also criticised the Board. The government accepted his advice that it be reconstituted as an Aborigines Welfare Board to administer a policy of assimilation for all persons of Aboriginal descent.

Soon after McLean's 1956 visit police had arranged committal of twenty-four children as State Wards. The whole community was disturbed, for they had always dreaded the removal of their children to institutions. As Aunty Ellen said, 'It would have been better to help their parents keep them. Those mothers were doing their best. You can't keep children clean on a rubbish tip, when you have to carry every drop of water half a mile.' In July 1957 the new Board enlisted police aid to control the Mooroopna camps. Huts on the rubbish tip were demolished in October, although the Rumbalara 'staging settlement' was not ready for occupancy until May 1958. The new Board's use of police to evict campers, and their employment of an official to supervise the domestic life of tenants in town homes reminded older Aborigines of the past and taught a new generation that government aid was not given without control and tutelage.

Innumerable reports over twenty years had attributed the squalor of the camps to the personal and 'racial' deficiencies of Aborigines. Some of this was caused by unwillingness to provide facilities and a hope that the campers would be put elsewhere, out of sight. Some of it was deserved. Aunty Ellen acknowledged and regretted the failings of some members of her community. She also understood that 'the younger ones never had what we had, our homes at Cumeroogunga'. Without the comfort of her faith she too might have 'gone like so many other women in drink and running around'. She had shared a lifetime of poverty and prejudice. She did not criticise those who had been broken by it.

During that long-ago summer she instructed me about the obligations of marriage: 'It's really the woman that holds a family together . . . a mother never stops battling, even for grandchildren'. She warned me that motherhood was not easy: 'You try to bring your children up right, and do your best for them, but you never know which way they'll go'. Aunty Ellen was proud of all her children. She saw their strengths and weaknesses clearly, as mothers do; she grieved for what life had done to them, as mothers must. In Geoff, her firstborn, she saw again Eddy's unassuming gentleness, his craving for education, his piety and musicianship. But Geoff's gifts could not find expression in a church career. For his generation, government housing and educational assistance had come too late:

Geoff never got help from the government. He made a home for himself and his family, working full time box-making at Don Howe's farm. His father Eddy was a bush carpenter, and his father Aaron before him. They built boats and everything, back at Cummera. Geoff used to play the violin, but his hands now with the box-making won't let him . . .

Poor Geoff, he's not an educated man, which you need to be a preacher. His father wasn't either, but Eddy had some education — he was taught by his uncle — more schooling than our children. Eddy sat up late, reading his Bible over and over. He never had training in the Church, but he used to attend ministers' meetings in Melbourne. He learned at conferences. We all went to one up near the Queensland border, with Maggie and her husband (he was a smart man), when Eddy was speaker . . .

Geoff hasn't had the education that's wanted for a pastor now. He studies, but he can't do it; he has no time working all day, and he can't leave his work. There wasn't the chance when he was young, and he can't get the education now. Geoff's a good man, like his father, but he's just a battler.

Only her grandchildren benefited from the changes in policy that her generation had fought for. I was glad that she lived to see a grandson attending a Melbourne grammar school, and that she learned before her death that Cumeroogunga would again be farmed by descendants of the pioneers.

There was no envy in Aunty Ellen. She rejoiced at any Aboriginal achievement, feeling 'proud when one of our own does well'. Of her own family she said, 'We've always been battlers, not successful like some. It's a hard go on women's wages and what our men can earn. But we've always had happiness.' She was pleased that 'my family has a good reputation as workers among the whites'. It mattered more to her that 'my family are proud of being Aborigines'.

A battler was a good thing to be in Mooroopna twenty years ago. Aborigines and other residents thought differently about many things. But all agreed that Aunty Ellen was 'a fine woman, a real battler'.

Additional reading

Barwick, D.E. (1972). Coranderrk and Cumeroogunga: pioneers and policy. In T.S. Epstein and D.H. Penny (eds), *Opportunity and response: Case studies in economic development,* pp. 10-68. Hurst, London
—— (1981). Cooper, William (1861?-1941). *Australian Dictionary of Biography,* vol. 8, 107-8
—— (forthcoming). *Rebellion at Coranderrk.* Australian National University Press, Canberra
Cato, N. (1976). *Mister Maloga: Daniel Matthews and his mission, Murray River, 1864-1902.* University of Queensland Press, St Lucia
Clark, M.T. (1965). *Pastor Doug: The story of an Aboriginal leader.* Lansdowne Press, Melbourne

14

Bandeiyama: She Keeps Going

Betty Meehan

They say of Bandeiyama that she is a 'good hunter', that 'you can't stop her from hunting', that she 'keeps going'. She is much more than that, for as a middle-aged Anbarra woman she makes a subtle but substantial contribution to the community in which she lives. The Anbarra are a community of Gidjingali-speaking Aborigines who own land and live at various home bases around the mouth of An-gatja Wana or 'big river' (Blyth River) in Arnhem Land. I got to know Bandeiyama not so much by talking to her — for she had little spare time for that — as by being with her and watching her. In a sense I am her apprentice and I learn my lessons by observation and participation; Bandeiyama has taught me most of what I know about the life of hunters. It has been my good fortune to have the perfect teacher, for she and I share an interest in food, in obtaining high quality products and preparing them carefully. Of the mature Anbarra women, Bandeiyama is regarded as *djindjana magun-gun* (a 'number one' gatherer). For a fifty-four-year-old (in 1982), delicately built woman (150 cm tall weighing 42 kg*) she tackles all foraging activities with skill and energy. She is always the perfectionist, intent on carrying out what she considers to be the correct method of collecting, cooking and serving food. 'Right way' is a comment she often uses. I am reminded repeatedly during my apprenticeship that she will not tolerate shoddy workmanship.

I first met Bandeiyama during 1958 at the government settlement called Maningrida, on the eastern bank of the Liverpool River in Arnhem Land. I was then a schoolteacher and the wife of research student Les Hiatt, who was there to carry out anthropological research. Maningrida had been established in May 1957, only twelve months before we arrived. Almost immediately Aborigines from the surrounding area had come to settle there. Bandeiyama, with other Gidjingali-speaking people, had

---

* 5ft, 6st 7lb.

joined the throng, leaving her own estate at the mouth of An-gatja Wana. By then she had married her second husband, the Djunawunya man Gurrmanamana, who later became a friend and teacher of my husband. In 1957, Bandeiyama had one daughter (by her first, then deceased, husband) called Djinbor who was then about ten years old and two sons by Gurrmanamana: Gumugun (five years old) and Nganmarra (four years old).

Bandeiyama comes from Madang-adjirra, a site distinguished by a cluster of large, shady fig trees and a deep, cool, freshwater well, which lies on the coast on the eastern bank of An-gatja Wana. One of her brothers is dead. The other, Mundrrug-Mundrrug, lives today in the same community as Bandeiyama. Her only other sibling, an older sister, Marrkoweitj, is also married to Gurrmanamana. Both women were previously married to an aged man, Anborama, to whom Marrkoweitj had borne a son, Aningarra. When Anborama died, some time before Maningrida had been established, Gurrmanamana became their husband.

My contact with Bandeiyama during 1958, and during my second trip to Maningrida in 1960, was only casual. One reason for this was that we were all living on a government settlement — a difficult social situation for any kind of interpersonal communication. Also, my substantial camp, luxurious compared with what I was to have in later years, tended to place a barrier between me and the Aboriginal community. I spent a lot of time with the three other European people who lived at Maningrida and with visitors who arrived occasionally by boat and later, when the airstrip was completed, by plane. My husband, whose intellectual interests lay in the area of social structure and kinship, carried out much of his research in our tent with one or two, sometimes more, consultants. These were nearly always men, and normally they came without their wives and families.

During 1958 I established the first school at Maningrida. Informal lessons were conducted in the bush structure made from corrugated iron and chicken wire or, more frequently, outside, either in the forest that surrounds the settlement or on the beaches that flank its northern boundaries. I was also responsible for much of the photography associated with my husband's work, and I became interested in the dancing performed by women, recording several local song cycles. With Ingrid Drysdale, the manager's wife, I regularly visited the leprosarium she had established a few kilometres to the west of the settlement and there helped her tend to the patients. These activities, plus the normal drudgery of household chores (made considerably more tedious because we were camping) kept me extremely busy.

At the end of our 1960 sojourn at Maningrida, Bandeiyama gave birth to her fourth child, Ngurraba Ngurraba, to whom she gave the additional name, Betty, after me though we had not yet established a close personal relationship. I was present at the birth, and somewhat over-awed by the experience, which took place in a tiny, one-roomed bark house in the Gidjingali portion of the settlement. It was a fully Aboriginal event; the European sister only saw the baby the next morning when Bandeiyama walked to the hospital to show it to her.

I cried as the old and rattling Lockheed aircraft took me away from Maningrida — cried for all my friends, but mainly for Gurrmanamana and his older brother An-gabarraparra because they were the people I had come to know best. I still regret that in 1958 and 1960 I did not get to know Bandeiyama and the other Anbarra women better than I did.

When I left Maningrida I did not think that I would ever return. Little did I realise how some future events would alter radically the lives of my friends there. These events, plus changes in my own life, meant that I eventually returned to Maningrida, where I became familiar with the

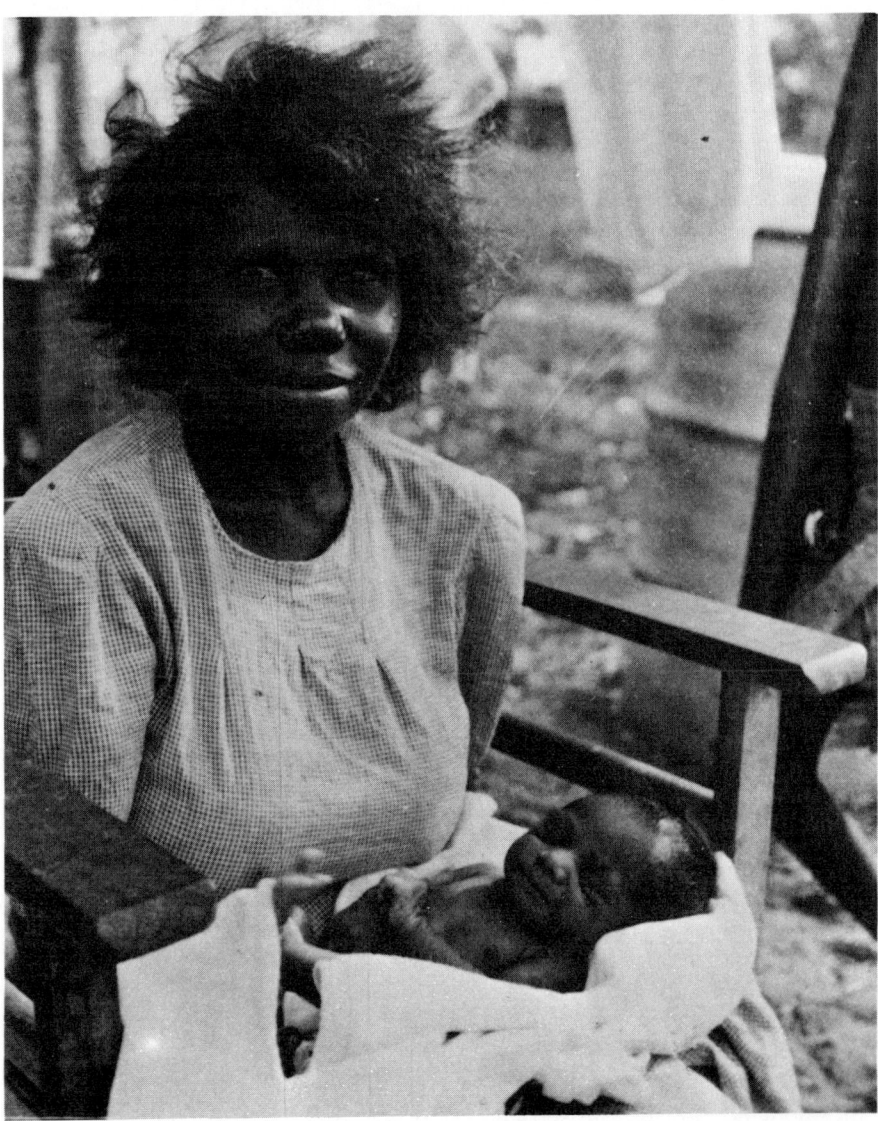

Bandeiyama with her newborn daughter Ngurraba Ngurraba at Maningrida in 1960 (Photograph by Betty Meehan and Les Hiatt)

Anbarra, Bandeiyama's community, in their own country. In this situation I grew to know and understand Bandeiyama in her own right, as a woman in her correct milieu, deeply immersed in the hunting life.

Between 1960 and my next visit to Maningrida ten years later, my marriage had ended and I had become an anthropologist myself. By 1970 I felt a strong urge to return to the north as an independent scholar to see again the people whose lives I had shared in the past. I also hoped that once there I would be able to discuss with them the possibility of carrying out some research on Anbarra territory. I had no notion then that I would be able to do this in their company for I knew that they still lived in the settlement, and I did not consider that this living pattern would change. I did hope, however, that Bandeiyama, Gurrmanamana and their family might be persuaded to camp with me for a few weeks at An-gatja Wana, to take a 'holiday', and to tell me about what life used to be like when they lived and hunted there.

I recall vividly the two hours it took to return me from Darwin to Maningrida in September 1970. The Connellan Airways flight was smooth; a heavy haze hung over the horizon as Aborigines below went about their annual practice of burning the countryside, producing a familiar patchwork pattern on the ground. I was apprehensive. It was nine years since I had been at Maningrida. Would the Anbarra people remember me? Would they allow me to visit their territory and would they want to come with me? More importantly, would they talk to me? I need not have worried. Bandeiyama was one of the first people to greet me when I arrived. Instantly I relaxed. She smiled at me in her warm, shy way and made me feel welcome, as did the men that I had known so well before. By now Bandeiyama had six children: two more girls, Gindjerrkama and Ngalimurra, and one more boy, Brama, had been born since 1960. None of the Anbarra had lived at the major Anbarra home base, Kopanga (said to be named after the Macassan town of Koepang), since I left Maningrida, and my friends were excited at the prospect of visiting their own country after such a long time.

Early on in my stay, Bandeiyama asked about my husband. I told her that he was well but that we were no longer married, that he had a new wife, and I a new husband, Rhys Jones. She appeared to take this news with disapproval and for some time I thought that she might reject me because of my changed status. I assured her that I was still 'good friends' with my ex-husband — that there was 'no trouble'. She grudgingly accepted my reassurances, but the matter was to be raised again when I came back to Maningrida in 1972 to work with Rhys.

There seems to be a belief amongst the Anbarra community that if a marriage breaks up, it is usually the fault of the woman, who has a boyfriend somewhere with whom she wishes to live. This view may be related to the fact that many Anbarra men have wives who are much younger than themselves and these husbands are constantly fearful that their wives are seeking young lovers. My own interpretation at that time of Bandeiyama's behaviour was that she assumed that I had left my husband for a younger man. The reverse situation did not seem to have occurred to her nor had the possibility that both parties in a marriage might have welcomed separation.

A few days after I arrived in 1970 I left Maningrida for Kopanga with a group of Anbarra people, including Bandeiyama. Perched on the back of a truck we all bounced along on tight Toyota springs over a track which had been made rough by the herds of buffalo which infest the area. We had some trouble proceeding. Logs had to be removed from the road and once we moved out onto the clay plains of An-gatja Wana, the thick, waist high grass made the going difficult. We arrived at our destination in the late afternoon and set up our camp. There were three hearth groups: Bandeiyama's contained her husband, three of her daughters, Ngurraba Ngurraba, Gindjerrkama and Ngalimurra, one of her sons, Brama, and me. On one side of us Bandeiyama's classificatory mother-in-law, Manalawula, camped with her young son; the other side was occupied by Marraginyaginya (Manalawula's daughter), her husband and their two daughters. We all slept beneath our mosquito nets on the sandy beach, just above the high tide mark. That first night, Bandeiyama wailed for her co-wife, her older sister, Marrkoweitj, who had chosen not to accompany us.

I was delighted with the few days I spent at Kopanga for it allowed me to begin the process of becoming re-acquainted with my friends — this time on their own land. The men went fishing with lines and spears. I saw pandanus plants collected and watched Bandeiyama manufacture an ingenious implement called a *djin-garngirra* which was used to remove the deeply embedded pandanus kernels. We gathered freshwater tortoises from the dry mud of the freshwater swamps. Crabs were roasted on the coals and Bandeiyama produced tasty dampers cooked in the ashes of our fires. We travelled on foot to Djunawunya, Gurrmanamana's country, where beneath the deep shade of a casuarina tree we cooked a wallaby. As the tide receded there, I accompanied Bandeiyama and Manalawula on my first shellfish gathering expedition. First we looked for the attractive tapestry bivalve, *diyama* (*Tapes hiantina*), which Bandeiyama said had been available here when last they visited the place. But we found none and collected mussels and crabs instead. On the return trip Bandeiyama carried a sugar-bag half full of mussels on her head, her youngest child, Ngalimurra, on her shoulder, a large billy-can full of shellfish in one hand plus all the paraphernalia that the women normally have with them: tomahawk, file, pipe and matches. I was horrified by the load that the tiny Bandeiyama was to carry 4 km, for Ngalimurra refused to walk. So I took the bag of shellfish and carried it on my head. This was the first time that I remember feeling a sense of responsibility towards my 'sister', as I had been taught to call Bandeiyama, and it marked the beginning of a deepening of our relationship. Sisters, real and classificatory, have a close and pleasant relationship in Anbarra society. They co-operate on gathering expeditions, give generously to each other and spend a lot of time together talking.

We returned to Maningrida after our short 'holiday' at Kopanga. Bandeiyama resumed her demanding job as a cook in the town's communal kitchen and Gurrmanamana once again took up his position with the settlement carpenter, though a few comments made by Bandeiyama and Gurrmanamana before I returned to Canberra indicated that they were somewhat disillusioned with their life at Maningrida. Bandeiyama had suffered several miscarriages and lost one full-term baby since she had moved there. They both thought that too many 'stranger' Aborigines occupied Maningrida, and they blamed their misfortunes and sickness on the over-crowding. In spite of their misgivings about town life I fully expected both Bandeiyama and Gurrmanamana to be living at Maningrida when I returned later to do my fieldwork.

In July 1972 when I returned to Maningrida to carry out some research, the 'outstation movement' was well underway. About 1970 many Aborigines in northern Australia who had for many years lived on church missions, government settlements or cattle stations began to move back into the bush, usually to their own territory, where they established what have become known as 'outstations'. On many of these outstations people hunted and gathered food for themselves as well as maintaining contact with the wider Australian society from which they derived some goods, and minimal medical and educational services. I was delighted to discover that Bandeiyama and her family, plus a considerable number of other Gidjingali people, were living on the eastern bank of An-gatja Wana at a site called Ngalidjibama, where the important ceremony Kunapipi had been in progress for about six months. Bandeiyama's two elder sons, Gumugun and Nganmarra, along with several other young men, were being initiated into the secrets of this cult, and Bandeiyama and Gurrmanamana were camped nearby to support them.

I was accompanied on this trip by Rhys and, as it transpired, Les Hiatt was also visiting the community for a few days just after we arrived. More discussion about my marital status ensued and much to my amusement (and a little to my chagrin) Gurrmanamana announced to the community that my first husband had given me to his 'younger brother', my second husband, and that he himself had acquired a younger wife; I had not caused any trouble. This story was totally acceptable to the Anbarra, who interpreted the supposed behaviour of my first husband as extremely generous and therefore commendable. After that the matter rested. I was exonerated; my second husband was accepted.

The next twelve months at An-gatja Wana were full of activity for me and the Anbarra community. Briefly, we lived at Ngalidjibama until August 1972, at Kopanga until the end of December 1972 and then at the wet-season site at Lalarr-gadjirripa until July 1973. During all of this time I was assisted and guided by Bandeiyama and members of her household. They accepted the responsibility for instructing me in the subtleties of their way of life and made sure that I did not get into any dangerous situations. Gurrmanamana was Rhys's older brother, and I was Bandeiyama's younger sister; I became her shadow whereas Rhys spent most of his time with the men. By now I had decided that I wanted to find out all I could about women's lives, particularly the details about their contribution to the economic life of the community. I learnt most of this under the tutelage of Bandeiyama and in the process developed a great respect for her knowledge and special talents.

She is what we would call in our society 'a good woman'. The Anbarra people recognise this quality in her too. Not only does she care for her family's needs exceedingly well, but she also participates in, and contributes substantially to all aspects of community life. In an Aboriginal setting this means providing food and craft items for mortuary and religious ceremonies as well as dancing when the schedule requires it and simply being in attendance. Bandeiyama possesses a highly developed sense of social responsibility.

Because of my special interest in diet this story about Bandeiyama is biased in that direction. I know more about her as a provider and preparer of food than I do about any other aspect of her life. This story is therefore only the first of several I hope to write about her.

During the year between July 1972 and July 1973, 7000 kg gross weight of shellfish were collected by the Anbarra people. Altogether, thirty species were chosen. One of these, *diyama*, was especially important, contributing about 4500 kg of the total weight. Anbarra women collected 2800 kg of that total weight.

When Bandeiyama's performance as a shell-gatherer is compared with that of other Anbarra women, she emerges as an outstanding provider. During a year, she collected *diyama* three times as often, gathered over four times the gross weight, walked three times as far to procure the species and spent four times as long engaged in that activity. The average weight she collected on each expedition was 6 kg greater than that accumulated by her colleagues. Bandeiyama's outstanding qualities as a provider of shellfish derive from a combination of her natural talent, her well-developed sense of responsibility towards the maintenance of her family and the obvious pleasure she derives from foraging activities.

By September 1972 we had all left the site of Ngalidjibama where the Kunapipi ceremony had taken place and were settled at Kopanga. The country was drying out, freshwater was becoming scarce and traditional plant foods, especially of the root and corm variety, were increasingly difficult to find. Most of the energy needs of the Anbarra during September were provided by European foods such as flour and sugar, but bush foods were also important in the diet. Bandeiyama provided a wide range of foods for the Anbarra cuisine during this month, including some European foods, but also fish, crabs, reptiles, fruits, nuts and vegetables. Her contribution represented 19 per cent of the total weight of all the food eaten by the Anbarra at Kopanga during that time, including that purchased from the store at Maningrida. Of the food derived from foraging activities alone, Bandeiyama procured 22 per cent. Anbarra women collectively contributed a massive 60 per cent of these non-European products; 35 per cent of this was provided by Bandeiyama.

Bandeiyama's outstanding performance as a gatherer is highlighted when it is examined in the total context of the events which affected her during the year. Her daughter, Djinbor, was pregnant when I arrived at Ngalidjibama in July 1972. Djinbor was still participating in shell gathering and other food gathering activities such as the collection and preparation of the plant food *natja (Cycas media)* but always in a low-key way, never exerting herself. Djinbor's baby girl, Gang-gabalinga, was born at Ngalidjibama on 11 August 1972, without complications. Henceforth the nursing mother gathered very little food and her family looked after her. Djinbor collected 9 kg of *diyama* early in September, but after that none at all until the middle of January 1973 when her baby was six months old. After this she began to participate increasingly in all foraging activities. Djinbor either carried her infant with her or left her in the care of one of the infant's grandmothers, Bandeiyama and Marrkoweitj, or with classificatory mothers, Ngurraba Ngurraba or Gindjerrkama. Between the middle of January and the middle of July 1973, Djinbor gathered *diyama* on twenty-two occasions as opposed to only once between July 1972 and January 1973.

By contrast, her mother, Bandeiyama, was a keen and persistent hunter during most of the year. She collected *diyama* eleven times up to the middle of January and nineteen more times until April 1973. After that, she gathered only small quantities though considerably more than Djinbor had done in the second half of 1972. Bandeiyama's foraging behaviour changed because she herself was pregnant.

At the end of December 1972, as the monsoon period approached, many people returned to the comforts of Maningrida to wait until the rain and winds had ceased. The rest of us, including Bandeiyama's household, moved to Lalarr-gadjirripa. Here we built a small waterproof and windproof settlement on the naked and exposed sand spit, which was flanked on its southern edge by a dense bank of dark-green mangrove trees. It was at this site that Bandeiyama's pregnancy became known. Early in May 1973 a boat arrived with the senior nursing sister from Maningrida aboard. She moved around the camp to see if anyone needed medical attention. Bandeiyama was pronounced to be about thirty-four weeks pregnant, though her advanced state was barely visible. The only indication that we had of her condition was that her foraging efforts had slackened slightly. The sister announced that Bandeiyama would have to go to Darwin because her blood pressure and haemoglobin were dangerously low. I was asked to discuss the matter with her and Gurrmanamana. I tried to explain the sister's position to them as clearly as possible. Both, however, were adamant that Bandeiyama should not go to Darwin, not even to Maningrida. They reminded me how she had lost several babies at Maningrida and how another one that had been flown to Darwin had died in the hospital soon after. They said that it was better for Bandeiyama to have her baby in the bush, in her own country, with all her relatives around her. I conveyed their decision to the nursing sister; she accepted it and left vitamin and iron tablets for Bandeiyama to take, which she did diligently and to good effect. When the sister again visited the outstation some weeks later she announced that Bandeiyama was in good health.

Pregnant Anbarra women were expected to slacken their foraging activities a little but Bandeiyama did so less than most others. Despite the fact that she no longer matched her earlier production efforts she still made a substantial contribution towards the subsistence of the Lalarr-gadjirripa community. She was never referred to as *djindjana mawa* ('lazy bugger'). In June 1973, Bandeiyama (in an advanced state of pregnancy) returned from the waterhole at Lalarr-gadjirripa carrying a flour drum containing 22 litres of water on her head. A few days later when a group of us were returning from the fish trap at Gunadjangga (2 km west of Lalarr-gadjirripa) Ngalimurra, Bandeiyama's youngest child (then aged four), insisted on being carried home on Bandeiyama's shoulder. A woman with us was disgusted, describing Ngalimurra as 'lazy'.

A few days before the end of July 1973 I visited Maganbal, another wet-season camp-site on the eastern side of An-gatja Wana, with Rhys and two young Anbarra men. On our way back in a canoe, late in the afternoon, we encountered a heavy squall. When we arrived at Lalarr-gadjirripa the Anbarra had already organised their houses to keep out the wind and rain. They were all 'cold'. Once more we were plunged into the wet season and again our little camp looked vulnerable. I recall with some distaste struggling along the beach in the dark carrying my pack and being hounded by platoons of mosquitoes that had obviously been revitalised by the change in the weather. Just as we entered our wind-torn tent and began to inspect the inevitable storm damage a gaggle of breathless children burst in wearing tragic expressions on their faces. Bandeiyama was sick; Bandeiyama wanted medicine for the baby pain in her belly; there had been a lot of blood. I felt weak with fear. All the sister's warnings about Bandeiyama's health came flooding back to me. Momentarily I lost my composure. If Bandeiyama had been so ill why had not someone gone to Maningrida? Why had they waited for me to return? There was nothing that I could do that they could not do. I went to see her. She lay in a specially constructed dome-shaped house draped with canvas and blankets. Its opening looked out to the sea. Inside, Bandeiyama was resting on her back with all but her head and shoulders hidden by a blanket. I questioned her about the 'bad pains'. She replied that they had only started as we arrived at Lalarr-gadjirripa. I asked her if she wanted me to call Maningrida on the two-way radio. She declined, saying that the sister could come to see the baby when it was born. She requested some 'cough medicine' and assured me that she was perfectly all right and told me not to worry. Her friend Dadbalak was tending to her needs and comforting her. Her husband, Gurrmanamana, her two eldest sons and a group of small children were sitting around a bright little fire which burned adjacent to the birth house. Their conversation was light-hearted and happy. The utter normality of the scene reassured me that all was well, that all present knew that everything was going as it should and that at this stage, at least, there was nothing to worry about. I decided that the young girls who brought me the erroneous news about Bandeiyama's condition were merely dramatising the event — something that young people in Anbarra society do frequently to create excitement.

Early next morning, after a night of fitful sleeping, I went to Bandeiyama's house. Her children were hovering around the door. A baby girl had been born during the night. Both mother and child were doing well and now this new member of the community was being inspected by the Lalarr-gadjirripa children. All were excited about the new *dalipa* (baby), each discussing what they would call her — 'mother', 'sister', 'daughter'? Bandeiyama was calmly allowing each child in turn to hold the dainty infant.

Jane, as Bandeiyama called her new baby, weighed 3 kg at birth. She was pretty with pink-grey coloured skin and thick, black, straight hair. Though I knew from conversations with Bandeiyama that she had not wanted another baby, she was a proud mother and Jane became the centre of attention in the little community at Lalarr-gadjirripa. I left within weeks of Jane's birth. Soon after my departure the Anbarra community moved to Kopanga. There, Jane died of influenza about six months later.

I returned to Kopanga briefly in October–November 1974. Bandeiyama did not look well; she was thin, and listless, very unlike the woman I had known a little over a year ago. Gurrmanamana said that she was still 'worrying for that baby' who had died.

I was shown the 'shade' (an open structure made from bush timber and roofed with branches) where the mortuary ceremonies for Jane had been held. The shelter stood abandoned at the northern end of Kopanga beach. I also saw the pandanus dilly-bag, kept in Bandeiyama's house, which held the baby's bones. Bandeiyama cried for her child most nights throughout my stay at Kopanga. She also suffered from headaches so much that I began to worry about her health. I discussed the matter with her husband. 'Same thing,' he said. He believed that her headaches were the result of the way she had struck her own head with axe and knife blades when she was mourning — a common way for women to show grief in Anbarra society. Bandeiyama's crown had become slightly bald and was criss-crossed with scar tissue from the many mournings she had been required to observe in her life. I also noted that she rarely carried things on her head anymore.

I do not wish to convey the impression that Bandeiyama had sat around moping during my 1974 visit to Kopanga. True she was not the lively, energetic, superior hunter that I remembered from 1973, but she was still a hard worker. It was rather that her style had changed. She continued to contribute substantially to the community, but I got the impression that she did so because it was her duty rather than because she derived pleasure from the activities and her mastery of them as she had done previously. It was obvious that the death of her baby had affected her; that physically and mentally she was demonstrating the severity of her grief.

Despite her generally depressed state of mind, we carried out some enjoyable hunting trips, some of which were new experiences for me. Bandeiyama seemed to brighten up during these expeditions and began to instruct me with her old skill and exactness. We gathered oysters from Matata-mayurripa, some inferior *diyama* from Ngatjarrabuka, and several times collected yams. All of these trips were satisfying as well as productive, and I felt relieved to see Bandeiyama behaving much more like her old self. But between trips her headaches and depression returned, making her low in spirits and uncommunicative. Sometimes she slept in camp all day, as if the exertion of a long and arduous hunting trip had left her exhausted.

Her eldest daughter, Djinbor, was also living at Kopanga at the time. She had a new baby called Cherylene. Increasingly, Bandeiyama was looking after Djinbor's small children, Polly, Cherylene and Olavi. Djinbor needed the assistance, but I think perhaps Cherylene had become for Bandeiyama a surrogate for her dead child Jane.

I was sad to leave Kopanga at the end of my fieldwork for again I did not know when I could return. Despite Gurrmanamana's insistence that Bandeiyama would soon be again a 'good hunter', I felt that in the months between July 1973 and October 1974 she had aged considerably. She had become frail and worn, more like her much older sister, Marrkoweitj. Perhaps she would be an 'old woman' when I next returned; perhaps she would be dead. But despite these uncertainties I derived some comfort from the fact that Bandeiyama was living on her own land, surrounded by a supportive group of close kin. There at least she possessed the basic necessities for what the Anbarra consider to be a good life.

It was 1978 before I returned to An-gatja Wana, though in the meantime Gurrmanamana came several times to Canberra as a member of the Australian Institute of Aboriginal Studies. On these visits I caught up on Anbarra gossip, the state of Bandeiyama's health and her family, and the identity of those Anbarra people who had died, as well as of those who had married and borne new babies. I picked up threads of my friendship with Bandeiyama quickly when I returned to Kopanga in 1978. Her situation had changed dramatically. Her family had grown in number — not because she had borne more children, but because she was fostering other people's. Djinbor had gone to live permanently in Darwin, leaving five of her children in her mother's care. In addition, Wanambi, son of Gurrmanamana's dead brother, had become a permanent resident in her camp. This meant that Bandeiyama's household now contained eight adults and seven children. Cherylene was the youngest and, Bandeiyama treated her as if she were her own child. Bandeiyama had regained much of the energy and enthusiasm she had so strikingly displayed during 1972–73, though her hair was now flecked with white and she seemed to tire more easily. This should have been no surprise, however: she was responsible for the day-to-day running of a large household. Her daughters, Ngurraba Ngurraba and Gindjerrkama, now adults, were able to give more help with household chores, but Bandeiyama still bore the main burden. Every day she carried water from the well, collected wood for household fires and made sure that each member of the family had enough to eat. Periodically there was a large wash to do. This was done with bar soap and a washing board at the waterhole. It often occurred to me as I watched her scrubbing away at a pair of Gurrmanamana's shorts or one of Ngalimurra's skirts that the Anbarra women had replaced one form of drudgery with another. Now that they had access to flour they collected their traditional vegetable foods less frequently. This meant that they had more leisure time. But with the acquisition of these new European foods they also began to wear clothes, use metal utensils and other household paraphernalia. The potential free time was now consumed by Western household chores.

By 1978 Bandeiyama was again participating fully in foraging pursuits. She was also producing a large quantity of craft in the form of mats and dilly-bags for her own use as well as for sale. She frequently held responsible positions in the major ceremonies such as Kunapipi, Badarra, and Rom that were being performed in the region.

It was during 1978 that I decided to record Bandeiyama's life history by interviewing her at night and taping our discussions. I made several attempts to initiate this but each time I was thwarted. I invited Bandeiyama to visit me after the evening meal when it was cooler and more peaceful in the camp, and when foraging for the day was over. I envisaged that then we would be able to drink tea, smoke a pipe and chat informally about her life. Each time we were interrupted by one of her small charges, usually Cherylene or Ngalimurra, who had become rivals for her attention. Although Bandeiyama seemed anxious to tell her story, the children's demands came first and the tape recordings were never made. In the end I gave up. The constant failure was worrying Bandeiyama; she felt that she was letting me down. I decided to wait until all her children were grown up. I would continue to learn about her as I had done up to now, by simply being with her as much as possible during the course of her daily routine.

Ironically, during 1978 I collected information about Bandeiyama from Gurrmanamana, who, being a man, could more easily extricate himself from informal family responsibilities. He loved to visit me after dinner to chat and tell me stories; he also liked to have them recorded on tape. Sometimes he brought one of his small children with him, usually his daughter Ngalimurra, but if she became difficult or demanding he merely handed her over to Bandeiyama, who once again had to relinquish her opportunity to reminisce about her life.

Gurrmanamana recalled for me the occasion on which Bandeiyama saw her first *balanda* (white man). He remembered that she was camping on the large earth mound at the swamp Djibadjirra when Gordon Sweeney, an officer of the Northern Territory Welfare Branch, came through Arnhem Land. This was in 1956, when she had three children — Djinbor, Gumugun and Nganmarra. Gurrmanamana also told of the cyclone that swept through Anbarra territory in the early 1950s when he and Bandeiyama had been camped at Lalarr-gadjirripa. A great wave from the sea had swept over the dune, almost washing Bandeiyama away, but Gurrmanamana had saved her. At that time, Gurrmanamana commented, Bandeiyama was wearing a traditional pubic covering made from string, manufactured from banyan tree bark.

Bandeiyama survived that cyclone, the scars of which can still be seen on the Anbarra landscape. She now wears European clothes, uses an iron digging stick, rides in motor vehicles and listens to rock and roll music on her transistor radio. But such past events are still close to her and impinge upon her as she moves around the countryside. With little difficulty she has reconciled herself to a changing environment and taken from European culture what she wants. She is able to do this because she is firmly attached to her own land, secure in the fact that its resources are hers and that its religious forces are fully intact and working for the benefit of her people.

In 1979, when I visited Bandeiyama and the Anbarra community, their outstation life was flourishing and she was again participating in it fully. Several times she joked with me saying that she was aging and that next time I came she would be an 'old woman'. Perhaps when she does at last settle into that role, we will both be old women with more time to spare and we will at last be able to sit down in some quiet place so that she herself can tell me about her life. Until then, I hope that the vignettes of that part of her past that I have shared here may provide some insight into the life of a hunting woman.

Bandeiyama (right), and her daughter Ngurraba Ngurraba, who is nursing her baby, Jackson. Taken at Maningrida in 1980 (Photograph by Kim McKenzie)

A few weeks after I left Kopanga in 1979 Bandeiyama's daughter, Ngurraba Ngurraba, gave birth to a son via a caesarean section carried out by European doctors in the Darwin hospital. My thoughts returned to that night, nearly twenty years ago, at Maningrida when Ngurraba Ngurraba herself entered the world in a tiny bark house. In many ways Bandeiyama is not willingly part of the European world though she copes with it admirably. She is one of the last generation of Aboriginal women who truly belongs to the bush — as does her special totemic animal, *birrabirraba*, the tiny fast-moving plover by whose name she is often and so aptly addressed.

During November 1982 Bandeiyama visited Canberra with twenty Gidjingali men and women. They came to perform a Rom ceremony for the Australian Institute of Aboriginal Studies. I feared that she might be over-awed by this experience because of the limited contact she had had with European society outside Maningrida. I should have had more faith in my friend's adaptability. She led the Anbarra women's dancing with flair, enjoyed meeting new people and found time and energy to indulge a lively interest in the life and sights of Canberra. She was present at the launching of my book about the collection of shellfish by the Anbarra people in which she features as a major actor, and she seemed pleased

Bandeiyama (right) with Betty Meehan and Gurrmanamana at the launching of the book *Shell Bed to Shell Midden,* taken in Canberra November 1982

with the result of what she had taught me. Bandeiyama came to Canberra to do a specific task. As usual she performed that task skilfully, while also deriving much pleasure from her effort.

Additional reading

Hamilton, A. (1981). *Nature and nurture: Child rearing in north-central Arnhem Land.* Australian Institute of Aboriginal Studies, Canberra

Hiatt, L.R. (1965). *Kinship and conflict: A study of an Aboriginal community in northern Arnhem Land.* Australian National University Press, Canberra.

Meehan, B. (1982). *Shell bed to shell midden* Australian Institute of Aboriginal Studies, Canberra

15

Mangkatina: Woman of the Desert
Isobel White

Alice Mangkatina worried about the white streak that had recently appeared in the front of her curly black hair, and asked me to send back some of 'that stuff you white-fellas use'. She meant hair dye, and I tried to persuade her that the white lock improved rather than spoilt her looks, that some European women, and even European men too, had a lock of hair in front whitened to make them look more distinguished. It was not from vanity that Alice wanted to conceal the white streak, but because she insisted it made her into a *minyma tjilpi* (an old woman — 'old' and 'white-haired' mean the same in her language), and she was not yet willing to accept this change in status. Now, a few years later, Alice has assumed fully the role of older woman and is adept at guiding and counselling girls and younger women.

When the white streak appeared, Alice was in her mid-forties, a handsome woman who looked younger than her age, in spite of being overweight by the standards of European Australian society. But the standards are different in the Western Desert, an area where in the old days the diet was usually so low in calories that it was hard to put on much weight. The word *kanpi* (fat) is used in the way we use 'sweet', or perhaps 'beaut', in Australian English; *tjitji kanpi, minyma kanpi* (a fat child, a fat woman), are words of high praise.

What I looked forward to most as I approached Yalata on each of my visits was Alice's beautiful welcoming smile. Not that I ever experienced anything but a warm reception from all the Yalata mob, but Alice's welcome was always something very special for me.

Mangkatina — or Alice Cox, as she is usually called — was one of the leading women in the community in 1969 when I first visited the Yalata Aboriginal Reserve and its Lutheran mission settlement in the far west of South Australia. I was then accompanied by Margaret Kartomi, an ethnomusicologist who wished to study Western Desert children's songs and ceremonies. As an anthropologist I studied women's lives and behaviour, with particular interest in their ceremonies, which I had already

Alice sewing, 1970 (Photograph I. White)

observed at other places in South Australia as part of a team led by Catherine Ellis.

The Yalata people were friendly and co-operative and invited us to pitch our tent in their camp, then 8 km from the mission headquarters. Alice was one of those who helped us most and on my subsequent visits to Yalata she became my closest friend. She was about forty-three years old when I first met her and still had young children, including a baby at the breast — and a grandchild as well. I also was a mother and grandmother and some years older than Alice; she called me *kangkuru* (older sister) and I called her *malang* (younger sister): thus I was placed in the kinship system which covered the whole community, and Alice instructed me in the proper behaviour to each category of kin. But young and old alike often called me *kapali* (grandmother), a title that can be used for any older woman, and until I got used to it I sometimes felt uncomfortably like a re-incarnated Daisy Bates.

Alice with her grandson, Martin, and Sally (Isobel White) 1980
(Photograph by Barbara Rentz)

Over the next four years I paid a number of visits to Yalata, for a month or two at a time. Although I have not stayed there since 1973, I have been able to visit my friends there quite often. I have accompanied my husband on his annual field trips to the vicinity of Kalgoorlie in Western Australia. We always call at Yalata and stay a few hours. In January 1977 we learnt that Alice and family were at Cundeelee mission settlement (north of the railway in Western Australia) and visited them there. In February 1980 I saw Alice on our way west, then met her daughter Effie and Effie's husband in Kalgoorlie. A few days after that, to my great surprise, there was Alice in the main street: she and others from Yalata had driven more than 1200 km to join the mourning rituals for a very old Yalata woman who had died in Kalgoorlie.

When I arrived in the camp at Yalata, Alice always invited me to put my tent within 20 m of her family dwelling. I was privileged to spend time sitting at her family fire, but I also kept a fire of my own alight, and around this a number of women would regularly gather. These were all closely related to Alice, and this presented a difficulty encountered by most anthropologists; namely, that one cannot live in a community without becoming part of a particular family, but this tie may inhibit communications with some other families, because among two or three hundred people there are bound to be separate groupings which do not mix very much. Consequently my knowledge of family life and behaviour is based on my experience with Alice's extended family group and their close kin. Fortunately almost all the women attended the women's ceremonies and thus I came to know them, but not as well as I knew Alice's immediate circle.

From her own account and from mission records I have been able to piece together Alice's life story. She was born between 1924 and 1928 in the ranges of north-west South Australia, which she describes as 'spinifex country' or 'proper Pitjantjatjara country'. The first years of her life were spent with her parents, grandparents and other close kin, who were still procuring their food by hunting and gathering. She remembers her maternal grandfather, who had three wives and many children and grandchildren. Many of his descendants live at Yalata today, so that Alice is surrounded by those she regards as 'close' sisters and brothers, nephews and nieces. (In the kinship terminology of the Western Desert, most of those we would call cousin are called sister or brother.) Here is her own account.

I was born in Black Hills [probably the Blackstone Range] goanna, *milbali*, country, so my dreaming *milbali*. We was hunting then; no white men. I saw white fella come spinifex. They bring us fruit and give us feed. We was all naked standing playing around. We were so glad to see the camels. We saw a string of camels coming. The whole people brought them dog scalp and they buy them and give us flour, sugar, golden syrup and some of clothes for children, and after that we all sat on the ground and the whole people cooking damper, funny sort of damper.

I saw Polly with them [Polly is another of my Yalata friends] — that white fella bringing Polly. They cooking damper for him [i.e. Polly] and his sister. We stop there a bit longer and the white fellas grows tomatoes and water melons and pumpkins and they make a well to stay there longer, and we stay there in spinifex camp. The white fella leave us and we were so sorry the boss gone.

We saw the native half-caste men come with camel and he looking for skin and they [her group] take him to west, spinifex way, and they look round and kill all the dog and take their scalp off and give it to the men for tucker [i.e. in exchange for food]. I was small girl then, we were all naked and playing around. When this white fella gone back to Ernabella, we came this way; we started walking to west coast [the Ooldea and Yalata area is called the West Coast], and the people said, 'Ah, missionaries over there. We can go and stay there.' We leave spinifex and we look for clothes. Margaret Williams' father, that one's father [Margaret was another friend at Yalata and her father was Alice's uncle], he bin tell 'em come down here. We get half way and a little boy called Peter Young was born there in spinifex, and his mother came carry little baby in the hand without blankets. After that coming up past another *kapi* [water hole] and another *kapi* and camp there. They have pussy-cat [this was an animal Alice had not seen before], and killing rabbits and tracking dingo; they keep the scalp. We walked through to Ooldea and Mr Green, cutting bread. We was naked, shy that time. We get there in the night time, shy, and Mr Green doing the windmill for water, fill our water and give us. We was real thirsty. Gave us water and bread and tea and sugar — everything he gave us feed. We fella was little that time and we was shy to see the white fellas dressed. Mr Green dressing we fellas with clothes. He didn't like to see us naked, and we was happy to go back to the fire having a feed of bread and jam. After that Mr Green call us 'Come and have a bath', and he bath us and cut 'em hair and take out all the loose [lice] — the children and the women.

We bin there along Ooldea, and Mr Green tell me to come, and he put me in a home for little girls and we grow there along Ooldea in the home. I see the Dais Bate [Mrs Daisy Bates] walking around in the siding and he [she] always cover him head and the umbrell' put up and he don't want to see the white people because they sell [buy] the kangaroos and boomerangs. He [she] went away in a train that old lady. She dressed in long skirt and long blouse — high neck — and dressing nice and hat and umbrell', and walking stick carry. He got sick and went away in a train that old lady.

Telegraph and railway development, and mining and pastoral leases on the desert fringes gradually caused the abandonment by the desert Aborigines of their hunting and gathering economy. Alice's people were no exception, though their own territory was not then involved in these enterprises; not until the 1960s and 1970s were mining leases granted. European food and material goods attracted the desert people, who gave up their freedom and their independence to live in the institutions that Europeans provided for them. Once they were in these institutions it soon became impossible for them to give up all they had come to value from European technology — security of water and food at first; later, other things such as tobacco, alcohol, vehicles, radios and medicines.

The importance of Ooldea to both Europeans and Aborigines was its permanent water, described by Daisy Bates as:

> one of Nature's miracles in barren Central Australia . . . Even in the cruellest droughts it had never failed. Here the tribes gathered in their hundreds for initiation and other ceremonies . . . On the steep hills about the soak, the visiting mobs camped, each in the direction of his own ground. Today, in a flintless country cut flints in millions are to be found on the surrounding sandhills and about the site of the native wells, and human bones and skulls are evidence of these great gatherings of long ago.

Ooldea was outside Pitjantjatjara territory but was on the border of Wirangu and Kokata country, people who spoke languages intelligible to Pitjantjatjara speakers, and who also shared ceremonies and other customs with them. Alice's people might have travelled to Ooldea previously, to join in ceremonies or to take refuge in times of drought. In order to help and serve the many Aborigines from the north who gathered at Ooldea, Mrs Daisy Bates lived near the railway at Ooldea from 1919 to 1935, and at another siding, Wynbring, from 1941 to 1945. The United Aborigines Mission sent a Miss Lock to found a mission at Ooldea in 1933, and in August 1934 a school was opened for the children. In April 1936 Mr and Mrs Harrie Green came to replace Miss Lock, and it is probable that Alice's family group arrived a year or two later, when Alice thinks she was about nine years old.

It is clear from Alice's description of the journey to Ooldea that, when they heard about the activities and possessions of the Europeans, the impulse was to go as quickly as possible to the intruders' settlements. Curiosity no doubt played a large part in these moves, but there was also the attraction of what has been called the 'super waterhole'. The stories of the food 'rations' — and the first experience of these which Alice remembers — were the main reasons for settling at missions. A number of Pitjantjatjara and their neighbours went east to Ernabella and others west to Warburton Range mission about the same time that Alice journeyed south to Ooldea.

Once they had moved into the alien world of Europeans, they were in a foreign country where they knew neither the language nor the customs. They needed interpreters and guides, needs which the missions were willing to supply in the hope that the Aborigines would be converted to Christianity. The reason why, at least until recently, Aborigines have made few moves to leave the mission and government settlements is that they feel totally insecure and unable to cope in what is still to them an alien world — even after two or three generations.

The missionaries recorded descriptions of Alice in the Ooldea days some years after her arrival:

> A bright girlish face looks up with a smile and shows a row of perfect teeth . . . Mungatina [sic] converses fluently in English . . . As a little child Mungatina had begged her mother to allow her to live in the Mission Home and go to school. The mother consented and the girl spent all her childhood under mission care . . . She was loved by everyone.

Separate dormitories had been built for the girls and boys and here Alice spent the years from about ten to sixteen. There seems to have been little attempt by the missionaries to force the children into the dormitories nor to keep those who lived there away from their parents. The dormitory children spent Sunday afternoons with their parents in the camp.

At that time Alice became a devout Christian, according to the missionary account. She was betrothed to an older man, over thirty, but:

> She had no affection for him and no joy in the prospect of marrying him, but the tribal laws were too strong for her . . . When she was fifteen years of age her parents asked permission to take her away for a fortnight's holiday. [Alice thinks she was older than fifteen.]

They promised to bring her back but did not do so:

> Whether Mungatina went submissively to her marriage or had to be cudgelled into obedience we do not know, but go she did . . .

And here is Mangkatina's own account:

> When I was a big girl I married. That old man there, my cousin, he made my marriage when I was baby. I always frightened of the men. I grabbed my mother by the hand and beg her not give me to that old man.

She returned as a married woman and she is described by the missionary after three years of married life: 'A bright-faced young woman with a fat little daughter toddling behind her.'

Alice at Ooldea, about 1946, with her first child, Elizabeth
(Photograph by the late Rev. Harrie Green, courtesy of Mrs Green)

After nearly forty years of marriage she clearly regards her husband with considerable affection. As an important ritual and secular leader he would have been entitled to take a second wife but has not done so. For many years he was probably the dominant partner in the marriage, being so much older than Alice. However, during the early 1970s, it was Alice, then in the prime of life, who appeared to dominate her husband in everyday affairs, though she still showed the greatest respect for his ritual importance. At that time he was showing signs of old age, mainly as an effect of failing sight. When I saw them in 1977, Alice was jubilant because, following a visit by the team of the Trachoma Eradication Programme, Jack Cox had undergone eye surgery and could see quite well again. When I saw Alice and Jack in February 1980, Jack was helping and waiting on Alice, who had a broken arm immobilised by a plaster cast.

Alice bore her first child, Elizabeth (Kuali), in September 1944 in the small mission hospital at Ooldea, helped by the mission nurse and her own mother. (This is the 'fat little daughter' mentioned in the missionary account.) Her second child, Effie (Manila), was born seven years later in the camp at Barton about 100 km east along the railway line from Ooldea. The 'Ooldea mob' still moved around the countryside, and particularly to various camps along the line so that they could beg from train passengers and sell them artefacts, and then buy flour, tea, sugar and tobacco at the railway settlements and from 'The Tea and Sugar' (as the weekly supply train for these remote settlements is called). They also travelled away from Ooldea for hunting, since the presence of 200 or so people made game scarce for a considerable distance in all directions. Rabbits had become plentiful, more so because the scalp bounty had reduced the dingo population, but even the rabbits were soon hunted out near the settlement.

The soak at Ooldea became an important water supply during construction of the railway line and was later used for the steam locomotives, as well as for the Aborigines living around the mission. Over-use of the soak for the needs of the railway led to its becoming brackish, so that by 1952 water was being railed to the siding and carted to the mission. More urgent was the radiation hazard from experiments at Maralinga, 40 km away, so the mission was abandoned.

While I was living in the Yalata camp, I set out more than once with a party of women to drive to Ooldea and see the old mission site, but each time we camped somewhere on the south side of the railway line. (The mission and soak were about 6 km north of the line.) Finally, one of the older men in the camp explained to me that the women did not really want to go to their former camping grounds because they were afraid of the spirits of the many people who had died there. I had heard so much about the Ooldea soak and the mission from my older friends at Yalata that I felt cheated. Finally, in 1974, I got there when travelling with my husband. The soak was hard to approach because the old road was covered with deep sand, and we had to abandon our four-wheel drive vehicle near the railway siding and walk in blazing heat up and down steep sandhills. The area surrounding the soak was inhabited by myriads of birds, which kept up a constant singing and chattering in the exotic trees that the missionaries had planted — pepper trees now grown to giant size, their roots penetrating deep into the underground water. One of the Yalata men remembered having to water them when he was a boy and they were seedlings. The ruined mission buildings are fast disappearing under the encroaching desert sand. The sandhills for hundreds of metres around are littered with innumerable stone tools, flakes and chippings, as well as the charcoal from old fires. But there is nobody there now.

When Alice's daughter Elizabeth and her two children were staying with me in Melbourne in 1972 we all visited Mr and Mrs Green, then living in retirement. Mr Green showed us colour slides of Ooldea and its inhabitants in the 1940s, which Elizabeth enjoyed, particularly as she recognised many of those in the photographs, though many had since died. She is of the generation that is willing to look at pictures of such people, but her mother is quite different. If she had been there we could not have looked at these slides.

Accounts given to me by Alice and other women nearly twenty years after the United Aborigines Mission's withdrawal from Ooldea suggest that a near panic was caused by the sudden departure of the missionaries. There seems to have been no consultation with the Aborigines beforehand, no explanation of what was going to occur, no long-term planning for the future in which they themselves could be involved. This is Alice's account:

> Mr Green pull everything away; he took away all the tucker; he go away. We was all alone — no missionaries. We do not know what can we do. We was very sorry when Mr Green went away. We was crying for him and for all of them — Mrs Green and Mrs Saxton, all nurses, all teachers — all gone. We go away on train. We get off at Tarcoola [300 km east of Ooldea] and we pool all the tucker, and we camp there one night. And the policeman come and tell us to go to Wilgena [20 km further east along the line] and not stay here all night. So we go walking, blankets and a lot of swag and the kids. Effie was a baby then and we took her along. Elizabeth had gone on the mail train to Wilgena. So we go walking; camp half way in the rock holes. After that night we saw another windmill and have dinner there. We saw a police car with Tommy Gibson on board. The policeman had caught him. He was a naughty boy and they were taking him back to gaol, and we cried for him. After that we go to Butterfield [?] and caught kangaroos. Then we saw the boss coming, Mr Dougall and the policeman. [This was probably Mr A. McDougall, the Commonwealth officer charged with ensuring that no Aborigines were on the range when rockets were fired from Woomera.] Mr Dougall said we could go north to Ernabella or to West Coast [i.e. of South Australia], and we said we'd like to go to West Coast, so he arranged for two trucks to pick us up and we went to Tarcoola, then back to Ooldea by 'The Tea and Sugar' train. And there were two trucks waiting for us — Koonibba trucks [Koonibba was a Lutheran mission near Ceduna, 200 km east of the present Yalata mission] — and they took us to some tanks north of here. [These were shed tanks on a track between Ooldea and Yalata, some 30 km north of the present Yalata Community

headquarters. The tanks are still a favourite place for hunting camps for the Yalata people.]

For a year following these events, they moved around what is now the Yalata Reserve, from water tank to water tank, hunting for their own meat and gathering vegetable food, occasionally getting government rations of flour and tinned food. I was told by the Lutheran missionaries at Yalata that the Lutheran Board of Missions offered to establish a mission settlement if the South Australian Government would provide a suitable reserve. In 1953 the government resumed the leases of Yalata and two adjoining pastoral stations to form a reserve of over 4500 square kilometres. In the next years the Lutheran Board of Missions built headquarters near the old Eyre Highway. Until a school was built, a mobile school in the bush was conducted by one of the mission staff, Margaret Tischler. At first she was also in charge of welfare and organised the distribution of rations — flour, sugar, tea and canned foods. But even after the headquarters were built, the 'Yalata mob', as they came to be called, preferred to camp at various places on the Reserve, from 2 km to 25 km away from European folk. And the camp was moved several times a year, sometimes following a death, sometimes for other reasons. I witnessed such moves a number of times.

After Effie was born, Alice had no more children for twelve years (which she was unable to explain) and then she gave birth to three in quick succession in the mission hospital at Yalata. First there were two daughters, Elaine and Evelyn, and finally, when she was over forty, in 1969, her only son, Neville, was born. In his first four years Neville was frequently sick and spent more time in hospital in Adelaide than at home with his mother, who was always grieving for him, wondering if she would ever see him again, and not even certain whether he was alive or dead. However, since the age of four he has maintained good health. Alice had previously suffered extreme anxiety about her second child, Effie, who had been born with a 'hole-in-the-heart'; but when she was seven, surgeons in Adelaide performed open-heart surgery.

Both Elizabeth and Effie have been married for many years. Alice supported Elizabeth in marrying the man of her choice rather than the man to whom she had been promised some years previously by her father, who was intent on fulfilling this promise and was supported by the adult men of the community. The women won, but Alice was speared by Elizabeth's rejected suitor, and shows the scars in her thigh with evident pride. (Although a father promises his daughter, it is the mother's responsibility to give her to her husband at the proper time.) Alice still calls this man Elizabeth's first husband.

Elizabeth has had three children, but two of them died in infancy, and Effie has never become pregnant. Both these situations cause great grief to Alice. She would love to have many grandchildren, like some of her 'sisters' in the community. Her closest 'sister' (her mother's sister's daughter) boasts at least ten grandchildren. In 1978 Alice's third daughter, Elaine, then an unmarried schoolgirl of fourteen, gave birth to a baby boy, Martin. Another woman told me that Alice was furious when she discovered that Elaine was pregnant, but forgave her after the baby was born and now dotes on the little boy, as I myself witnessed in 1980.

Alice always seemed to me to represent the ideal of what a Pitjantjatjara woman should be, and was so regarded by both Aborigines and Europeans. She explained many aspects of behaviour and set me an example of how I should behave. Together with her children and her 'close sisters' she helped me to improve my understanding and speaking of Pitjantjatjara.

The freedom that Alice possessed during her girlhood, which enabled her to move from mission dormitory to family camp, taught her two contrasting lifestyles. Though she spent much time in a European-style building, she is adept at all the skills required for camp life. Ever since her marriage she has been responsible for constructing the family dwelling (*wiltja*), a framework of poles cut from trees, covered with a thatch of leafy branches. Today this is covered with one of the family's few possessions, a large tarpaulin which is more efficient than traditional materials at keeping out rain and wind. Each time the camp is moved Alice has to rebuild this dwelling, and I have seen her rebuild it at other times in order to move to a preferred site within the camp. In very hot weather, she and her family live in the open and she then builds a simple windbreak. In 1972 at the request of the Yalata Council, Alice built a beautifully neat old-style *wiltja* in the middle of the village to show tourists how Aborigines lived in traditional style.

She used to add to the family's meagre income in two ways. The welfare worker entrusted her with the care of several blind or senile pensioners whose immediate families could not look after them. In exchange for seeing to their fire, food and safety, Alice was paid part of their pensions. She took this responsibility very seriously and seldom left them alone unless she could find some other responsible person to watch over them. She also earned a fairly regular weekly sum by making artefacts. Yalata artefacts, made from the wood of the western myall, are well known for their excellent quality. I have seen them for sale in gift shops in San Francisco and New York, as well as all over Australia. Alice made several boomerangs each week and taught her craft to her daughters. It is skilled and tedious work and I could always raise a laugh from friends by attempting to help them.

Alice's cooking was of the simplest, and consisted mostly of putting pieces of meat on the open fire. Occasionally she would use a saucepan to make a stew, but like other similar possessions, saucepans had but a short life under the camp conditions. She excelled in making damper, a mixture of flour, salt, baking powder and water cooked in the hot ashes. It is delicious eaten hot with butter, jam or golden syrup, and I used to look forward to the times she made it, as I always came in for my share. In general we shared our food: she would give me some meat (lean mutton from the mission store) and damper, and I would provide something extra, such as butter, jam or fruit. For breakfast I would make a large saucepan full of porridge. This the children loved, and the adults too. (I hung on to my saucepan and made it clear that I wasn't very willing to lend it.) For lunch we shared bread or damper, and of course there was a billy of tea on the fire all the time, into which the bread or damper was dunked.

I was surprised to find out one day that Alice could sew quite well, and others in the camp would sometimes bring a badly torn garment for her to mend. Moreover, she was one of the few women in the camp who, with a little help in cutting-out from one of the mission staff, could sew together a dress by hand. She could also crochet, and any scraps of coloured wool she could collect were made into crocheted caps for herself and her children. She possessed great skill at spinning human hair into string, rubbing it on her thigh with her right hand while twirling in her left hand a spindle she had made of two crossed sticks. She and another woman once performed for me a series of complicated string figures, some of which they used to illustrate myths.

One of the returns I could offer Alice and the other women who helped me was to take them hunting. Their main target was wombats, though once the hunting dog who accompanied us killed a kangaroo. The Land Rover would fill to capacity with excited women and their younger children and we would set out for the edge of the Nullarbor Plain, a distance of about 30 km. We enjoyed taking off from the track and driving across the Plain in order to find the most likely wombat mounds to dig up. Each pair of women would choose her particular burrow and then we would return to the trees at the Plain's edge to camp for the night. However cold it was (winter nights on the Plain are frosty), we would keep warm when asleep by using the old trick of first lighting a big fire right across the intended sleeping area, letting it burn down and then raking all the hot coals away and laying blankets on the warm ashes. In the meantime we cooked a wombat in the hot ashes for supper and boiled a billy of tea. Before we went to sleep the women performed one of their ceremonies, perhaps one of the most secret, because of the safe distance from possible male interference. In the morning the women turned to the heavy work of digging out the wombat mounds, a task in which Alice was often the most active and successful.

During her girlhood in the dormitory at Ooldea, Alice became a practising Christian — and still maintains she is one, though she almost never goes to the Lutheran services — but she is also fully conversant with the ritual life of her people, the women's own ceremonies and the rituals in which both sexes participate. In the mission she learnt to speak English and this was most useful when she and the other women were translating song texts for me and explaining the meaning of the myths and ceremonies. She and her 'close sister' once told me an important myth about the 'Two Men', this time in the manifestation of mallee fowl (*nanamara*). Although this was a myth belonging to men, my two friends had been told it by their fathers, both of the 'Two Men' totem, and they were now old enough to tell it themselves. However, they told it in whispers while we three were quite alone. It was important to me in the context of current archaeological research because it explained the origin of the underground fresh-water lake in Koonalda Cave (200 km west of Yalata).

Alice showed understanding of what my research entailed. Often when I was puzzled by some item of everyday behaviour or by some details of the ceremonies, Alice surprised me by volunteering an explanation before I had even posed a question. Despite her apparent seriousness she has a great sense of humour and is a particularly good mimic. After she had discovered that I was not closely associated with the European staff at the mission headquarters she used to imitate one or the other mercilessly until we were helpless with laughter.

Alice Mangkatina's life history is typical of many of her people — birth in clan country in pre-contact times, then the move to European settlement, often followed by several moves to other centres. The Yalata people seem particularly unfortunate. They are displaced and landless, because the Yalata Reserve is not in what they regard as their own territory. It is 'orphan country', since all the original Wirangu owners have died out. There is no outstation movement, no return to clan lands, since these are far away, although they are in the North-West Reserve and not occupied by Europeans. Of the older people who came to Ooldea forty to sixty years ago, only a few have ever been back to their birthplaces. The community maintains a strong ritual life, but this lacks its old physical tie to the land. However, they rejoice, together with their kin in other Pitjantjatjara settlements, at the recent granting by the South Australian Government of title to their ancestral land.

Alice is a woman of the desert still. She has but once visited the sea coast, which is only 20 km from Yalata village, and one of the most beautiful and spectacular in Australia, with rocky cliffs alternating with beaches of pure white sand. But she hates and fears the sea, and would not join us when I took a party of younger people and their children there. Once, when I was driving a group of women from Yalata to Ooldea, we stopped for a picnic at Pedinga, where the earth is bright red, unlike the orange-red soil of the coastal plain. Alice knelt on the ground, almost weeping. She picked up some red sand and let it run through her fingers, saying 'This is like my home country, this red sand'.

Additional reading

Bates, D.M. (1938). *The passing of the Aborigines.* Murray, London
(This book is flawed because Mrs Bates accuses the Western Desert Aborigines of cannibalism, cruelty, and immorality. In my fieldwork amongst these people and their descendants, I found her allegations untrue.)

Gale, F. (ed.) (1970). *Woman's role in Aboriginal society.* Australian Institute of Aboriginal Studies, Canberra

White, I.M. (1972). Hunting dogs at Yalata. *Mankind 8,* 201-5

—— (1975). Sexual conquest and submission in the myths of Central Australia. *In* L.R. Hiatt (ed.), *Australian Aboriginal Mythology.* Australian Institute of Aboriginal Studies, Canberra

—— (1977). From camp to village. *In* R.M. Berndt (ed.), *Aborigines and change.* Australian Institute of Aboriginal Studies, Canberra